The Disney Way
Fieldbook

The Disney Way Fieldbook

How to Implement Walt Disney's Vision
of "Dream, Believe, Dare, Do"
in Your Own Company

Bill Capodagli
Lynn Jackson

McGraw-Hill

New York   San Francisco   Washington, D.C.   Auckland   Bogotá
Caracas   Lisbon   London   Madrid   Mexico City   Milan
Montreal   New Delhi   San Juan   Singapore
Sydney   Tokyo   Toronto

Library of Congress Cataloging-in-Publication Data

Capodagli, Bill
    The Disney way fieldbook : how to implement Walt Disney's vision of "Dream,
believe, dare, do" in your own company / Bill Capodagli, Lynn Jackson.
       p.   cm.
   Includes index.
    ISBN 0-07-136106-5 (pbk.)
    1. Industrial management. I. Jackson, Lynn. II. Title.
HD31.C3432 2000
658—dc21   00-055431

McGraw-Hill

*A Division of The **McGraw·Hill** Companies*

8 9 10 IBT/IBT 1 9 8 7 6 5 4 3 2

ISBN-13: 978-0-07-136106-4

ISBN-10: 0-07-136106-5

McGraw-Hill books are available at special quantity discounts to use as premiums and sales promotions, or for use in corporate training programs. For more information, please write to the Director of Special Sales, McGraw-Hill, Two Penn Plaza, New York, NY 10121-2298. Or contact your local bookstore.

This publication is designed to provide accurate and authoritative information in regard to the subject matter covered. It is sold with the understanding that neither the author nor the publisher is engaged in rendering legal, accounting, futures/securities trading, or other professional service. If legal advice or other expert assistance is required, the services of a competent professional person should be sought.
          —From a Declaration of Principles jointly adopted by a Committee
          of the American Bar Association and a Committee of Publishers

DEDICATION

To Alan from Dad and Lynn—the guy with two ages, 27 and "5," and it's no secret which one we enjoy the best! No one else can say to us, "What's the plan, guys?" and evoke an instant smile like Alan does. He lives to embrace life and people every day, and he accepts both as he finds them.

To Jaimie from Aunt Lynn and Uncle Bill—our bold, bright, and beautiful 10-year-old niece whose "can do" attitude spells wisdom beyond her years.

And to Cassandra ("Cassie") from Grandpa Bill and Nana Lynn—that darling angel of a 2-year-old whose charm with people causes us to forget about her being "that age."

These three children, leaders in their own right, teach us to keep in perspective whatever success comes our way, and to grasp hold of the fun in every new venture.

CONTENTS

Act III: Dare   147

Act IV: Do   213

PREFACE

This year, we have been fully engaged in life on the road and have felt inspired by so many who are embracing the *Dreamovations* principles, *Dream, Believe, Dare, and Do*, with great vigor and enthusiasm. When practiced on a regular basis, these four simple elements make for a powerful credo that provides the rock on which you can build your passion, your business, your castle.

As consultants, we encounter the naysayers who seem to tire of hearing yet another "Disney success story." According to some, Walt just got lucky. Period. Recently, we heard a caller on our favorite national talk radio show echo this mindset. His opening comment was, "I'm one of those people who are tired of hearing the name Tiger Woods." For an instant, we just looked at one another. You see, we are among those who believe there can never be enough said about leaders like Walt Disney, Tiger Woods, Vince Lombardi, or Phil Jackson. They all define the formula for winning with their talent, long-term vision, determination, unrelenting spirit, and, let us not forget, strong team values.

Remember this: Success breeds success. It's an old and often overused cliché, but it will always ring true. Time and time again, the happiest people are those who get "hooked" by a dream and get out there and just do it. Oh yeah, and they keep doing it!

As for the two of us, we share a common vision: to live each and every day to the fullest, and to experience some laughter and fun along the way. And, of course, *Dream, Believe, Dare, Do* are the principles that keep us focused. We are grateful and privileged to be survivors, both personally and professionally, but most of all we embrace the challenges of life itself. We believe the journey is worth it. It is our sincere hope that this *Fieldbook* will help you in pursuing your own life's work.

Bill Capodagli and Lynn Jackson

ACKNOWLEDGMENTS

Years ago, before embarking upon our first book project, we naively thought that we would write the manuscript, wrap it up, and deliver it to the publisher, and show up for the signings. The reality was a far cry from our dream. In the '90s, we all had the line, "It takes a village to raise a child" drilled into our psyches. Well, we're not sure about that, but we do know that it takes a village to get a book launched!

Our village of people is special for many reasons, with passion for their work right at the top of the list. Ever since we visited Seattle's famous and phenomenally successful Pike Place Fish Market, we have come to see teaming in a new light. Their staff talks about their work with enlightening terms such as: "It's not about fish," "You gotta make it fun," "Make their day," and "Anyone can do this." Yes, yes, yes! It can happen anywhere when people come together for any common goal, rally around it, and get it done. In our case, it's a book, but it didn't have to be.

The point guard, Audra Kieffaber, whose fearlessness and diplomacy totally embody the Believe section. Audra maintains the course and never, never gives up on us. Without Audra, nothing gets totally done!

The star intern, Pete Fairfield, from the Butler University Internship Program, whose clear, long-term goal to be in the book business has been a great gift to us at the right time. Pete is a fine editor and a stabilizing force in our office.

The creative illustrator, Cassandra Smiley, whose dramatic representations, particularly in the *Dare* section, make people want to jump right in!

Our editing consultant, Martha Lawler, who has been a great ally on both of our *Disney Way* books.

Our editor, Peter Maeck, whose show-business flair breathes life into the *Fieldbook* exercises.

Our senior editor at McGraw-Hill, Mary Glenn, whose adoption of the *Dream, Believe, Dare,* and *Do* principles inspires us to forge ahead with our writing projects!

A sincere thanks to Ken Blanchard, a legend in the field of leadership development, for his encouragement, support, and letting us share *The Disney Way* message at his *Gung Ho* seminar in Indianapolis in December 1999.

And certainly, we would be remiss if we let the opportunity slip away without saluting the hundreds of teams who have participated in and contributed to many of the *Fieldbook* activities, and who believe that fun and business results run hand-in-hand.

We thank you all.

WHY A FIELDBOOK?

Make everyone's DREAM come true; BELIEVE in your people, your guests, your partners; DARE to make a difference; then just DO it!
—Walt Disney

It is said of the Disney empire that, "It all started with a mouse." That's not true. It all started with Walt's *dream* of a mouse—a mouse that his belief, daring, and spirit of can-do brought to glorious and hugely profitable life.

What's your dream? Do you have one? We bet you do, though you may not have expressed it yet, even to yourself. Do you want to express it, flesh it out in verbal and visual form, discuss it, enhance it, refine it, test it, refine it some more, and then spring it full-blown upon the world?

Sure you do. How do we know that? You picked up this book. We've also written another one for you—*The Disney Way: Harnessing the Management Secrets of Disney in Your Company*. That volume, combined with *The Disney Way Fieldbook* you hold in your hand, can launch you toward the stars of success.

You may be saying, "I'm not in the entertainment industry. How can Walt Disney's show business principles work for me?"

Our answer is, they'll work beautifully. How do we know? Because in our decades of consulting we've seen them do so in companies from investment banking to publishing to hotel management, plus businesses in between and beyond. The truth is, *all* business is show business. That's why principles that originated in show business apply to your business, too.

What do we mean when we say, "All business is show business"? We mean that whatever the concrete benefits of your products or services, your biggest reward from a customer is a smile—a smile that means they've had a great experience, they trust you, they've gotten full value for their money, and most importantly, they'll come back for more.

You can't generate that smile all by yourself. Your customers don't come for a solo act; they want a full-cast performance with complete production values. They want lights, camera, and action. They're not out for a recitation of product features and a little demo; they want a mind-stirring, heart-grabbing *show*.

The *Dream, Believe, Dare, Do* spirit is infectious. Our book, *The Disney Way*, has inspired readers worldwide to ask us:

- How can we begin making our own dreams real?
- How do we put "show" in our business—for ourselves and for our guests?
- How do we engage all our team members in storyboarding?
- How can our teams work together with more energy and excitement toward a common goal?

For these readers, and for you, we've created *The Disney Way Fieldbook: How to Implement Walt Disney's Vision of "Dream, Believe, Dare, Do" in Your Company*, as a compendium of thought-provoking, skill-building, motivation-enhancing exercises that will help you assimilate the *Disney Way* principles and use them to practical, profitable effect.

Practice and profit, of course, don't come overnight, especially if you spend every day just staying afloat.

So get away. Breathe some fresh air. Look through new windows at new landscapes. Unzip your mind. Instead of meeting deadlines and filling quotas, do something really wild: Dream. Walt Disney did that in the 1950s with his top creative thinkers—"Imagineers," he called them. You can do it, too. Where? In a *Dream Retreat®*. Here, over the course of a day or a week, you'll have the time and freedom to be a dreamer yourself, and to inspire your team members to be dreamers too.

Of course, dreams and ideas gain bottom-line value as they progress through the mills of design, manufacturing, and marketing. At a *Dream Retreat®*, you'll plot the course of your inspiration on a business map, too.

Here's your kit:

- *The Disney Way: Harnessing the Management Secrets of Disney in Your Company*

- *The Disney Way Fieldbook*
- *Dream Retreat*®

Does your *Dream, Believe, Dare, Do* journey sound like the challenge of a lifetime? Does it sound like fun?

It's both. *The Disney Way Fieldbook* will help you to "Make dreams come true, believe in yourself and your coworkers, dare to make a difference, and just do it."

The Disney Way
Fieldbook

Showtime

We are such stuff as dreams are made on.
—Shakespeare

If a picture is worth a thousand words, imagine the worth of a thousand pictures.

Walt Disney did just that, staking his initial vision for $500 in 1923. His investment is now worth two million times that amount. The saying, "There's no business like show business," seems to be literally true.

*Dream*ovations is a visionary, holistic management approach based on Walt Disney's credo: Dream, Believe, Dare, Do. It cannot promise a two millionfold increase in your company's worth, but it can help your organization put on a much more crowd-pleasing and profitable show.

How?

By pulling you out of the old problem-solving wrestling ring, and placing you on a brightly-lit management stage where creativity, courage, and a bit of magic can make personal and organizational dreams come true.

Don't worry; you won't live the actor's nightmare of facing an audience without knowing your lines. *The Disney Way Fieldbook* prepares you with checklists, diagnostic tools, team building and team "fun" activities, and demonstrations of the Dream, Dare, Believe, Do principles—in short, with the text, direction, and rehearsal you need to be a management star.

Dreamovations is a certified hit, but there's another long-running show in town. To choose which production you want to be a part of, check the critics' reviews below.

"Traditional Strategic Planning"
The Classic Drama

"Attempts to make the best of existing situations. Often ends up recycling the status quo."

"Focuses on solving problems instead of creating solutions."

"Obsesses about reducing costs. Bottoms out on the bottom line instead of soaring to new heights."

"Dreamovations"
A High-Flying Journey into Business Blue Sky

"Establishes a culture of collective commitment involving all employees at every level."

"Generates a mutually enriching synergy between employees, customers, guests, and suppliers."

"Spurs innovation, bolsters courage to take risks, strengthens belief in organizational values, catalyzes positive change, and facilitates planning for future growth and success."

"Creates customers for life."

"Encourages and enables team members to constantly reinvent themselves and their work."

Of course, reviews can only hint at a show's quality. The proof is in the play itself, and the play, as Hamlet said, is the thing.

DREAMOVATIONS: WHO'S WHO IN THE CAST

Your Organization:

The overall corporate structure within which your team works.

Your Team:

The work group under your direct supervision.

Your Team Members:

Your most important resources—the individual people who get the job done.

You:

Team leader, facilitator, counselor, coach. When your team succeeds, you succeed, and your organization does, too.

DREAMOVATIONS: SYNOPSIS

ACT I: DREAM

Long-term and short-term *visions* are born out of pulsing ambitions, realistic appraisals, and blue-sky hopes.

A picture of your company's future is sketched by using the *story* technique.

ACT II: BELIEVE

Each department learns to align its own *mission* and *values* with those of the overall corporation.

You, as leader, strengthen your bonds with your *teams*.

You also discover new ways to forge mutually beneficial, long-term relationships with *customers, guests,* and *suppliers*.

ACT III: DARE

You learn to create an environment of creative conflict in which failure is recognized as a valuable step toward *change* and *empowerment*, with improved quality and higher profits as the results.

ACT IV: DO

You practice techniques of project *planning* and *communication of details* to *develop* the project awareness, readiness, and preparedness of your employee *"cast."*

Overview of the *Dreamovations* Process

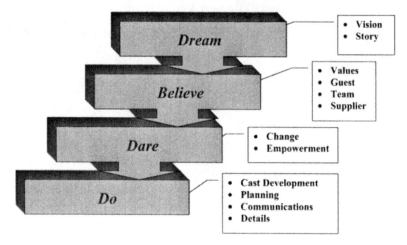

HOW TO LEARN AND PLAY YOUR ROLE

Though the *Fieldbook* follows The Disney Way's four-part structure, it can be used in whatever measure or sequence you wish.

Think of the *Fieldbook not as a script to be performed straight through from beginning* to end, but as scenes to be rehearsed, with priority given to those that need the most work. To do this, determine which, if any, of the Dream, Believe, Dare, Do principles are currently in effect in your organization. (You may be using different terms, of course.) Then focus on the concepts, tools, and techniques you need to achieve maximum managerial success.

The *Fieldbook* exercises are dynamic, interactive activities that will engage you heart, mind, and soul. You won't just be taking notes. All business is show business, and you are not a passive member of the audience; you are a live, performing member of an onstage cast.

You are not, however, a chorus member. You are a lead player with supervisory responsibilities to your team. *The Disney Way* and *The Disney Way Fieldbook* are founded on the belief that the best leadership does not dictate behavior, but inspires peak effort for optimum results.

These beliefs have been tested and confirmed over our collective consulting experience spanning 40 years. In seminars ranging from one hour per week, conference room team meetings to weeklong, mountain lodge *Dream Retreats*®, individuals, teams, and total organizations have been transformed time and time again. Participants have come from companies of all types and sizes, in industries ranging from manufacturing to public utilities to health care, to name a few. Business-as-show-business does not apply only to the entertainment field. In truth, "All the world's a stage."

The curtain is rising on a new management era, and *your* show is about to begin.

Using The Disney Way Fieldbook to Achieve the Best Team Experience

- **Choose** exercises that are relevant to the team's work situation. In doing so, assess the team members' backgrounds, their current roles, and their plans for the future. Consider the length of time they have been together, how well they work as a team, the risks they are facing, and their specific mission and goals.

- **Be Sure** that you can answer "why" you have selected each exercise, and that you are prepared to discuss your rationale with the team.

- **Practice, practice, practice** each exercise before administering it to the team. Do not begin until you are totally comfortable with the procedures and materials. We feel so strongly about this that we devote an entire chapter to it in *The Disney Way*.

- **Define** your role in the exercise before you present it to the team. Are you to be a facilitator, an observer, or an active participant? When the team assembles, make it clear to them what your role will be.

- **Explain** each exercise to the team in clear and precise detail. Their understanding is essential for a successful result.

- **Debrief** each exercise thoroughly by asking questions such as, How does this apply to our team?; What can we take away from this experience?; and What did you observe during the exercise? Respond to feedback in nonjudgmental terms.

- **Encourage** each team member to try new activities, take risks and think "outside the box." Present the exercise environment as one in which each individual is secure within a safety net of mutual support. Permit any person to decline participation in any exercise for any reason, no questions asked.

The following icons will help you understand the nature of each exercise in the *Fieldbook*.

 This icon designates a Checklist exercise.

 This icon designates a Fun, Team-Building exercise.

 This icon designates a Diagnostic or Questionnaire exercise.

 This icon designates a Demonstration or Operational exercise.

Act I: Dream

Somehow I can't believe there are many heights that can't be scaled by a man who knows the secret of making dreams come true.

—Walt Disney

SCENE 1: DREAMOVATIONS: IMPLEMENTING DREAM, BELIEVE, DARE, AND DO

Have faith in your dreams and someday your rainbow will come smiling thru.

—Cinderella, *Cinderella*

AUTHORS' NOTES

From acorns great oaks grow. Walt Disney's four-word credo—*Dream, Believe, Dare, Do*—spawned an entertainment empire comprising the movies, songs, and attractions we know and love so well. How did Walt produce hit after hit? By consulting his principles before starting each one.

First, he would say, I *dream* of characters, stories, and ways of doing business that have never been dreamed of before.

Second, I *believe* in the values that guide me and my company.

Third, I *dare* to take risks to pursue my dreams.

Fourth, I *do* everything necessary to make my dreams come true.

Walt didn't *Dream, Believe, Dare, and Do* all alone. He created an organization populated with like-minded cast members, and instilled his guiding principles in every single one. "The organization must be with you," he said, "or you don't get it done."

Walt was the embodiment of a great leader, which we define as "a person who inspires, motivates, and brings to fruition individual and team effort in an environment of creativity, trust, and mutual respect."

That's a wide-ranging definition—holistic one, we might say. By "holistic" we mean, to quote the dictionary: "Characterized by the fundamental and determining components of reality creating an existence beyond the mere sum of their parts."

A holistic approach is all-inclusive. Top management must commit to it totally, embracing all four *Dream, Believe, Dare,* and *Do* principles and engaging all departments and all teams at all levels in planning, resource allocation, and training.

Fine, you say, but how long will it take to get results? We have to answer: Don't expect them overnight. After all, your present situation wasn't created in a day. Years can pass before the transforming effects of *Dream*ovations are fully felt. Hard work, a common focus, and team commitment to the plan will score short-terms gains; while long-range vision, steady direction, and discipline will hold you on course toward making *Dream*ovations a way of organizational life.

In our book, *The Disney Way,* we cite numerous top-flight companies that adopted the *Dream*ovations model. Among their great successes are:

- Product development time cut from 150 to 100 weeks.
- 5,167 work-team ideas implemented, resulting in $10.06 million in savings in one year.
- Cycle time reduced by 90 percent.
- Purchasing process costs lowered by $800,000 in one year.

Transforming your culture holistically is a long-term venture. The exercise presented in Scene 1 is the first step.

PLOT

To infuse and energize an entire organization with the Dream, Believe, Dare, Do principles—and thus launch them toward previously unimagined success.

RUNNING TIME

Unlimited

KEY PLAYERS

- Chief Executive Officers
- Department Heads
- Team Leaders

PROPS

Dreamovations Creating the Dream, Believe, Dare, Do Culture handout (Exhibit 1-1)

DIRECTOR'S SCRIPT

LIGHTS ...

1. Predistribute the *Dreamovations* Creating the Dream, Believe, Dare, Do Culture handout to all Leadership Team Members.

CAMERA ...

2. Assemble the Leadership Team.

ACTION!

3. Champion and discuss the following guidelines for implementing *Dreamovations*: Dream, Believe, Dare, Do. Don't conduct the session as an academic lecturer, but rather as a fervent believer, supporter, and promoter of "business-is-show-business" passion.

Act I—Setting the Stage: Dream

- Invite the team to share their achievements, disappointments, hopes, ambitions, and blue-sky visions of the future they would love to see.
- Help kindle and maintain a spirit of "united we stand, divided we fall."

- Promote a free-flowing exchange of ideas and dreams, now and every day.
- Validate the ideas of all team members.

Act II—Reaffirming the Values: Believe

- Demonstrate your own confidence in the team's ability to achieve ultimate success.
- Affirm that core beliefs and values are a team's compass, guiding them to find the knowledge, wisdom, and courage to make the best decisions every time.
- Help new team members immerse themselves in the team's beliefs and values.

Act III—Launching the Dream: Dare

- Grant team members creative freedom to take risks.
- Evaluate every project that goes "wrong" in terms of:
    - What problems did we face?
    - How can we readdress and solve those problems as a team?
    - Can we resurrect this project?
    - How can we do this better in the future?
- Be ready, willing, and able to accept and embrace change; it's the only way to grow.

Act IV—Getting Things Done: Do

- Generate plans that involve all team members, foster cooperation, and instill mutual trust.
- Attend carefully to team members' individual development, because each person's own progress is essential for team success.
- Celebrate every checkpoint and milestone reached, remembering that the longest journeys begin with single steps.

4. Return to the *Dreamovations* Creating the Dream, Believe, Dare, Do Culture handout.

Champion and discuss its recommendations for:
- initial leadership activities and actions;
- the next level of leadership implementation activities.

5. Make plans for an initial *Dream Retreat*®. (See Scene 3.)

CURTAIN CALL

Walt Disney, the shrewd, bold businessman, began his career as a commercial artist. Only a businessperson with the soul of an artist and a dreamer's heart could have brought us ...

When you wish upon a star,
Your dreams come true.

Dream	Activity	Desired Outcomes	Follow-up Actions	Responsibility
	Dream Retreat® - Leadership	Identified: • Vision or Story • Core Strengths • Values • Objectives • Stakeholders	Communicate vision, core strengths, values, and stakeholders to all coworkers	Leadership Team
		Identified potential barriers to accomplish vision	Require all departments to submit feedback	
		Best of Show Action Plan to remove barriers	Revise vision and action plans based on feedback	
		Team member appreciation of unique personality styles; having fun		
		Initiate benchmarking study, if needed		

Believe – You Better Believe It	Activity	Desired Outcomes	Follow-up Actions	Responsibility
	Dream Retreat® - Departmental	Mission completion		Department Managers
		Aligned department missions and tactics with company vision	Measure decisions against missions	
Never a Customer, Always a Guest	Dream Retreat® - Customer Service	Identified Customer Service Policy: • Guest • Setting • Delivery • Service Goal	Communicate customer service policy to all	Leadership Team
		Defined system for every coworker to collect customer feedback	Analyze customer feedback and encourage coworker participation	

EXHIBIT 1-1 (CONTINUED)

All for One and One for All	***Dream Retreat®** - Organizational	• Elimination of functional departments; creation of a process-focused organization • Colocated teams • Individual rewards linked to team achievements	Conduct periodic team-building activities	Leadership Team
Share the Spotlight	***Dream Retreat®** - Partnering	• Key suppliers identified • Potential customer problems identified • Initial supplier retreats scheduled	Conduct supplier retreat	Designated Product Teams

Dare	*Activity*	*Desired Outcomes*	*Follow-up Actions*	*Responsibility*
	Crazy Idea Presentations	One "Crazy Idea" implementation per quarter	Promote "Crazy Idea" concept to all coworkers	Leadership Subteam
	Celebrate failures	Evaluation of failed projects; celebration for effort		Leadership Subteam

EXHIBIT 1-1 (CONTINUED)

Do – *Capture the Magic with Storyboards*	*Activity*	*Desired Outcomes*	*Follow-up Actions*	*Responsibility*
	Annual Storyboard Feedback	Ideas from all regarding the progress of the organization	Communicate changes that occur as a result of storyboard activity	Leadership Team
	Dream Retreat® - Communication Plan	Formal communication plan that defines who, what, when, and how communications are made to all	Monitor implementation of the communication plan	Leadership Team
Practice, Practice, Practice	*Dream Retreat*® - Orientation	Implementation plan for reinventing the orientation process for all new hires	Monitor implementation of the new orientation process	Leadership Team
	Dream Retreat® - Development Planning	Identified processes for: • Ongoing "Good Show"/ "Bad Show" Feedback • Annual 360° feedback for all • Development planning process for all	Begin implementation with Leadership Team; become a role model for the processes	Leadership Team
Make the Elephant Fly – Plan	*Dream Retreat*® - Project Planning	Process for project implementation that is used by all	Provide training on the process and champion the use of inexpensive prototypes	Leadership Subteam
Give Details Top Billing	*Dream Retreat*® - Details	"Details Squad" appointed to: • Evaluate effectiveness of processes • Reinvent processes as necessary	Monitor and act on "Details Squad" recommendations	Leadership Team

SCENE 2: TRUE NORTH

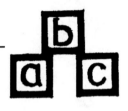

It's kind of fun to do the impossible.
—Walt Disney

AUTHORS' NOTES

One might ask, however: Isn't it futile to dream of the impossible? Isn't it a waste of time? We say no: Dreams ignite the spirit, put fire in the belly, provide a compass heading to orient you in your quest. Dreams unite and align you with your team members in a common pursuit. Dreams are Oz, Olympus, Elysium, and Disney. Dreams are true north.

Without dreams, we settle for the status quo instead of imagining "what could be." Walt Disney imagined what a carnival really could be. His dream resulted in hundreds of millions of people experiencing the fantasy and larger than life experience of what is widely known as the Theme Park.

Still, you could dream all day long and never get past your front gate.

That's where the *Dreamovations* process comes in: mapping the route, provisioning the expedition, and budgeting time, materials, and fuel.

Dreams are just dreams, until *Dreamovations* makes them come true.

The True North exercise is adapted from Stephen R. Covey's *Seven Habits of Highly Effective People* seminar, October 1991.

PLOT

To become aware that a team's collective success requires the orientation of all team members toward a common goal.

RUNNING TIME

5 minutes

KEY PLAYERS

- Natural Work Team Leaders

PROPS

- Compass (optional)

DIRECTOR'S SCRIPT

LIGHTS, CAMERA ...

1. Assemble the team in a workshop setting.

ACTION!

2. Ask everyone to stand up and close their eyes.

3. While their eyes are closed, ask them to point and turn to face north.

4. Ask everyone to open their eyes. In most teams, individuals will be facing toward nearly every point on the compass. (See Illustration 2-1.)

5. On the compass, show that the needle points to true north.

Illustration 2-1

CUT!

6. Discuss:

■ the use of true north by navigators and commercial airline pilots to track airborne progress against a flight plan;

■ similarities between piloting an airplane and conducting a team project;

■ similarities between true north and a team's guiding vision;

■ the difficulty, if not impossibility, of accomplishing missions and goals when teams lack a collective orientation toward the results to be achieved.

CURTAIN CALL

The importance of every team member having focused, true north expectations may be illustrated by many successful teams, but none better than Whirlpool's Global No-Frost Team. Leader Jerry McColgin decided to launch his team's project by holding a strategic *Dream Retreat*. During those five days in the snow covered hills of Brown County, Indiana, this dedicated team of people developed their game plan. Jerry had specific ends in mind: to establish a culture; for team members to understand his expectations; and most of all, to inspire a 100 percent focused effort by every member. Jerry's True North navigation was the key to his team's phenomenal success.

SCENE 3: DREAM RETREAT®

"If you dream it, you can build it."
—Walt Disney

AUTHORS' NOTES

Build what? Shared vision. Sustaining values. Mutual cooperation, trust, and respect. Alignment between individual, team, and corporate goals.

How? By coming together to exchange ideas, knock heads, shake hands, brainstorm, have fun, reexamine team and corporate values, break down barriers, have fun, formulate strategy, redesign processes, venture beyond the comfort zone, have fun, plot change, push the envelope, have fun.

... Did we say have fun? (If the exercises don't pump you up enough, the nightly karaoke, dart tournaments and laser tag games will.)

This *Fieldbook* contains the exercises that are the core of a typical *Dream Retreat®*—though in fact there is no "typical" *Dream Retreat®*. Each one is as unique as its participants. What *is* typical is everyone relaxing and feeling safe enough to share what is uppermost in their minds and deepest in their hearts.

Shakespeare's Hamlet said, "To sleep, perchance to dream."

We say, "To *retreat*, perchance to dream."

Correction: Forget "perchance"—it's a sure thing.

PLOT

To engage in blue-sky thinking to generate effective business strategies.

RUNNING TIME

Two days to a full week

KEY PLAYERS

- Any team with one or more of the following goals:
  Visioning
  Project planning
  Problem solving
  Decision making
  Goal setting or team building

PROPS

- Storyboard materials (see Scene 30)
- Team-building exercise materials as needed
- Proposed outcome statement (one for each participant)

DIRECTOR'S SCRIPT

LIGHTS ...

I. Prepare a document containing your thoughts on the desired outcome of the retreat, or a definition of the problem to be solved by the team.

CAMERA ...

2. Distribute copies of the document to the team members at least five working days prior to the retreat.

3. Reserve a retreat location where your team will be totally removed from their daily work environment.

Notes:

- An off-company site liberates participants to brainstorm, strategize, and solve problems in ways they never imagined before. Such innovative thinking and planning can literally revolutionize a culture.

- "Dreaming" in this context is not a solitary occupation. Instead, the power of communal intelligence, team spirit, creative conflict, storyboarding, and group fun creates a fertile atmosphere in which collective dreams arise.

ACTION!

Overture

4. Start the *Dream Retreat*® by reviewing your own desired outcomes for the retreat as contained in the document you previously distributed to the team.
5. Invite team members to share their individual, personal goals for the retreat.
6. Record the team members' goals on a flip chart.
7. Invite the team members to express team goals for the retreat.
8. Ask the team members to consider their individual, personal goals in context with the overall team goals.

Act I: Dream

9. Collate, synthesize, and formalize the desired outcome(s) in one of the following forms:
   - a vision statement,
   - a mission statement,
   - a definition of the culture, or
   - a story of what the organization might look like in five years.

The Storytelling and Storyboarding sections of the *Fieldbook* (see Scenes 5 and 30) are useful tools to encourage input from all stakeholders.

10. State that the desired outcomes as expressed above are the team's *Dream*.

Act II: Believe

11. Compare and contrast the team's *Dream* with the values or beliefs of the organization. If a formal set of organizational values or beliefs does not exist, use Storyboarding to identify them.

12. Use the Vision Align® exercise (see Scene 7) to analyze how the team's *Dream* can contribute to the overall success of the organization.

Act III: Dare

13. Identify risks and barriers that might hinder or prevent the realization of the *Dream*. Use Storyboarding to quickly identify, record, and prioritize barriers and risks.

Act IV: Do

14. Help the team establish plans to reduce or remove barriers and to minimize or eliminate risks.

15. Establish time frames for the completion of each task and the achievement of the ultimate goal.

16. Identify required resources.

17. Assign individual team members to specific tasks.

18. Confirm *who* will do *what* by *when*.

CUT!

19. At the conclusion of the *Dream Retreat*®, lead the team in reflecting upon their experiences by asking these questions:

- What did we accomplish?
- What new insights, strategies, and techniques did we gain from this process?
- Could or should we have done anything different as a team?
- What will be our next step?
- What are our most exciting upcoming opportunities?

CURTAIN CALL

Dreams can be shared with your team members,
Compared with their dreams,
Sharpened, modified, strengthened, and enhanced,
Then used to help create a team vision,
To be aligned with organizational goals
That are strategically plotted and pursued
And cheered when they are achieved,
So you can go back to your own private place
And dream again.

Walt Disney's stellar accomplishments might suggest that he had no difficulty in taking whatever action was needed to bring his dreams to fulfillment.

SCENE 4: DEVELOPING THE "BEST SHOW" EXPERIENCE FOR YOUR GUESTS

In the beginning was the plan.

And then came the assumptions.

And the assumptions were without form.

And the plan was completely without substance,

And darkness was upon the faces of the workers.

And they spake unto their marketing managers, saying,

"It is a pot of manure, and it stinketh."

And the marketing managers went unto the strategists and saith,

"It is a pile of dung, and none may abide the odor thereof."

And the strategists went unto the business managers and saith,

"It is a container of excrement, and it is very strong,

and such that none may abide by it."

And the business managers went unto the director and saith,

"It is a vessel of fertilizer, and none may abide its strength."

And the director went to the vice president and saith,

"It contains that which aids plant growth, and it is very strong."

And the vice president went unto the senior vice president and saith,

"It promoteth growth, and it is powerful."

And the senior vice president went unto the president and saith,

"This powerful new plan will actively promote the growth and

efficiency of the company and the business in general."

And the president looked upon the plan and saw that it was good.

And the plan became policy.

—Author Anonymous

AUTHORS' NOTES

The author of that poem has apparently observed many of the same organizations we have encountered, where lofty visions, vague strategy statements, and proforma financial statements bear little resemblance to actual day-to-day operations. Self-flattering companies forget that they are indebted first and foremost to their customers, not to their own self-image. In contrast, since 1928 the Walt Disney Company has been steadfast in the pursuit of their ultimate goal, "To provide the finest in family entertainment."

Businesses today have two choices:

- Offer a commodity product, compete on price alone, and pray that a profitable cost structure can be maintained; or ...
- Create a unique experience that far surpasses customers' basic requirements, and thus fulfills their dreams.

The first option is cheaper and simpler. It's the house brand, plain vanilla approach. The second way demands a full commitment of thought, time, and effort—and serious money, too. It's more a Ben and Jerry's Cherry Garcia banana split approach.

It boils down to this: You can just show up, or you can put on a "good show"—then work overtime to make it the "best."

The Disney organization epitomizes "best show." They and all of their cast members are fully committed to business-as-show-business, giving equal attention to the guest experience, the cast experience, and bottom-line business results.

Other companies, operate on a piecemeal basis, cutting costs in slack seasons and helping the cast only when times are good. They don't bow to the customers until the booing starts, and by then it's too late. The "strategy of the month" tactic mortgages the future for fleeting short-term results.

The future belongs to those who *Dream, Believe, Dare,* and *Do.*

PLOT

To develop and fine-tune an organization's performance so that it balances the guest experience, the cast experience, and the financial results.

RUNNING TIME

Two to five days

KEY PLAYERS

■ Leadership Team

PROPS

■ Developing the "Best Show" Experience for Your Guests Overview handout (one per participant) (Exhibit 4-1)

■ Developing the "Best Show" Experience for Your Guests Management Structure handout (one per participant) (Exhibit 4-2)

■ Appropriate guest survey results

■ Cast ideas and suggestions storyboard or document

■ Financial information

■ Competitive benchmarking data

■ Process Evaluation team data

DIRECTOR'S SCRIPT

LIGHTS, CAMERA ...

1. Assemble the Leadership Team.

ACTION!

2. Discuss the "Best Show" planning concept.

3. Discuss the "Best Show" Experience for Your Guests Overview.

Act I: Dream

■ Thoroughly review your guests' experience with your organization. Focus on:

- Guests' main problems with your product or service.
- All contacts between guests and cast members—the "moments of truth."
- Benefits you can expect when guests enjoy and applaud your "Best Show" performance.

Act II: Believe

- Thoroughly review your cast's experience with your organization. In addition to employees, include consideration of potential partners with whom strategic alliances have been or may be forged. Focus on:
  - Cast members' views of the main barriers blocking achievement of legendary service.
  - Your most important potential or existing strategic partnerships.
  - Benefits you can expect from improving your performance.

Act III: Dare

- Assess the risks and the benefits of striving to put on a "Best Show" performance.
- If appropriate, undertake Competitive Benchmarking or Process Evaluation studies. (See Scenes 39 and 40.)

Act IV: Do

- Generate a "Best Show" plan, including methods for all departments to receive and deliver feedback. (See Exhibit 4-3.)
- Develop a system to monitor improvements in the following areas:
  - quality of the guest experience,
  - quality of the cast experience, and
  - key financial results.
  4. Review the Developing the "Best Show" Experience for Your Guests Management Structure handout.

5. Assign team leaders to the following subteams:

- Guest Experience
- Cast Experience
- Competitive Benchmarking (if needed)
- Process Evaluation Team (if needed)

6. Ask subteam leaders to estimate the time they will need to obtain data in their respective areas.

Notes:

- Significant time will be needed if the subteam members have not gathered this type of information before. To save time, the leadership team may use preliminary results to prepare a "Best Show" Plan.
- Gain the subteams' commitment to regularly monitor and update their data.

7. Plan a *Dream Retreat*® (see Scene 3) with the following agenda:

- Review and discuss the subteams' reports.
- Revise strategy and plan actions to make the improvements recommended in the reports.
- Assess the costs and benefits of making these improvements.
- Develop or reaffirm the guiding vision.
- Prepare the "Best Show" Plan and include the following:
  - Guest Experience Measurements
  - Cast Experience Measurements
  - Improvement Goals
  - Financial Results Tracking
- Budget sufficient time to implement the plan

Note: The subteams may expect to spend 60 to 80 percent of their time in this effort.

8. Determine how the subteams will communicate the "Best Show" Plan to all departments, and how they will gain feedback. Determine how each department will provide this feedback. Ensure that team and departmental goals align with overall corporate objectives.

Note: The *Vision Align*® tool (see Scene 7) is very effective in meshing team, departmental, and corporate goals.

CUT!

9. Meet with the Leadership Team two months after implementation of the plan has begun. Check the leaders' focus on the plan's objectives and reaffirm their dedication to success.

Thank everyone for committing 60 to 80 percent of their time to this effort, which is critical to achieve continuous long-term improvement.

CURTAIN CALL

What drives your strategic planning? Finances, market share, and new product development? Do you genuflect to stockholders alone?

Take note: Only when you enable your cast to give the "best show" to your customers and guests will your company achieve full vitality, stability, and growth.

The Technical Assistance Research Program in Washington, D.C. reports that over two-thirds of customers—68 percent—leave suppliers due to poor service. Poor quality is the reason in only 14 percent of cases. High price is cited just 9 percent of the time.

These numbers tell the tale, but too many companies are tuned out. Even those paying lip service to the "best show" ideal proceed as if cutting costs and tweaking products are all that customers really want. They treat their customers merely as buyers, instead of as honored guests. They ask them to part with their money, instead of showing them the time of their lives.

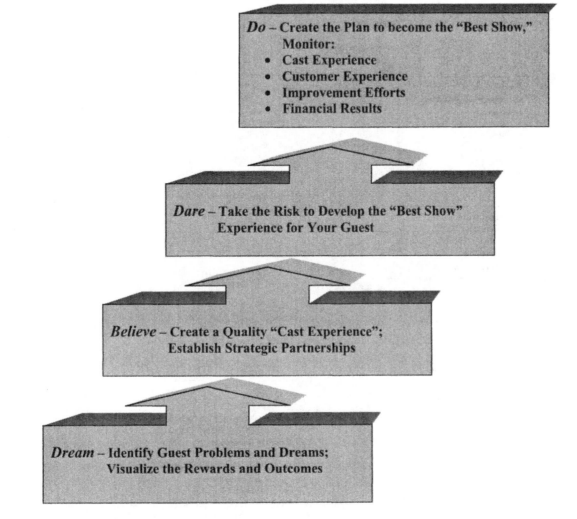

Do – Create the Plan to become the "Best Show,"
Monitor:
- Cast Experience
- Customer Experience
- Improvement Efforts
- Financial Results

Dare – Take the Risk to Develop the "Best Show"
Experience for Your Guest

Believe – Create a Quality "Cast Experience";
Establish Strategic Partnerships

Dream – Identify Guest Problems and Dreams;
Visualize the Rewards and Outcomes

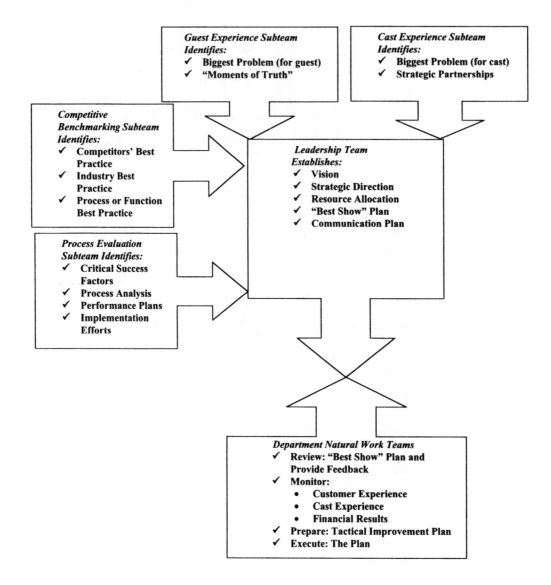

Guest Experience Subteam Identifies:
- ✓ Biggest Problem (for guest)
- ✓ "Moments of Truth"

Cast Experience Subteam Identifies:
- ✓ Biggest Problem (for cast)
- ✓ Strategic Partnerships

Competitive Benchmarking Subteam Identifies:
- ✓ Competitors' Best Practice
- ✓ Industry Best Practice
- ✓ Process or Function Best Practice

Leadership Team Establishes:
- ✓ Vision
- ✓ Strategic Direction
- ✓ Resource Allocation
- ✓ "Best Show" Plan
- ✓ Communication Plan

Process Evaluation Subteam Identifies:
- ✓ Critical Success Factors
- ✓ Process Analysis
- ✓ Performance Plans
- ✓ Implementation Efforts

Department Natural Work Teams
- ✓ Review: "Best Show" Plan and Provide Feedback
- ✓ Monitor:
  - • Customer Experience
  - • Cast Experience
  - • Financial Results
- ✓ Prepare: Tactical Improvement Plan
- ✓ Execute: The Plan

EXHIBIT 4-3
DEVELOPING THE "BEST SHOW" EXPERIENCE
FOR YOUR GUESTS

The "Best Show" Plan

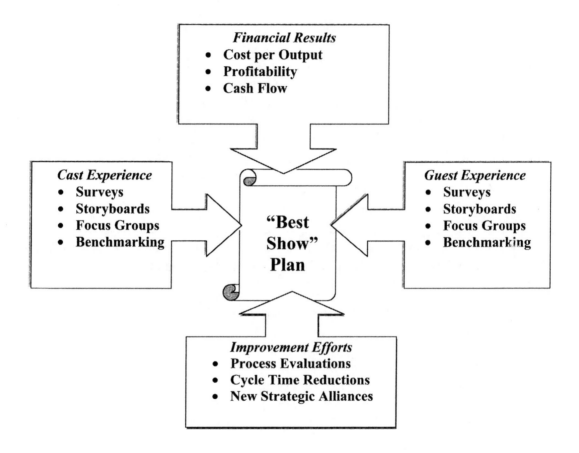

Financial Results
- **Cost per Output**
- **Profitability**
- **Cash Flow**

Cast Experience
- **Surveys**
- **Storyboards**
- **Focus Groups**
- **Benchmarking**

"Best Show" Plan

Guest Experience
- **Surveys**
- **Storyboards**
- **Focus Groups**
- **Benchmarking**

Improvement Efforts
- **Process Evaluations**
- **Cycle Time Reductions**
- **New Strategic Alliances**

Achieving "Best Show"

A certain manufacturing company was facing bankruptcy due to runaway warranty costs, high turnover, and massive customer complaints. Desperate, they sold their plant. The new owners made virtually no changes in personnel or equipment, and after five years showed these results:

- Warranty costs were reduced from $22 million to $3.5 million.
- Complaints (within the first 90 days of purchase) were down from 70 percent to 7 percent.
- Personnel turnover was lowered from 30 percent to 1 percent.

How did the new management work this "magic"? First, by honoring their "cast members" as proficient, highly motivated self-starters who could upgrade the quality of their own work. (In one example, line workers were trusted to manage the assembly production process, and to improve it as they saw fit.) With the "cast" in high gear, the whole "show" gained new life. Customers who had suffered from the old management's shoddy service now felt like guests invited to a command performance. Pretty soon the line for tickets stretched around the block. This "revival" was a hit.

Disney's Commitment to Balance the Cast Experience and the Guest Experience with Business Results

In 1994, Frank Wells, president of the Walt Disney Company, was killed in a helicopter crash during a ski vacation. Later that year, Chairman and CEO Michael Eisner suffered a near-fatal heart attack.

At that time, Michael Ovitz was a very successful Hollywood talent agent and one of Eisner's best friends. As an agent, Ovitz's single-minded focus was on getting the best business deals; he had little concern for cast members or guests. This was a very un-Disney-like attitude, to say the least. Nevertheless, Eisner asked Ovitz to be the new Disney president, to fill Wells's place. Apparently, he thought his friend could suddenly switch from a business-first mentality to one in which cast and guests were the stars of the show.

Vain hope. Ovitz brought his short-term, bottom-line obsessions with him and wouldn't let them go. After 18 months, his myopic strategies threatened the whole Disney culture and ethic, in Eisner's view. Eisner had no choice but to fire him before more damage was done.

What was Ovitz's biggest regret? Being unable to realize he couldn't change Disney's organizational culture. Contrast this with Eisner's main fear upon becoming chairman: that he might not uphold the longstanding, successful culture that was already in place.

Ovitz had the last laugh in one sense: He won a $120 million contract buyout settlement in court. But with Ovitz gone from Disney, Eisner was the one breathing the big sigh of relief.

Checklist for Transforming the Cast Experience into "Best Show"

✓ Using the Storyboarding Technique (see Scene 30), ask cast members:
- What are the barriers that prevent you from providing legendary customer service?
- Who are your most important outside suppliers?

✓ Conduct storyboard sessions at least once a year. Conduct at least one session for each key business process.

✓ In large organizations, avoid unmanageably large groups by assembling representative employees.

✓ Analyze the information. Identify:
- common barriers to providing legendary customer service;
- quick fixes to remove barriers;
- key supplier partnership relationships that need improvement.

Checklist for Transforming the Guest Experience into "Best Show"

✓ Review internal perceptions of guests' concerns.

✓ Identify potential service and product quality problems.

✓ Develop a field survey program:
- Designate distribution channels.
- Select market segments (regional, metropolitan).
- Select customers (from an overall pool of current, past, and non-customers).
- Determine specific information to be obtained.
- Determine preliminary survey techniques (written, Internet, phone, and in-person interviews).
- Field-test survey techniques with selected customers.
- Revise and finalize the survey instrument.

✓ Perform the field study.

✓ Analyze the information:
- Identify common factors that influence buying preference.
- Identify common factors that do not influence buying preference.
- Identify common problems your customers experience regarding your product or service.
- Identify common dreams and desires of your customers.
- Develop profiles of customer problems and requirements.
- Distinguish profiles by regions, metropolitan areas, distribution channels, or specific customers.

SCENE 5: TELLING THE STORY

The fable is the best storytelling device ever conceived.
—Walt Disney

AUTHORS' NOTES

Parents tell their young children stories at bedtime to prepare them for sleep and sweet dreams. At our seminars and *Dream Retreats*®, storytelling also brings sweet dreams: of new products, ventures, and processes, even of entire new corporate cultures. But far from inducing sleep, these stories jolt and awaken everyone's creative faculties.

Clearly, this isn't business as usual. Instead of receiving mandates from on high, team members are involved in gestating initiatives from the start, fleshing them out in storyboards and planning their implementation. What a departure from traditional management by decree!

Our Telling the Story exercise isn't simply theoretical. We turn participants into employees of a fictitious company, Swings and Things, and challenge them to create a new, imaginative product to revive lagging sales. Don't just recycle old ideas, we encourage them; dream large! The concepts that emerge are always astonishing, and in most cases, practical enough to actually work.

Most striking of all, though, is the immediate and fervent commitment of all team members to the project. Within 15 minutes of starting, they're all acting like full-fledged Swings and Things employees.

Walt Disney engaged his cast members in storytelling, and their commitment was—and is—legendary.

Storytelling isn't magic. It just produces magical results.

PLOT

To allow participants to engage in the Dream principle without the fear of being laden with the typical business paradigms, such as project planning, cost containment, and feasibility studies.

RUNNING TIME

Two to four hours

KEY PLAYERS

- Any team with the will and desire to dream

PROPS

- Assorted colored paper
- Crayons
- Markers

DIRECTOR'S SCRIPT

LIGHTS, CAMERA ...

1. Assemble the team in a comfortable and casual environment, preferably at an off-site location.

2. Describe the following fictional company:

   Swings and Things is a manufacturer of steel swings and slides. Founded in 1953, the company scored early success selling playground equipment to schools. In the 1980s they added the day care and municipal park markets. In the past two years, though, sales have declined. The marketing department believes that a new product line based on some theme or story will reverse the downward trend. They have enlisted your team to help create the product line.

   Note: Working in a fictional company allows participants to feel safe about experimenting and thinking creatively, as opposed to potentially falling into the traditional mind set of a real-world company.

3. Challenge the team to develop a theme or story that will be the basis for the new product line.

4. State that each team member should be assigned a specific role in the group creative process.

5. Inform the team:

- Colored paper and markers may be used for sketching ideas.

- The team's theme or story will be shared aloud at the end of the session.

- A picture is worth a thousand words.

ACTION!

6. Allow 15 minutes for the team to work on this exercise.

7. When time is up, invite the team to present its theme or story to you.

8. After you have heard the team's theme or story, share the following Swings and Things Story with them:

In a land where children reign and adults are merely occasional visitors, a playground emerges. First come swings that seem to soar above the clouds; then come slides that gently transport their tiny passengers to earth. One day, the children invite the neighboring adults to help them create a new land: One in which King Arthur, Casey Jones, Jules Verne, and Walt Disney are likely visitors; one whose pleasures far surpass mere swinging and sliding; one where creativity and a fanciful sense of fun prevail for kids and grownups alike.

Note: As an alternative, you may create and share a story of your own.

9. Compliment the team on creating a story for a company they knew nothing about just 15 minutes ago. Challenge them to imagine how creative they could be with the products, processes, or services of their own company, which they know through and through!

10. Challenge the team to develop a story for their own real company. The story may be to revive an existing product, process, or service, or it may be to create something brand new.

11. Tell the team to develop the story without regard to any business obstacles, limitations, or restraints.

12. Allow unlimited time for this activity, but tell them you will check their progress after 45 minutes have elapsed.

13. Have the team predetermine how they will present their story to you, and potentially to others in their organization.

14. Tell the team to begin.

15. After 45 minutes, check progress and permit a 10-minute break.

16. Reconvene the team to complete the story.

17. When the story has been completed, ask the team to share it aloud with you.

CUT!

18. Help the team determine the next steps. Ask them:
   - What barriers might prevent your story from coming true?
   - How could you remove these barriers so your Dream becomes reality?

19. Remind the team that Walt Disney once said, "If you can Dream it, you can Do it."

CURTAIN CALL

There is nothing as powerful as an idea whose time has come. Your job is to make sure that when the time comes, the ideas do, too.

Time comes (and goes) on it's own, of course. Ideas often need help. By Telling the Story, you can sow great ideas, fertilize them, and watch them blossom forth.

In the end, your success is the real story, and the author is *you*.

SCENE 6: MISSION DEVELOPMENT

Reflect before you act.
—Mulan, *Mulan*

AUTHORS' NOTES

In the above context, you might ask, "Reflect on what?" In successful companies, people align their actions with the focus of the mission. The dictionary defines "mission" as:

1. A specific task that a person or group of persons is sent to perform.

2. An assigned or self-imposed duty or task.

3. Military: An operational task, usually assigned by a higher headquarters.

4. Rocketry: a. A rocket flight or trip. b. The tasks, tests, experiments, etc. that such a flight or its astronauts are to perform.

Let's hold onto that rocketry-astronaut image. As a team leader, you are something of a NASA controller, launching and guiding your cast members on missions into business blue sky.

Before launch, though, you must plan the flight. This means enlisting your team to help write a Mission Statement that boldly and concisely articulates:

- Who we are.
- What we are doing.
- What value we are creating for our guests or customers, or partners, our organization, and ourselves.
- Where we are headed.

Without such a Mission Statement, your team will lose trajectory and fall out of orbit.

With a Mission Statement, your course will lead, as the astronaut Buzz Lightyear says in *Toy Story*, "to infinity and beyond."

PLOT

To create a "living" mission statement by answering a structured set of key questions.

RUNNING TIME

Two to four hours

KEY PLAYERS

- Natural Work Team Leaders

PROPS

- Flip chart
- Blue and red markers
- Tape or pins

DIRECTOR'S SCRIPT

LIGHTS ...

1. At the top of four respective flip chart pages, write the following questions:

Page 1
What function does the team perform?
What products or services does the team provide?

Page 2
Who are the team's ...
- Customers?
- Guests?

- Partners?
- Critical stakeholders?

Page 3

How does the team go about fulfilling its function?

What methods are being used?

Page 4

Why does the team exist?

What is the payoff for the team?

CAMERA ...

2. Assemble the team in a comfortable environment far removed from their daily responsibilities.

ACTION!

3. Post the flip chart pages side by side.

4. Starting with Page 1, ask team members to answer the questions on the pages. Write the answers on the flip charts.

5. Ask the team which questions and answers are most important to them in their work. Mark the ones they identify with an asterisk.

6. Ask for volunteers to draft a mission statement based on the flip chart data. Set a date for completion of the draft.

CUT!

7. On the mission statement completion date, reassemble the team and review the first draft of the statement.

8. Evaluate the mission statement using the following criteria:

- Does it cite an "end result" as well as a "means"?
- Does it involve all critical stakeholders?
- Does it address key areas of need (e.g., economic, psychological, "walking the talk")?

- Will it stand as a "living" document that will ensure buy-in from all affected stakeholders?

9. Make revisions with the entire team, or ask new volunteers to write a second draft. Repeat the process until the team is satisfied with the result.

10. Challenge the team to consider:

- how the mission statement will be communicated to all stakeholders;

- what method(s) will be used to "cement" the statement into the organization.

CURTAIN CALL

I think, therefore I am.

We think, therefore we are.

We write a Mission Statement, therefore we *know* who we are, as well as:

- what we are doing;

- what value we are creating for our guests or customers, our partners, our organization, and ourselves;

- where we are headed.

SCENE 7: VISION ALIGN®

Alignment is the essence of management.
—Fred Smith, CEO of Federal Express

AUTHORS' NOTES

Fred Smith gets it. Unfortunately, too many managers in America do not. As Fred Smith further observes, "Most managers don't know what management is about."

Part of the problem, we believe, is that managers have lacked an effective diagnostic tool for evaluating departmental missions so that they fit with and thus promote their organizations' visions and values.

Vision Align® changes all that. As leaders who have used this tool attest, *Vision Align®*:

■ helps integrate short-term activities with longer-term visions;

■ allows an organization's overall objectives to cascade down through the various staff levels to the natural work teams;

■ eliminates top-down interference, thus promoting seamless change;

■ creates a detailed process for executing a strategy;

■ provides a basis for sharing information and authority;

■ fosters team creativity;

■ keeps employees focused;

■ establishes a mechanism for timely and accurate feedback on problem issues;

■ enhances teams' sense of their own contributions to organizational success, thus increasing morale and commitment to achieve project goals.

Aligning departmental and organizational missions is a skill that takes practice to acquire. Our *Vision Align®* exercise gives you the practice you need to start.

PLOT

To ensure that departmental missions and projects are directed toward accomplishing the visions and objectives of the overall corporation.

RUNNING TIME

One-half to one full day

KEY PLAYERS

■   Natural Work Team Leaders

PROPS

■   *Vision Align®* Worksheet Example (Exhibit 7-1)

■   Pleasure Island Original Vision Worksheet (blank) (Exhibit 7-2)

■   Pleasure Island Original Vision Worksheet (precompleted) (Exhibit 7-3)

■   Pleasure Island New Vision Worksheet (Exhibit 7-4)

■   *Vision Align®* Worksheet (blank) (Exhibit 7-5)

DIRECTOR'S SCRIPT—VISION ALIGN® WORKSHEET EXAMPLE

LIGHTS ...

1. Organize the overall group into teams of 7 to 10 members.

CAMERA ...

2. Distribute the *Vision Align®* Worksheet Example to all team members.

ACTION!

3. Explain:

- The elements entered under each of the column headings (Core Strengths, Values, Objectives and Stakeholders) are for demonstrational purposes. Only one element is shown here in each column. An actual *Vision Align®* Worksheet would have multiple elements in each.
- The elements entered under the column headings Core Strengths, Values, and Objectives should come from the corporate leadership team.

Note: These elements can be extracted from the corporate strategic plan, vision statement, or annual report.

- Each departmental team can determine for itself what elements to enter under the last column heading, Stakeholders.

4. The matrix is completed by:
- discussing the intersection of each row and column;
- determining whether the two intersecting elements are:
  a) an obvious fit,
  b) a potential fit,
  c) an area of concern, or
  d) totally unrelated (leave blank);
- recording the appropriate icon for each intersection.

For example, a smiley face was entered at the intersection of "Better Quality" and "Customer Service Lab," since a customer service lab will likely contribute to better quality.

DIRECTOR'S SCRIPT—PLEASURE ISLAND WORKSHEETS

LIGHTS ...

1. Maintain the same teams.

CAMERA ...

   2. Distribute the blank Pleasure Island Original Vision Worksheets.

ACTION!

   3. Explain:

- Pleasure Island, a nightclub complex at Disney World, opened in 1989. Shortly after opening, guests began to complain about alcoholic beverages being served to teenagers. This practice, they felt, undermined Disney's wholesome family image. Disney took immediate action by assembling a group of cast members who used a worksheet similar to *Vision Align*® to analyze the problem.

   4. Discuss Disney's:

- Core Strengths
- Values
- Objectives
- Stakeholders

   5. Explain the Key Mission Points of the Original Pleasure Island:

- *Entire Family Experience*: Ensure an enjoyable time for all family members.
- *Increased Evening Revenues*: Attract the many Disney guests who seek evening entertainment at non-Disney properties.
- *Nighttime Entertainment in the Disney Image*: Enable guests to continue their Disney experience during the evening hours.
- *Nonsecured, Walk-in Environment*: Maintain Pleasure Island as a non-gated, walk-in attraction open to anyone.

   6. Instruct team members to assume the roles of Disney cast members in 1989, shortly after Pleasure Island has opened. Have them complete the worksheet matrix by:

- discussing the intersection of each row and column;

- determining if the two intersecting elements are:

  a) an obvious fit,

  b) a potential fit,

  c) an area of concern, or

  d) totally unrelated (leave blank);

- placing the appropriate icon in the intersection boxes.

Note: For illustration, the first intersection has already been filled in: The smiley face icon symbolizes that "Provide Legendary Service" and "Entire Family Experience" are obvious fits.

7. Allow 15 minutes to complete the exercise.

Note: As long as several icons are showing at intersections by the end of the time, not all boxes need to be discussed.

8. Distribute the completed Pleasure Island Original Vision Worksheets.

9. Compare each team's own completed worksheet with the precompleted worksheet you have just distributed.

Note: Make the point that many of the Areas of Concern were concentrated on the Nonsecured, Walk-in Environment and the Entire Family Experience.

10. Distribute the Pleasure Island New Vision Worksheets.

11. Explain that this diagnostic tool helped Disney change Pleasure Island in the following ways, as reflected in the revised Vision/Mission Key Points:

- "Entire Family Experience" became "Adult Experience."

- "Provide Nighttime Entertainment with the Disney Image" became "Provide Nighttime Entertainment for Ages 22 to 45." (Also, several nightclubs that did not meet the Disney image standards were closed.)

- "Nonsecured, Walk-in Environment" became "Secured, Gated Environment."

Note: The actual detailed Pleasure Island alignment diagnostic tool appears on page 53 of *The Disney Way*.

DIRECTOR'S SCRIPT—VISION ALIGN® WORKSHEET (BLANK)

LIGHTS ...

1. Maintain the same teams.

CAMERA ...

2. Distribute the blank *Vision Align®* Worksheets.

ACTION!

3. Instruct the teams to identify 3 to 5 respective Core Strengths, Values, Objectives, and Stakeholders of their own company. Have them enter this information under the appropriate column headings on the blank *Vision Align®* Worksheet.

Note: The corporate leadership group should provide most of this information.

4. Instruct the teams to identify the key 4 or 5 points of their department's vision or mission, and to record these on the *Vision Align®* Worksheet under Vision/Mission Key Points.

5. Ask the teams to examine each row and column intersection, and to determine the degree of fit.

Note: Encourage open and honest expression of differing views and opinions.

6. Allow several hours, as needed, to complete the exercise.

7. Call a time-out when the teams need a break.

8. If the teams need reenergizing, engage them in a brief, fun exercise, as time permits.

CUT!

9. When the matrix is completed, debrief by asking these ....
   - Are there many areas of concern in the intersections?
   - Are you fully utilizing your core strengths?
   - Are you supporting all your values?
   - Do you have sufficient means to meet all your objectives?
   - Are you meeting the needs of your stakeholders?

10. Ask how the teams might revise their team or departmental missions or launch new projects as a result of this analysis. Have the teams assign responsibilities for achieving these new goals, including initial and follow-up actions and documentation of results.

CURTAIN CALL

Question:
What are the three keys to successful management?

Answer:
- Alignment.
- Alignment.
- Alignment.

Question:
What is the prime operational benefit of alignment?

Answer:
- Maximally effective contribution of departmental initiatives to organizational objectives.

Question:
What are the bottom-line benefits of alignment?

Answer:
- Optimized efficiency and economy.
- Industry-leading quality.
- Dramatic boosts in revenues, profits, and growth.

HANDOUT

EXHIBIT 7-1
VISION ALIGN® WORKSHEET EXAMPLE

☺ Obvious Fit ? Potential Fit X Area of Concern Vision/Mission Key Points	Core Strengths	Values	Objectives	Stakeholders
	Customer Focus Lab	*Innovation*	*Foster Coworker Development Planning*	*Coworkers*
Better Quality	☺	☺		?
Faster Cycle Times		☺	X	
Lower Costs	?	?	X	
Fun Place to Work		?	☺	

HANDOUT

EXHIBIT 7-2
PLEASURE ISLAND ORIGINAL VISION WORKSHEET

☺ Obvious Fit
? Potential Fit
X Area of Concern

Vision/Mission Key Points	Core Strengths	Values	Objectives	Stakeholders
	Provide Legendary Service	Dare to be Different	Protect the Image	Entire Family
Entire Family Experience	☺			
Increase Evening Revenues				
Provide Nighttime Entertainment with the Disney Image				
Non-secured, Walk-in Environment				

EXHIBIT 7-3
PLEASURE ISLAND ORIGINAL VISION WORKSHEET

HANDOUT

Obvious Fit ☺ / Potential Fit X				
Area of Concern Vision/Mission Key Points	Core Strengths *Provide Legendary Service*	Values *Dare to be Different*	Objectives *Protect the Image*	Stakeholders *Entire Family*
Entire Family Experience	☺		☺ X	☺ X
Increase Evening Revenues	☺		☺	☺
Provide Nighttime Entertainment with the Disney Image	☺	☺	☺ X	☺
Non-secured, Walk-in Environment	☺ X	☺ X	X	

55

EXHIBIT 7-4
PLEASURE ISLAND NEW VISION WORKSHEET

	Core Strengths	Values	Objectives	Stakeholders
Area of Concern / Vision/Mission Key Points	Provide Legendary Service	Dare to be Different	Protect the Image	Entire Family
Provide an Adult Experience	☺	☺	X	?
Increase Evening Revenues	☺		☺	?
Provide Nighttime Entertainment for ages 22 to 45	☺	☺	?	
Provide a Secured, Gated Environment	☺			

Legend:
☺ Obvious Fit
? Potential Fit
X

EXHIBIT 7-5
VISION ALIGN® WORKSHEET

☺ Obvious Fit ? Potential Fit X Area of Concern **Vision/Mission Key Points**	Core Strengths	Values	Objectives	Stakeholders

57

SCENE 8: DEMONSTRATING DREAMOVATIONS

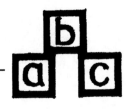

A journey of a thousand miles must begin with a single step.
—Lao Tzu

AUTHORS' NOTES

Even minor business changes can be slow to take effect. No wonder full-scale cultural transformations can try the patience of even managerial saints. Be forewarned, therefore, that the metamorphoses driven by the *Dreamovations* principles will not culminate overnight, or even next week. In fact, if your company is large and encrusted with old paradigms and attitudes, it may take three to five years for the new culture to permanently take root.

It's worth the wait.

Remember, Dream, Believe, Dare, and Do is not a hot new paradigm of the month. It has guided the Disney organization for many decades. The time it takes to revolutionize your company will be time well spent.

PLOT

To demonstrate how values and principles must be incorporated into daily activities in order to develop long-lasting, positive work habits.

RUNNING TIME

5–10 minutes

KEY PLAYERS

- Natural Work Team Leaders

PROPS

- One two-quart container with lid, filled to within 1" of the top with aquarium gravel
- One empty two-quart container with lid
- Four Ping-Pong balls, labeled respectively:
    - Dream
    - Believe
    - Dare
    - Do

DIRECTOR'S SCRIPT

LIGHTS, CAMERA ...

1. Seat the team around a table.
2. Place the empty container on the table.
3. State that the empty container represents a vessel to hold all the things we do in a typical day.
4. Place the filled container on the table. State that the gravel-filled container represents all the tasks we accomplish in a typical day.

ACTION!

5. Ask the team members to call out some of their own daily tasks (e.g., answering phones, filling customer orders, etc.).
6. For each task called out, add some gravel to the empty container.
7. When the container is filled, put on the lid.
8. Observe aloud that everything seems to fit very well into a typical day.
9. Take the lid back off the container.
10. Now say the team will have to fit four new things into their day—the four Ping-Pong balls, representing:

- Dream of all the possibilities that haven't been tried before.
- Believe in the values of the organization.
- Dare to make a difference.
- Do create plans to achieve the dreams.

11. Have the team place the balls on top of the gravel in order of Dream, Believe, Dare, Do. (See Illustration 8-1.)

12. Try to put the lid back on the container. Clearly, it won't close.

13. Ask: "What can we eliminate from the typical day so these balls will fit?"

14. Pick up the empty container. State that we will now begin applying the Dream, Believe, Dare, Do principles in all areas of our work.

Illustration 8-1

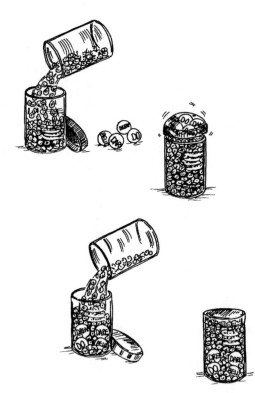

15. Place the four Ping-Pong balls in the empty container.

16. Pour the gravel over the Ping-Pong balls.

As you pour, recite the list of the team members' daily activities.

17. When the jar is full, close the lid. (See Illustration 8-1.)

CUT!

18. Observe aloud that the Dream, Believe, Dare, Do principles serve best not as an overlay but as the underlying, internalized foundation of our daily activities and our lives.

CURTAIN CALL

Early on, Walt Disney infused his work with the personal values that also came to define his company. To assure the most efficient transformation, management must model the desired behavior from the start. They must make all forward progress palpable to employees, and make the benefits concrete. Transformation cannot be viewed in the abstract. The *Dreamovations* principles must be assimilated and internalized so they are fuel for action, not just food for thought.

Act II: Believe

When we consider a new project, we really study it—not just the surface idea, but everything about it. And when we go into that new project, we believe in it all the way.

—Walt Disney

SCENE 9: BRIDGE BUILDING

Every guest is a VIP.
—Disney Traditions

AUTHORS' NOTES

At Disney, this is not a meaningless slogan. It comes as little surprise to us how often organizations say they put the customer first, but they have no clue what the customer wants, or worse, who the ultimate customer is. Far too many companies produce magnificent products that ignore customer specifications, and provide services that nobody wants. In the end, their work is for naught.

How does this come to pass? Many teams tell us they are made to work to management's specifications instead of the customer's. We've even heard of production being started before anyone knew who the customer was—or if the customer existed at all!

One pharmaceutical company had been conducting a major nutritional testing program for years. No one knew who the testing was for, when it had begun, or why it should proceed. A retiree was asked to identify the original customer, but he had no clue. When the company halted the program, no customer came forth to protest. Apparently there never was a customer! The company's embarrassment was only exceeded by its sense of relief.

Walt Disney knew instinctively what his guests wanted. Disney's understanding of his guests coupled with his innate drive for perfection meant that audiences got more than they ever knew they wanted, whether in watching his stories unfold on the silver screen or visiting his magical Theme Parks.

If your company is never confused about its customers' needs and specifications, you can sit out the Bridge Building exercise. However, if you need to clarify and strengthen your relationships with customers and suppliers, it's time to rally your team.

PLOT

To plan, design, and construct a bridge that meets a customer's needs.

RUNNING TIME

One hour

KEY PLAYERS

- Any team responsible for developing strong customer relationships

  Note: A team for this exercise should have 10 members maximum and 4 members minimum. If there are more than 10 individuals in the overall group, form an additional team or teams.

PROPS

- Tinker Toys, separated into bags containing:
  - 12 red rods
  - 11 purple rods
  - 9 orange rods
  - 5 blue spools
  - 9 green connectors
  - 10 blue rods
  - 24 yellow spools
- Two tables plus one table per team
- Tape measure or yardstick
- Tonka truck weighing five pounds
- Tub with a lid large enough for the truck to be hidden from the team
- Bridge Building General Instructions handout (one per participant) (Exhibit 9-1)

- Bridge Building Cost Factors sheets (one per participant plus two for exercise leader) (Exhibit 9-2)
- Bridge Building Template sheets (one per participant) (Exhibit 9-3)
- Bridge Building Team Results Summary sheet or overhead transparency (Exhibit 9-4)
- Stopwatch or watch with second hand
- Overhead projector and screen (optional)

DIRECTOR'S SCRIPT

LIGHTS ...

1. Hide the Tonka truck in a nearby location outside the meeting room.
2. Hide the Tinker Toys within the room.

CAMERA ...

3. Assemble the team around a large table. If you have more than one team, each team should have its own table.
4. State the objective of the exercise: To design and build a Tinker Toy bridge that will support five pounds of weight at its center.
5. Distribute to all team members:
   - Bridge Building General Instructions handouts; (The General Instructions are intentionally vague and are intended mainly to prompt questions.)
   - Bridge Building Cost Factors sheets; (Keep a master copy for yourself.)
   - Bridge Building Template sheets.
6. Do not say anything about the Tonka truck.
7. Announce that you will allow 10 minutes for initial planning, during which the team must do the following:
   - Choose certain members to design the bridge and certain other members to build it according to the design.

- Complete the first 5 items on the Bridge Building Cost Factors sheets, estimating costs according to:
    - Design time @ $500 per minute
    - Construction time @ $300 per minute
    - Construction Pieces @ $100 to $600 each, as itemized at the bottom of the Cost Factors sheet.

8. When the team has finished planning, instruct the Designer group to do the following:
    - Produce two "blueprint" views of the bridge.
    - Adhere to the following minimum bridge dimensions: 18" long × 3" wide.
    - Vacate the construction site during the construction phase.

9. Instruct the Constructor group to do the following:
    - Use only one hand while building the bridge;
    - Vacate the Designers' area during the design phase.

ACTION!

Design phase

10. Tell the Constructors to vacate the Designers' area, and the Designers to begin their work.
11. Begin timing the Designers.
12. When the Designers have completed two "blueprint" views of the bridge, stop timing.
13. Announce the elapsed design time and record it on your own Cost Factors sheet.
14. Collect the Designers' Cost Factors sheets.
15. Record the Designers' Cost Factors estimates on your master Costs Factors sheets, and then on the Bridge Building Team Results Summary sheet or overhead transparency.

Construction phase

16. Give the Constructors one bag of Tinker Toys.

17. Tell the Designers to vacate the construction site, and the Constructors to begin their work.

18. Begin timing the Constructors.

19. Remind Constructors that they can only use one hand to build the bridge.

20. Make sure that construction follows design specifications.

21. If the Constructors have too few pieces to build the bridge according to the design specifications, tell them they have two options:

■ Ask the Designers to modify the design so the bridge can be built with the number of pieces available. If this option is taken, time the additional design work and record this time on your own Cost Factors sheet.

■ Buy all extra construction pieces from you at a rate of $200 per shipment or request.

22. When the Constructors have completed the bridge, stop timing.

23. Announce the elapsed construction time and record it on your own Cost Factors sheet.

24. Complete your Cost Factors sheet by filling in all actual costs.

Note: Actual design and construction costs are per worker. (This is for your own awareness. Do not clarify it now for the team.)

25. Transfer all data on your Cost Factors sheet to the Bridge Building Team Results Summary sheet or overhead transparency.

CUT!

26. If you have an overhead projector, project the Bridge Building Team Results Summary onto the screen.

27. Debrief the exercise by asking:

■ Did you lose money on this job? If so, why?

69

Teams usually have many excuses for losing money. (Very few teams come out ahead!)

- Who was your customer for the bridge?

  You will see a lot of blank stares, and hear comments like:

  - "We never saw the customer."
  - "You didn't tell us about the customer."

28. Retrieve and show the Tonka truck for everyone to see. (See Illustration 9–1.)

29. Reveal that this is the customer's truck, and the bridge was meant to support its 5-pound weight.

30. Ask:

- What do you notice about the truck?

  Typical comments will be:

  - "It's a whole lot bigger than three inches wide!"
  - "It's not what we were expecting!"

Illustration 9-1

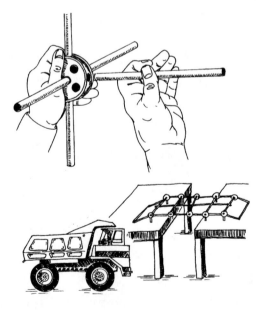

31. Ask:

- Why didn't you ask to see and speak to the customer? Almost always, they will say, "We thought you were the customer!"

32. Ask:

- What other assumptions did you make? Other assumptions may be:
- The Tinker Toy template was to scale. (Which they now realize it was not.)
- The design and construction costs were per team and not per individual worker.

33. Discuss:

- What happens when we act based on what we assume the customer wants?
- What happens when we forget about the customer altogether?

If more than one team participated in the exercise:

34. Ask:

- Which team would have been awarded the job? The likely answer will be: The team with the lowest estimated costs.

35. Put two tables together, 18" apart.

36. Place the Tinker Toy bridge so it spans the tables.

37. Set the Tonka truck on the center of the bridge.

38. Applaud the team's design and construction efforts whether the bridge holds the truck or collapses under its weight.

CURTAIN CALL

If you don't know your customers or what they want, the only way to achieve legendary customer service is by accident.

EXHIBIT 9-1
GENERAL INSTRUCTIONS

HANDOUT

Once the estimate is prepared, the Designers will prepare the design. They may not start designing the bridge until the Construction workers are out of the room.

Design a bridge with a minimum length of 18" and a minimum width of 3" that will support a weight of five pounds at its center. You have been given a blank design sheet and a template.

The design, with at least two views complete, must be finished along with cost estimates, before you take it to the construction workers. The design should be clear to the construction workers, but exactness is not necessary.

Once the design is completed, the construction time begins when the Designers leave the room. Remember, the bridge must be able to support a five-pound weight at its center, and you can only use one hand to construct.

Follow the design, but if you feel it will not work, is not strong enough, is too expensive, or is too time consuming, you may ask the designers to change it. (They may not change the material and labor cost estimates, but they may change the design itself.) You are not finished until the design and the model match.

There are three cost factors:

- Design time costs $500 per minute
- Straight-time construction labor costs $300 per minute
- Materials cost from $100–$600 each

Each construction worker may use only one hand during the construction. Construction workers cannot design and designers cannot build. The team will select designers and construction workers. While the design is being prepared, the construction workers cannot be in the room. Likewise, when construction is taking place, the designers cannot be in the room.

EXHIBIT 9-2
BRIDGE BUILDING COST FACTORS

Team # _____

Factor	
1) Estimated material cost	
2) Estimated design cost	
3) Estimated construction cost	
4) Total	
5) Total estimate	
6) Actual material cost	
7) Actual design cost	
8) Actual construction cost	
9) Total actual cost	
10) Profit (loss)	

Construction Piece	Cost Per Piece
Spool	$200
Connector	$100
Rod, Red	$300
Rod, Blue	$400
Rod, Purple	$500
Rod, Orange	$600

73

EXHIBIT 9-3

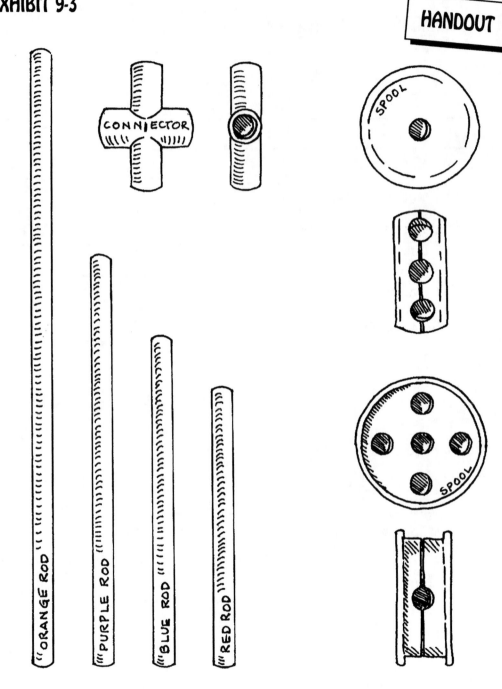

EXHIBIT 9-4
BRIDGE BUILDING TEAM RESULTS SUMMARY

	1	2	3	4	5	6
Estimated Material Cost						
Estimated Design Cost						
Estimated Construction Cost						
Total						
Total Estimate						
Actual Material Cost						
Actual Design Cost						
Actual Construction Cost						
Total Actual Cost						
Profit (Loss)						

SCENE 10: CUSTOMER SERVICE CHECKUP

If you're not serving the customer, you'd better be serving someone who is.

—Karl Albrecht and Ron Zemke

AUTHORS' NOTES

What's the difference between a gazelle and an antelope? Don't ask us. Ask any of Disney's Animal Kingdom Park cast members. With three days of animal identification training under their belts, they can answer you on the spot. With a smile.

Have they been trained in how to smile, too? No, that comes naturally. Disney hires people who truly like people. But since good nature alone does not create a "good show" for guests, Disney thoroughly orients its personnel in all aspects of Disney services, products, and images.

This is no "meet and greet" briefing like so many organizations provide before sending their troops out to sell. That's because Disney cast members are not "selling" the Disney experience, they are enabling guests to enjoy it to the fullest—which in the end means seeing them smile.

Would you like to see more smiles on your customers' and guests' faces? Do you wish you could give them more of what they want?

What *do* they want? How profound and detailed is your awareness of their needs and dreams?

The Customer Service Checkup will help you find out.

PLOT

To learn a structured approach to evaluating customer service.

RUNNING TIME

One hour

KEY PLAYERS

- Any team that seeks to develop long-lasting relationships with customers by continuously striving to roll out the welcome mat

PROPS

- Flip chart
- Storyboard materials
- Hotel Chain Seminar Lunch Example (one per participant) (Exhibit 10-1)
- Six Steps to Create Your "Whole Show" handouts (blank; one per participant) (Exhibit 10-2)

DIRECTOR'S SCRIPT

LIGHTS ...

1. On the first page of the flip chart, prepare two columns titled Positive and Negative.
2. On the second page of the flip chart, write the heading: Ideal Doctor's Visit.

CAMERA ...

3. Assemble the team in an area conducive to creativity.

ACTION!

4. Ask team members to think of their last trip to the doctor's office.
5. Have the team members record their "images" of their doctor's visits on a piece of scrap paper.
6. Allow one minute for recording of images.
7. Ask for volunteers to share their images with the team.
8. Record the participants' images under the appropriate column on the first flip chart page. Typical negative responses will include "Long wait," "Doctor never on time," etc.

9. Ask the team to imagine the "ideal" doctor's visit.

10. Record responses on the flip chart page headed "Ideal Doctor's Visit."

11. Discuss:
    - The image that doctors project to patients.
    - How doctors could improve their image, and thus promote patient satisfaction with their services.

12. Ask the team to describe its own customer image.

13. Ask if the team's sense of its image is purely subjective, or is based on customer feedback on their performance.

14. Discuss customer service in general, with attention to the following:
    - The importance of customer expectations.
    - That creating legendary service goes beyond taking care of customers' expressed needs and demands.
    - That customer service means creating an environment that encourages listening to every customer's problems and dreams.
    - That every business is really show business, because nearly every customer, or guest, perceives even the most "hidden" aspects of your operations and forms lasting impressions of your entire "show."

15. Distribute the Hotel Chain Seminar Lunch Example handouts to the participants.

16. Describe the Six Steps to Create Your "Whole Show" that this hotel chain used to evaluate its lunchtime service to seminar participants:

Know the Customer
- Who are your customers or guests?
- What are their problems and needs?

Know the Service
- What are your values associated with providing the finest service?

Know the Setting
- How does your environment promote a "good show"? (i.e., how does it positively affect the service?)
- How does your environment promote a "bad show"? (i.e., how does it negatively affect the service?)

Deliver the Service
- What aspects of your service most require evaluation?
- By what criteria will you evaluate them?
- How will you conduct the evaluation?

Train the Cast
- Which employees, or cast members, need to learn new skills?
- How will you train them?

Remove the Barriers
- What complaints are you hearing from customers or guests?
- What actions are you taking to address the complaints?

Note: This six-step approach is similar to the one used by the Disney organization.

17. Distribute the blank Six Steps to Create the "Whole Show" handouts to the team.
18. Ask the team to consider its own real-world services, and to select the two that are most important to their customers.
19. Instruct the team to fill in the "Whole Show" handouts with regard to the two services they have selected.
20. Give team members the option of either filling in the handouts individually, then discussing them as a team, or completing the exercise as a team from beginning to end.
21. When the "Whole Show" handouts have been completed, discuss:

- How can we improve our customer service image regarding these services?
- What actions must we take to make these improvements?
- By what date must these improvements be made?
- Who will be responsible for taking the required actions to make the improvements?
- Does our image regarding other services need to be reviewed and improved?

CURTAIN CALL

Do the math:

Knowledge of customers' needs and dreams
+ Well-rehearsed cast
+ Service with a smile
= "Good Show"

EXHIBIT 10-1
HOTEL CHAIN SEMINAR LUNCH EXAMPLE

Know the Customer—Who are your customers or guests? What are their problems and needs?

Customer	Service	Customer Needs	Customer Problems	Comments
Seminar Participant	Lunch	Tasty Nutritious	Have personal time to check with office	

Know the Service—What are your values associated with providing the finest service?

Service	Desired Image	How is Service Delivered	Service Values (in priority order)	Competitive Advantage/ Disadvantage
Lunch	Service meets quality of fast food	Hotel staff delivers lunch to participants	Safety Courtesy Quality Efficiency	Heart healthy menu /limited number of entrees

Know the Setting—What are the elements of your environment in terms of "good show" (positively affect the service) or "bad show" (negatively affect the service)?

Your Values	"Good Show"	"Bad show"	On Stage or Backstage	Comments
Safety	Tray Racks		On and Back	
Quality		Warm Iced Tea	On	

Deliver the Service — What criteria are worth measuring, and what method(s) will you use to measure them?

Service	What to Measure	How is Service Measured	Ideas to refine measurements and involve all cast members in guest feedback
Lunch	Did participants like food?	Participant evaluation	Cathy to conduct focus group with participants

EXHIBIT 10-1
HOTEL CHAIN SEMINAR LUNCH EXAMPLE (CONTINUED)

HANDOUT

Train the Cast--Which cast members or employees need to learn new skills? How will you provide their training?

Service	Skill	Training Method	Who Attends
Lunch	Communication	Team role plays; feedback	Conference Center Staff

Remove the Barriers--What complaints are you hearing from guests or customers? What actions are you taking to remove existing barriers?

Most Frequent Customer Complaint	Barrier to Meeting Customer Needs	Actions to Remove Barriers
Slow Service	Hotel staff failed to communicate a ten minute delay in serving lunch, and how they were resolving the problem	1. Inform seminar leaders any problem which may negatively affect their session, and let them know how the hotel staff will rectify the situation.

EXHIBIT 10-2
SIX STEPS TO CREATE YOUR "WHOLE SHOW"

Know the Customer--Who are your customers or guests? What are their problems and needs?

Customer	Service	Customer Needs	Customer Problems	Comments

Know the Service--What are your values associated with providing the finest service?

Service	Desired Image	How is Service Delivered	Service Values (in priority order)	Competitive Advantage/ Disadvantage

EXHIBIT 10-2
SIX STEPS TO CREATE YOUR
"WHOLE SHOW" (CONTINUED)

HANDOUT

Know the Setting--What are the elements of your environment in terms of "good show" (positively affect the service) or "bad show" (negatively affect the service)?

Your Values	"Good Show"	"Bad Show"	On Stage or Backstage	Comments

Deliver the Service--What criteria are worth measuring, and what method(s) will you use to measure them?

Service	What to Measure	How is Service Measured	Ideas to refine measurements and involve all cast members in guest feedback

EXHIBIT 10-2
SIX STEPS TO CREATE YOUR
"WHOLE SHOW" (CONTINUED)

Train the Cast--Which cast members or employees need to learn new skills? How will you provide their training?

Service	Skill	Training Method	Who Attends

Remove the Barriers – What complaints are you hearing from guests or customers? What actions are you taking to remove existing barriers?

Most Frequent Customer Complaint	Barrier to Meeting Customer Needs	Actions to Remove Barriers

Getting Intimate with Customers

Fred Wiersema, coauthor of *The Discipline of Market Leaders*, believes that superior customer service is a requisite for market leadership. Fred, who also wrote the foreword to our best-selling book, *The Disney Way: Harnessing the Management Secrets of Disney in Your Company*, warns that unless customer intimacy is achieved, a company's operational excellence and product leadership may be for naught.

Becoming intimate with customers starts with learning their "stories." According to a 1997 article in *Fortune* magazine, highly successful companies gain more from customer storytelling than they do from focus group sessions and other traditional market research.

Intuit customers, for example, told stories that suggested their need for a new money management system. Intuit software writers took note and produced just the product these customers had in mind. (This proves that non-entertainment companies can indeed profit from Disney's "show business" storytelling approach.)

Kimberly-Clark visited parents of children of toilet training age and heard that "older" toddlers were embarrassed to wear diapers. Huggies Pull-Ups was the company's immediate and wildly successful response.

Unfortunately, many companies don't listen this carefully to customers' stories. They spend more on marketing efforts to attract new business than on protecting the existing customer base. This makes no sense, because gaining one new customer costs five times as much as keeping an existing one. In fact, many studies show that a 1 percent rise in customer retention boosts profits by 4 percent.

How can you keep customers happy and loyal? Here's our advice:

Treat your employees as well as you treat your customers.

Employees enjoy solving customers' problems and helping them meet their dreams. They're flattered and empowered when management trusts them to do so, and gives them the leeway to do it in their own way.

Employees who are happy in their work transmit their joy to customers, engendering loyalty along the way. And happy employees stay with their organizations. Why leave a place that honors your special talents and clearly needs you for its own success?

Listen to your customers' stories and dreams.

Teach your employees to solicit and make notes on everything customers say. Customers' response to your performance can be the most important feedback you ever get.

Make customer retention your employees' number-one priority.

Your customers are your guests. Your relationship with them is gold. All your employees must preserve, protect, and defend that relationship with every smile, gesture, and word.

SCENE 11: CODE OF CONDUCT

The first thing in a visit is to state your name and business. Then shake hands.

—Tweedledum, *Alice in Wonderland*

AUTHORS' NOTES

In Disney's famous Traditions orientation where cast members learn the origin of the rich fabric upon which every Disney attraction is based, they learn something equally important: Cast members are an integral part of the total performance. However, they cannot be left totally to their own devices in dealing with each other and with guests. It is the leader's job to communicate to them clearly and concisely how he or she expects them to behave.

Does this mean the leader is a dictator decreeing how they should act?

Think of it this way: Is the person in the theater who helps actors learn their parts and rehearses them thoroughly so they're prepared for opening night a dictator?

No, that person is a director, whose mission is not to suppress individual talent, but to let it shine.

One example of how Disney cast members practice their code of conduct "treat your customers as you would a guest in your own home, and always refer to them as a guest" occurred when we were visiting Walt Disney World with a group of clients.

After checking into the hotel, we quickly departed for dinner. While riding along in one of the Disney Transportation buses, the driver asked us if we liked our rooms. One guy in our party mentioned to the driver that his bar sink had a continual drip that he feared might keep him awake at night, but said that he didn't have time to call maintenance. The driver quickly replied, "Sir, I'll take care of it for you."

After returning from dinner late that evening, our colleague discovered that his bar sink was perfectly dry. This level of service is expected behavior for cast members, all with a ready smile. The bus driver had truly learned to live the Disney code of conduct.

PLOT

To create a set of working principles to guide the quest for customer service excellence.

RUNNING TIME

One-half to one full day

KEY PLAYERS

- Leaders
- Team members

PROPS

- Storyboard supplies
- Flip chart
- Markers

DIRECTOR'S SCRIPT

LIGHTS, CAMERA ...

I. Assemble the team in a comfortable location, preferably away from the company site.

ACTION!

2. Provide the following Code of Conduct examples:

We Create a Friendly Atmosphere

- We always wear a smile.
- We use friendly, courteous phrases when we speak.
- We maintain a neat, professional appearance.

- We never complain or mention operational or personal problems in the presence of customers.

We Give the Personal Touch

- We treat each guest as a special individual.
- We know that a single good or bad experience can form a guest's impression of our overall performance.
- We address guests by their names whenever possible.

We Know the Answers

- We respond cheerfully to all questions: immediately when we know the answers; as quickly as possible when we need to seek additional information.
- We do not send guests in circles or pass the buck when responding to customers' requests.
- We respond directly to telephone queries, and transfer calls only when absolutely necessary.

We Are a Team

- We maintain a friendly, informal atmosphere.
- We take our jobs seriously, but not ourselves. By having fun we help our guests have fun, too.
- We communicate freely and openly with each other and with our guests.

3. Ask team members to share examples of their own Code of Conduct behavior.

4. Write the examples on the flip chart.

5. If you wish, work with the team to create a Code of Conduct Storyboard (see Scene 30).

- Invite team members to answer the question: "What should our Code of Conduct be?"
- Have them write their answers on Storyboard cards, one answer per card.
- Allow 10 to 15 minutes of quiet time for this activity.

- Complete the storyboard by categorizing and prioritizing the cards.

6. Prepare a working draft version of the team members' proposed Code of Conduct.

7. Formulate a plan to:
   - Communicate the Code of Conduct to all stakeholders.
   - Receive stakeholders' feedback on the Code.
   - Disseminate the Code to employees (e.g., on laminated pocket cards, one per week, each focusing on one particular Code).
   - Establish a reward and recognition system for employees who memorize the Code of Conduct or whose on-the-job performance shows exemplary adherence to the Code.

8. Schedule a subsequent meeting to share and discuss stakeholders' feedback, and to prepare a final draft of the Code of Conduct.

CUT!

9. At the subsequent meeting, prepare the Code of Conduct final draft. Agree on a plan to communicate the final Code of Conduct to all stakeholders.

CURTAIN CALL

An effective Code of Conduct recognizes that everyone in the team or organization has a stake. This recognition, as reflected in the specific guidelines for behavior, promotes buy-in and faithful adherence in all groups.

Though a Code of Conduct cannot be a top-down decree, it is wise when setting behaviors for an entire organization to have the senior management team attend discussions from the start.

SCENE 12: LASTING PARTNERSHIPS

A good, strategic partnership can double the value of your company.

—James Attwell, Managing Partner, Private Equity
Venture Capital Practice, Price Waterhouse Coopers

AUTHORS' NOTES

Before James Attwell made that statement, his company researched 436 emerging businesses in the $50 to $100 million sales range. Their discovery: Only 43 percent of the businesses had strategic partnerships. Further investigation showed that those companies grew 31 percent faster than nonpartnering companies, introduced 79 percent more new products, and recouped their investment almost 20 percent faster.

EPCOT is a testimony to long-term partnerships. Even when CEO Michael Eisner and the late president Frank Wells assumed the leadership of the Walt Disney Company in 1984, Walt's original partnerships with Exxon, AT&T, and General Motors were still making great contributions to the Disney coffers.

With this proof of the benefits of dancing together, why tango alone?

Long-term partnerships forge mutual trust and commitment, and pool resources and strength; but ultimately they work for the partners because they work for the partners' guests. At the end of the day, if the guests aren't happy, the partners can't rejoice.

For most companies, the term "partner" means a supplier or customer. For especially progressive companies, strategic partners are cast members, guests, suppliers, schools, benchmark companies, and the community at large.

The Lasting Partnerships exercise puts you in the progressive class.

PLOT

To establish a partnership that will help create a "Best Show" experience for your guests and cast, and will lead to profitable financial results.

RUNNING TIME

One hour to discuss and develop a plan

KEY PLAYERS

- Leadership Team
- Any Natural Work Team wishing to establish a partnership

PROPS

- Workflow to Develop Lasting Partnerships (Exhibit 12-1)
- Storyboard materials (see Scene 30)

DIRECTOR'S SCRIPT

LIGHTS ...

1. Collect information on existing and potential partnerships. (See Scene 4.)

CAMERA ...

2. Assemble the Leadership Team.
3. Distribute the information on existing and potential partnerships.

ACTION!

4. Storyboard potential strategic partnerships with customers and suppliers. Use priority dotting to select the three partnerships that would most benefit the organization.

5. Discuss the merits of establishing or improving strategic partnerships with schools or the community.

6. Select strategic partnerships that will most benefit the organization.

7. Designate a Partnership Team Leader.

8. Draw up a preliminary budget for each potential strategic partnership.

9. Arrange for the Partnership Team Leader to meet with the Leadership Team.

10. Discuss Workflow to Develop Lasting Partnerships. Emphasize the importance of establishing compatible values with your partners. Be aware that:

   ■ If your organization values teamwork and your partner's company values individual competition, it may be difficult to develop a long-term partnership.

   ■ If compatible values are not achievable, your team should look for a new partnership.

11. If a partner's values are compatible with your company's values, determine the partner's willingness to commit the resources needed to create a "Best Show" experience. If the partner is unwilling or unable to commit the resources needed, your team should seek an alternative partnership.

CURTAIN CALL

Businesses of any type can form partnerships, but only parties that are willing to commit significant resources and that share similar values will achieve long-term success.

EXHIBIT 12-1
WORKFLOW TO DEVELOP LASTING PARTNERSHIPS

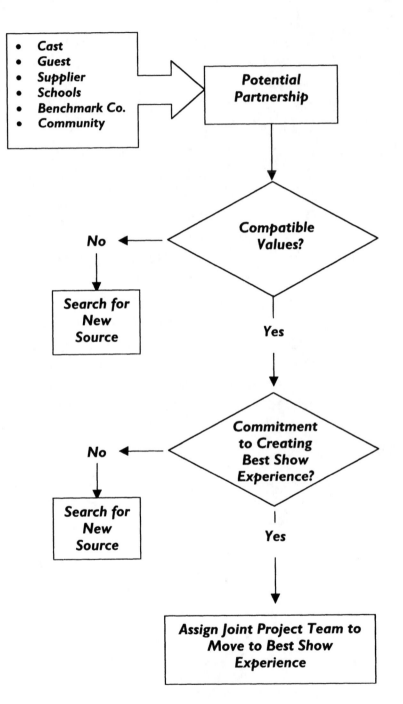

Supplier Partnership Case Study

The Situation:

- Packaging Material
- 20 Million per year
- $3 Million Direct Labor
- $2 Million Products per year
- 50,000 damaged products per year

The Values:

- Focus on Packaging As a Priority
- Team Approach
- Best of the Best
- Empowered to Make Change

The Process:

- Team Identification and Commitment
- Key Process Identification
- Process Workflow Diagrams Completed
- Process Improvements Approved
- Implementation Planned

The Results:

- Direct Labor Savings $160,000
- Service Call Reductions $570,000
- Material Reductions $1,133,000
- Cycle Time Reductions   5 Weeks

Why Partner with Schools

- Only 3 out of 4 high school students graduate.
- American business spends $30 billion on training workers in rudimentary reading and mathematics skills.
- By the end of the seventh grade, more than 50 percent of students view their teachers as adversaries.

SCENE 13: GROUPTHINK

Disney respects the ideas of all cast members, regardless of their level in the organization.
—A Disney Stores Manager

AUTHORS' NOTES

In a society and culture focused on individuality, it is amazing how often we are admonished to stay with the group ...

"There is safety in numbers."
"Get with the program."

Of course, we must act together to survive. But what is survival? Just going with the flow? And who controls the flow? Who steers its course?

Many people do, of course, but the many are comprised of individuals, each of whom has the ability, the power, and the *right* to think and act creatively.

Your team members are such individuals. So are you.

We're not advocating anarchy or preaching an ethic of "I, me, mine." We are, though, warning against groupthink, in which a herd mentality holds sway and consensus is compelled, or worse, faked.

In the early 1970s, Dr. Irving Janis of Yale defined groupthink as "a mode of thinking that people engage in when they are deeply involved in a cohesive in-group, when the members' striving for unanimity overrides their motivation to realistically appraise alternative courses of action."

A work team must ultimately reach a consensus, but that consensus must be a synthesis or distillation of varying inputs, not a stage-managed fait accompli. As a leader, your job is to solicit these multiple inputs and then guide discussion, moderate dispute, and negotiate compromise. The idea to expand the Walt Disney Company's retail presence into malls and shopping centers came from a member of Eisner's staff, Steve Burke.

Originally, Eisner didn't like Burke's suggestion, but he listened to the arguments and decided to give it a shot. His willingness to consider all points of view, particularly when they differed from his own, resulted in over 100 million dollars a year in revenues from Disney stores throughout the world.

PLOT

To provide an understanding of the danger in abiding by the old paradigm, "Silence facilitates consent"; to encourage teams to make decisions in a climate of openness, trust, and mutual respect.

RUNNING TIME

One to two hours

KEY PLAYERS

- Any team with the responsibility for making decisions

PROPS

- Flip chart
- Markers

DIRECTOR'S SCRIPT

LIGHTS ...

I. At the top of a flip chart page, write: Janis's Eight Symptoms For Identifying Groupthink.

Below this, write the symptoms:

- Illusion of Invulnerability—the feeling of power and authority
- Belief in Group Morality—the conviction that the team's actions are "right"
- Rationalization—understanding but downplaying the facts

- Shared Stereotypes—a belief in the character or nature of an outside group based on conjecture and unverified perception
- Self-Censorship—committing to a course of action simply to show team spirit or to support company policy
- Direct Pressure—open criticism of team members' differing opinions
- Mindguards—pertinent data withheld from decision-making consideration (by individuals inside or outside the team)
- Illusion of Unanimity—a belief that no doubts remain, and all team members are in agreement

2. On a separate flip chart page, write: Methods to Avoid Groupthink. Below this, write the methods:
   - Create an open climate where people are free to make candid comments and raise relevant questions.
   - Allow objective outsiders to meet with the team and challenge their decision-making process.
   - Ask for team volunteers to function as critical evaluators who challenge how the decision is being made.
   - As a team leader, refrain from pressuring the team or any member to make a quick decision or to agree with your viewpoints.
   - Offer to excuse yourself from one or more meetings during the decision-making process.

CAMERA ...

3. Assemble the team in an environment conducive to open discussion.

ACTION!

4. Present Janis's Eight Methods for Identifying Groupthink, using the previously prepared flip chart. Check for understanding of each of the eight symptoms before proceeding to the next step.

5. Share the following powerful historical examples of Group-think:

■ The Space Shuttle Challenger disaster of January 1986

Frustrated by highly publicized shuttle launch delays, NASA project managers met privately with engineering contractors in an attempt to accelerate their work. The contract engineers were concerned that the seals be-tween the SRB (solid rocket booster) joints might not withstand the low temperatures expected on the scheduled launch day. Accordingly, they proposed a fur-ther delay. NASA said no. Fearful of damaging their re-lationship with NASA, the contractor senior staff capit-ulated—with catastrophic results.

■ The Bay of Pigs Invasion

In April 1961, the Kennedy Administration landed 1,500 CIA-trained Cuban expatriates at a swampy site on the southern coast of Cuba. Their mission: to attack and overthrow Fidel Castro. The result: 300 expatriates killed and 1,100 taken prisoner after three days of futile fighting. This human disaster was a massive humiliation for the Kennedy Administration. At the time, Kennedy himself was viewed as the unwitting victim of poor ad-vice, but documents released in the 1990s suggest oth-erwise. Numerous advisers, in fact, told the President that the plan was risky at best, with only a 50 percent chance of success. Kennedy disdained these warnings and relied instead on overly optimistic CIA memos that were crafted to persuade the President to authorize the invading force.

6. Invite the team to share instances of groupthink symptoms and results from their own work experiences. Record their responses on the flip chart.

7. Challenge the team to consider what they might have done differently to avoid groupthink, and how they will act to avoid it in the future.

8. Present Methods to Avoid Groupthink, using the previously prepared flip chart.

9. Discuss the methods and compare them to those the team proposed to avoid groupthink in the future.

CURTAIN CALL

Question
What is groupthink?

Answer
In-group, conformist thinking that strives at all costs for unanimity and willfully ignores alternative points of view.

Question
What causes groupthink?

Answer
The human instinct to please other people and to remain included in the group.

Question
What are the benefits of groupthink?

Answer
None.

Question
What are the negative consequences of groupthink?

Answer
Tunnel vision, lackluster performance, reduced productivity, and lowered morale.

Questio
As a leader, how can you prevent groupthink?

Answer
By soliciting multiple inputs, honoring differing points of view, guiding discussion and moderating disputes impartially, and gaining true and willing consensus on the best course of action to take.

SCENE 14: THE DIME EXERCISE

Superior performance not only does not require competition; it seems to require its absence.

—Alfie Kohn, author of *No Contest: The Case against Competition*

Winning isn't everything, it's the only thing.

—Vince Lombardi, former Green Bay Packers coach

AUTHORS' NOTES

The two speakers don't seem to agree. Which one of them is right?

Considering the competitive ethic—the thrill of victory, the agony of defeat—Lombardi's view would seem to ring true. But think a minute: What is victory? The vanquishing of an opponent? Why not a job well done on its own terms? Why make some people losers? Why can't everyone win?

In fact, Vince Lombardi did make everyone win—every Packer, that is. Instead of spurring competition among his team members, he compelled intrateam cooperation so that the team as a unit could go out and trample the rest of the league. Boston Celtics coach Red Auerbach did the same thing, as do all great coaches, mentors, and leaders of human endeavor.

Indeed, Alfie Kohn cheers this approach. His research reveals that intrateam competition—between separate groups or within one group—hurts a team's ability to compete in the wider world.

David and Roger Johnson of the University of Minnesota concur. Their analysis of over 50 years of performance data in both competitive and cooperative environments leads them to conclude that cooperation produces far superior results.

"United we stand, divided we fall" could be Lombardi's, Kohn's, and the Johnsons' common rallying cry.

Walt Disney said, "Many hands, and hearts, and minds generally contribute to anyone's notable achievements."

PLOT

To determine which work environment—competitive or cooperative—produces more positive and lasting results.

RUNNING TIME

10–15 minutes

KEY PLAYERS

- Natural Work Team Leaders with teams of 8 or more

PROPS

- Four dimes
- Flip chart
- Marker

DIRECTOR'S SCRIPT

LIGHTS ...

1. Create two columns on the flip chart titled Group 1 and Group 2.

CAMERA ...

2. Divide the overall team into two groups. Ask the groups to form circles in opposite corners of the room.

Note: During this exercise, it is important to use the term "groups" instead of "teams."

3. Ask each group to select a leader. Explain that each leader will moderate the discussion within his or her group and communicate the group's decisions to you. If a group cannot reach consensus, the leader will make the decision.

4. Explain that as facilitator, you will:

- State the objective of the exercise.
- Present the rules of the exercise.
- Answer any questions before, but not after, the exercise begins.

5. Introduce the exercise by explaining and demonstrating that:

- You have four ordinary dimes.
- There will be four rounds. You will start each round by asking Group 1: "How much will you give me for this dime?" (Rounds 2 and 4 will start with Group 2.)
- Responses must be in increments of at least a penny.
- A group will have 1 to 2 minutes to decide upon a response, which may only be communicated to you by the group leader.
- After Group 1 responds, you will ask Group 2, "What will you give me for this dime?" Group 2 can raise Group 1's offer, or it can pass. If it raises the offer, you will return to Group 1 and ask the same question. The sequence will continue until one of the groups passes, at which point the process will stop.
- When one group passes, you will collect the money offered by the other group.
- You will record the money amount on the flip chart in the appropriate group's column. (See Illustration 14-1.)
- Ask the groups if they have any questions regarding the rules.

Remember:

a) Use the term "groups," not "teams."

b) Do not use the term "bidding."

c) Refer to this activity as an "exercise," not a "game."

6. When all questions are answered, state the exercise's objective: "To win as much as you can!"

Write the objective on the flip chart.

Illustration 14-1

ACTION!

7. Ask Group 1: "What will you give me for this dime?"

8. Proceed with the exercise as described above.

Note: Encourage the groups to discuss their strategies before making decisions on what amount to pay. If a group does not reach consensus after two minutes, call time and ask the leader for an immediate response. Create an atmosphere of excitement and urgency. Ignore any additional questions.

CUT!

9. Ask each group how much it won. (See Illustration 14-2.) Winnings are the net gain after subtracting what the group spent.

10. Ask each group: "How much could you have won?"

Note: The maximum a group could possibly have won is $.36, by paying only $.01 per round to win $.10, and thus paying $.04 over 4 rounds to win $.40. The $.04 expenditure, deducted from the $.40 won, would leave a $.36 net winning gain.

Illustration 14-2

11. If the groups did not win the maximum, ask: "Why didn't you win the maximum $.36?" Typical "excuses" are:

"We were competing with the other team."

"They kept bidding."

"You put us in a competitive situation."

"You put us on different sides of the room."

12. Remind the groups that you never used the terms "team," "bid" or "game." Point out that their "excuses" reflect a competitive attitude.

13. Discuss how competitive attitudes have been instilled in all of us since childhood.

CUT!

14. Debrief by discussing these ideas:

- Cooperating instead of competing with the other group would "win" the Dime Exercise, as well as win in a real-world work environment.

- The two groups are not opponents, but members of an overall team. (See Illustration 14-3.)

Illustration 14-3

- Working together works!
- Cooperation is the best practice for attaining healthy goals and achieving ultimate success.
- Teams must continuously be encouraged to engage in activities that lead to mutual goals and demonstrate mutual respect and trust.

CURTAIN CALL

Question
What are the three keys to a team's collective success?

Answer
- Intrateam cooperation.
- Intrateam cooperation.
- Intrateam cooperation.

Question
What are the prime internal benefits of intrateam cooperation?

Answer

- Peak individual performance.
- Coordination and mutual enhancement of individuals' work.
- Single-minded team focus.

Question

What is the prime external benefit of intrateam cooperation?

Answer

- Industry-leading competitive unit strength.

SCENE 15: MYERS-BRIGGS TYPE INDICATOR TEAM "BULLET"

Bee yourself.
—The Genie, *Aladdin*

AUTHORS' NOTES

Shades of teamwork are everywhere in Disney films, but none better illustrates Walt's belief in the value of collaboration than Snow White and the Seven Dwarfs. For many of us, those seven individual characters—Happy, Sleepy, Doc, Bashful, Sneezy, Grumpy, and Dopey—are treasured childhood friends. We remember them as a true team, always going off to work each morning whistling a happy tune. Walt intentionally embedded the concept of teamwork and cooperation into the script, with the dwarfs illustrating how different talents and personalities can be brought together to accomplish shared goals. Imagine if Snow White and the Seven Dwarfs had compared Myers-Briggs Type Indicator (MBTI® assessment tool) results.

Now imagine if David and Goliath had compared MBTI results.

Or the Road Runner and Wile E. Coyote.

Or John Dillinger and Elliot Ness.

Would the world have turned out differently? Perhaps not, but if differing personality preferences cause friction and disrupt communication in your workplace, the MBTI can make the future brighter for you.

Differing personality preferences can prematurely obstruct even the best potential relationships. Upon first meeting, people with opposite preference letters on all four MBTI scales typically experience some communication disconnects. While we concede that some relationships take more time and energy to develop than others, we know many people with opposing MBTI preference letters who have established harmonious and productive partnerships at work. They've done it by acknowledging their differences; identifying at least one value, interest, or activity shared by both; being good listeners; and providing constructive feedback from their respective points of view.

PLOT

Team members use awareness of their respective Myers-Briggs Type Indicator (MBTI® assessment tool) personality types to promote mutual understanding and communication.

RUNNING TIME

One-half to one hour

PLAYERS:

- Team members who have completed the Myers-Briggs Type Indicator and want to use their similarities and differences to build and strengthen their mutual relationships

PROPS

- Myers-Briggs Type Indicator results for all team members
- Master Team "Bullet" (one master copy plus one copy for each team member) (Exhibit 15-1)
- Myers-Briggs Characteristics Frequently Associated with Each Type (Exhibit 15-2)

DIRECTOR'S SCRIPT

LIGHTS ...

1. Confirm that all team members have completed the Myers-Briggs Type Indicator. Gather all members' results.
2. Thoroughly familiarize yourself with the theory and application of the Myers-Briggs Type Indicator.

Notes:

- Consulting Psychologists Press, Inc. is the exclusive publisher of the MBTI and maintains a strict code of ethics and procedures for purchasing, learning, and using the instrument.
- A few organizations that are quite helpful in providing resources on the MBTI instrument are: The Center for Application of Psychological Type (CAPT), a nonprofit organization in Gainesville, Florida, founded by the creators of the Myers-Briggs Type Indicator, provides invaluable resources to those who seek additional support in MBTI.
- The Association for Psychological Type (APT) provides a comprehensive Qualifying Workshop for those needing to equip themselves with the basic knowledge necessary for effective and ethical application of the MBTI.

CAMERA ...

3. Assemble the team.

4. Review the MBTI personality types:

E/I (Extraversion-Introversion)

People prefer either:

- *Extraversion*—Tending to derive their energy from their environment, including the people in it.

  Or

- *Introversion*—Tending to derive their energy from within themselves, which they often deem a safer environment.

S/N (Sensing-Intuition) (problem-solving scale)

People prefer either:

- *Sensing*—Tending to focus on the present reality.

  Or

- *Intuition*—Tending to focus on future possibilities.

T/F (Thinking-Feeling) (decision-making scale)

People prefer either:

- *Thinking*—Tending to focus on facts and evidence rather than feelings; tending to view issues in right-and-wrong or black-and-white terms, with no shades of gray.

Or

- *Feeling*—Tending to be sensitive to other's feelings and opinions.

J/P (Judgment-Perception)

People prefer either:

- *Judgment*—Tending to plan their schedules logically and systematically, with time a prime consideration.

Or

- *Perception*—Tending to allow room for schedule changes, even at the last minute.

5. Distribute copies of the "Bullet" to all team members. (Exhibit 15-1)

6. Review the 16 personality types from the Myers-Briggs Type Indicator Characteristics Frequently Associated with Each Type. (Exhibit 15-2)

7. Instruct team members to write their names in the left-hand column of boxes on the "Bullet."

8. Create a team master copy of the "Bullet."

9. Describe the MBTI "dominant," as follows:

- A "dominant" is any given person's preferred behavioral mode, or the person's strongest preference on either the problem-solving scale (S or N) or the decision-making scale (T or F).
- Each of us has a dominant area.
- Dominant areas begin developing early in life.

10. Describe the following easy method for determining one's "dominant":

111

- For **E—J** and **I—P** combinations (1st and 4th letters), the "dominant" is the 3rd letter. For example, the "dominant" of an **ENTJ** is **T**.

- For **I—J** and **E—P** combinations (1st and 4th letters), the "dominant" is the 2nd letter. For example, the "dominant" of an **ENTP** is **N**.

ACTION!

11. Ask each team member to circle his or her dominant letter on the "Bullet."

12. Explain that the energy needed for persons to communicate with each other depends on their mutual similarities and differences, as indicated in their respective Myers-Briggs preference letters.

Illustrate with this example:

- Person A prefers **E N T J**. Person B prefers **I N T P**. They have two letters in common, **N** and **T**. Thus, they will expend a Medium (M) degree of energy when communicating with each other.

13. Explain that the dominant is also a factor in how easily people communicate with one another. Illustrate with this example:

Communication between opposite dominants (**S—N** and **T—F**) may entail frustration or even end in failure if both dominants are not utilized.

14. At the intersection of all team members' names on the "Bullet," ask team members to write the abbreviations for the Energy Expended:

- H (High)
- MH (Medium High)
- M (Medium)
- ML (Medium Low)
- L (Low)

CUT!

15. After each team member has completed his or her "Bullet," debrief by asking:

- What have you observed about your team?

Note: Most comments will probably concern similarities and differences.

- What will you have to do to compensate for differences? For similarities?
- How can you use the strengths of each team member?
- How can awareness of team members' respective dominant preferences be used to achieve ultimate team success?

16. Ask for a volunteer to share a team example of communication difficulty, failure, or particular success. Do not prod anyone to volunteer. Team members will share stories when they are sure that there is a healthy feeling of mutual respect and trust.

CURTAIN CALL

The Myers-Briggs Type Indicator "Bullet" isn't just a feel-good tool; it's a versatile, practical, "living" instrument for self-development, relationship building, and healthy team development. As such, it's a tool to uncover individual and team potential, and thus help the team to achieve breakthrough business results.

We don't all eat only vanilla ice cream. We don't all buy only white bread. Variety is the spice of life.

The "Bullet" reminds us that our differing personalities make us strong as a group.

EXHIBIT 15-1
MYERS-BRIGGS TYPE INDICATOR TEAM "BULLET"

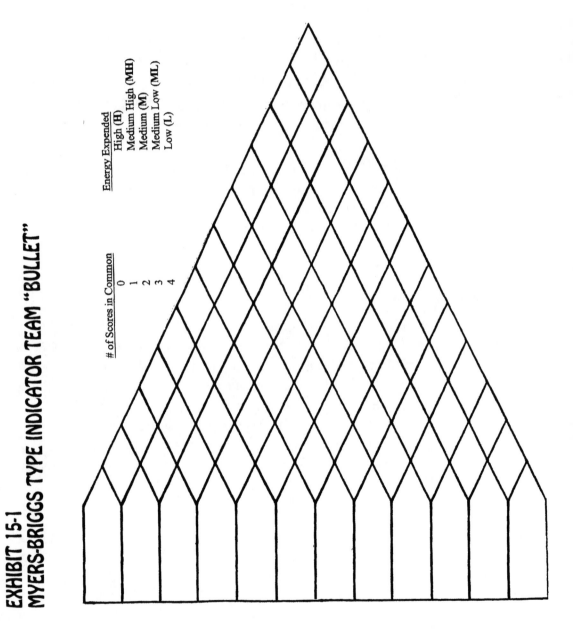

# of Scores in Common
0
1
2
3
4

Energy Expended
High (**H**)
Medium High (**MH**)
Medium (**M**)
Medium Low (**ML**)
Low (**L**)

EXHIBIT 15-2

HANDOUT

	Sensing Types		Intuitive Types	
Introverts	**ISTJ** Quiet, serious, earn success by thoroughness and dependability. Practical, matter-of-fact, realistic, and responsible. Decide logically what should be done and work toward it steadily, regardless of distractions. Take pleasure in making everything orderly and organized—their work, their home, their life. Value traditions and loyalty.	**ISFJ** Quiet, friendly, responsible, and conscientious. Committed and steady in meeting their obligations. Thorough, painstaking, and accurate. Loyal, considerate, notice and remember specifics about people who are important to them, concerned with how others feel. Strive to create an orderly and harmonious environment at work and at home.	**INFJ** Seek meaning and connection in ideas, relationships, and material possessions. Want to understand what motivates people and are insightful about others. Conscientious and committed to their firm values. Develop a clear vision about how best to serve the common good. Organized and decisive in implementing their vision.	**INTJ** Have original minds and great drive for implementing their ideas and achieving their goals. Quickly see patterns in external events and develop long-range explanatory perspectives. When committed, organize a job and carry it through. Skeptical and independent, have high standards of competence and performance—for themselves and others.
Introverts	**ISTP** Tolerant and flexible, quiet observers until a problem appears, then act quickly to find workable solutions. Analyze what makes things work and readily get through large amounts of data to isolate the core of practical problems. Interested in cause and effect, organize facts using logical principles, value efficiency.	**ISFP** Quiet, friendly, sensitive, and kind. Enjoy the present moment, what's going on around them. Like to have their own space and to work within their own time frame. Loyal and committed to their values and to people who are important to them. Dislike disagreements and conflicts, do not force their opinions or values on others.	**INFP** Idealistic, loyal to their values and to people who are important to them. Want an external life that is congruent with their values. Curious, quick to see possibilities, can be catalysts for implementing ideas. Seek to understand people and to help them fulfill their potential. Adaptable, flexible, and accepting unless a value is threatened.	**INTP** Seek to develop logical explanations for everything that interests them. Theoretical and abstract, interested more in ideas than in social interaction. Quiet, contained, flexible, and adaptable. Have unusual ability to focus in depth to solve problems in their area of interest. Skeptical, sometimes critical, always analytical.
Extraverts	**ESTP** Flexible and tolerant, they take a pragmatic approach focused on immediate results. Theories and conceptual explanations bore them—they want to act energetically to solve the problem. Focus on the here-and-now, spontaneous, enjoy each moment that they can be active with others. Enjoy material comforts and style. Learn best through doing.	**ESFP** Outgoing, friendly, and accepting. Exuberant lovers of life, people, and material comforts. Enjoy working with others to make things happen. Bring common sense and a realistic approach to their work, and make work fun. Flexible and spontaneous, adapt readily to new people and environments. Learn best by trying a new skill with other people.	**ENFP** Warmly enthusiastic and imaginative. See life as full of possibilities. Make connections between events and information very quickly, and confidently proceed based on the patterns they see. Want a lot of affirmation from others, and readily give appreciation and support. Spontaneous and flexible, often rely on their ability to improvise and their verbal fluency.	**ENTP** Quick, ingenious, stimulating, alert, and outspoken. Resourceful in solving new and challenging problems. Adept at generating conceptual possibilities and then analyzing them strategically. Good at reading other people. Bored by routine, will seldom do the same thing the same way, apt to turn to one new interest after another.
Extraverts	**ESTJ** Practical, realistic, matter-of-fact. Decisive, quickly move to implement decisions. Organize projects and people to get things done, focus on getting results in the most efficient way possible. Take care of routine details. Have a clear set of logical standards, systematically follow them and want others to also. Forceful in implementing their plans.	**ESFJ** Warmhearted, conscientious, and cooperative. Want harmony in their environment, work with determination to establish it. Like to work with others to complete tasks accurately and on time. Loyal, follow through even in small matters. Notice what others need in their day-by-day lives and try to provide it. Want to be appreciated for who they are and for what they contribute.	**ENFJ** Warm, empathetic, responsive, and responsible. Highly attuned to the emotions, needs, and motivations of others. Find potential in everyone, want to help others fulfill their potential. May act as catalysts for individual and group growth. Loyal, responsive to praise and criticism. Sociable, facilitate others in a group, and provide inspiring leadership.	**ENTJ** Frank, decisive, assume leadership readily. Quickly see illogical and inefficient procedures and policies, develop and implement comprehensive systems to solve organizational problems. Enjoy long-term planning and goal setting. Usually well informed, well read, enjoy expanding their knowledge and passing it on to others. Forceful in presenting their ideas.

Source: From *Introduction to Type* (6th ed., p. 13), by J. B. Myers with L. K. Kirby & K. D. Myers, 1998 Palo Alto, CA: Consulting Psychologists Press.

SCENE 16: MYERS-BRIGGS TYPE INDICATOR TEAM "BREAKOUTS"

We've never had a cat in our gang before, but we can use all the help we can get.

—Fagin, *Oliver and Company*

AUTHORS' NOTES

The critical work of problem solving and decision making is challenging enough without personality issues getting in the way.

On the other hand, what if personalities were not "issues" but advantages instead? What if we could understand each other well enough to use our differences to stake out common ground? What if, not *despite* but *thanks* to being many, we are one?

Are we dreaming? Yes, but the dream is made real every day. In the 1930s, the mother—daughter team of Katharine Briggs and Isabel Briggs Myers had the dream and set about realizing it by creating a method for using personal preferences to identify behavioral types. Their intent was not to underscore and widen divisions between people, but to illuminate them and let people create harmony out of diversity while standing in shared light.

Their efforts produced the MBTI that, for our purposes, clarifies and strengthens communication between work team members, animates a vibrant camaraderie, and engages everyone's individual efforts toward the achievement of collective goals.

In "Breakouts," members of MBTI subgroups share their common behavioral preferences and then compare these preferences with those of other subgroups. What develops is not just a deeper mutual understanding, but a communal bond.

Our greatest pleasure after the exercise is hearing someone exclaim, "Oh, now I understand why you act that way," or, "No wonder you get so frustrated when we ask you for all those details," or, "So that's why we don't communicate very well when we're facing deadlines." We're thrilled when team members who arrive with condescending, even arrogant attitudes depart proclaiming their newfound awareness that a multiplicity of personality types makes the world a better place.

PLOT

Team members use awareness of their respective Myers-Briggs Type Indicator (MBTI) personality preferences to promote mutual understanding and communication.

RUNNING TIME

One to two hours

PLAYERS

- Any team that has completed the Myers-Briggs Type Indicator and wishes to build and strengthen relationships among its members

PROPS

- Myers-Briggs Type Indicator results for all team members
- Flip chart
- Markers (4)
- Tape or pins (for posting flip chart pages)

DIRECTOR'S SCRIPT

LIGHTS ...

1. Confirm that all team members have completed the Myers-Briggs Type Indicator. Gather all members' results.
2. Thoroughly familiarize yourself with the theory and application of the Myers-Briggs Type Indicator.

Notes:

- Consulting Psychologists Press, Inc. is the exclusive publisher of the MBTI and maintains a strict code of ethics and procedures for purchasing, learning, and using the instrument.

- A few organizations that are quite helpful in providing resources on the MBTI instrument are: The Center for Application of Psychological Type (CAPT), a nonprofit organization in Gainesville, Florida, founded by the creators of the Myers-Briggs Type Indicator, provides invaluable resources to those who seek additional support in MBTI.

- The Association for Psychological Type (APT) provides a comprehensive Qualifying Workshop for those needing to equip themselves with the basic knowledge necessary for effective and ethical application of the MBTI.

CAMERA ...

3. Assemble the team.

4. Introduce the exercise by explaining to the team that:

- People typically behave in consistent and predictable ways.

- There are four combinations of sensing, intuition, thinking, and feeling. Sensing and intuition may be related to how people solve problems: emphasizing details and facts, or emphasizing the possibilities of what could be. Thinking and feeling may be related to how people make decisions: emphasizing the concrete evidence or emphasizing how people might be affected by the outcome.

  - SF (Sensing/Feeling)
  - ST (Sensing/Thinking)
  - NF (Intuition/Feeling)
  - NT (Intuition/Thinking)

- Team members will be divided into four groups according to their respective preferences. In the groups they will answer a series of questions, after which they will share their answers with the other groups.

5. Break the team into SF, ST, NF, and NT groups.

6. Give each group a sheet of flip chart paper and a marker.

7. Ask the groups to write the following questions on their flip chart sheets:

   - What activities motivate you as a group?

   - What activities demotivate you as a group?

   - What aspect of your group's personality preference is of greatest benefit to the overall team?

   - What does your group expect from other groups when working on projects as a team?

8. Tell the groups they will have 20 minutes to write their answers to the questions.

ACTION!

9. Tell the groups to start. Begin timing the exercise.

10. Observe the groups discussing and writing their answers; pay special attention to these expected behaviors:

    - **SFs** respond in systematic detail, then make sure everyone agrees upon the answers.

    - **STs** objectify their responses by putting answers in the form of lists.

    - **NFs** and **NTs** take time to "play with" the wording and meaning of questions and answers before reaching consensus on the most accurate responses.

11. After 20 minutes, stop the exercise.

12. Ask each group to post its flip chart sheet on the wall.

13. Ask the SF group to share its responses with the other groups. Ask the other groups to hold their questions and comments until the SFs are through.

14. After the SFs have shared their answers, take a blank flip chart sheet and write SF, ST, NF and NT as column headings across the top.

119

15. Post the sheet.

16. Ask the ST, NF, and NT groups: "What theme seems to be common in all of the SF group's answers?"

17. Record the responses under SF on the flip chart sheet.

Note: Do not object to any responses, even if you strongly disagree with what you hear.

18. Repeat the procedure with each of the other groups.

CUT!

19. Review the themes that have been cited as common within each group.

20. Comment that while all groups share some characteristics, this exercise highlights their distinctive group approaches to problem solving and decision making.

21. Share your own observations on how each group approached answering the questions. For example:

- SF—Discussed detailed questions but checked for consensus along the way.
- ST—Produced straight facts and detailed answers.
- NF—Discussed many ideas, and considered how they might "sell" or communicate them to others.
- NT—Discussed many ideas, then put them into a logical plan.

22. Invite discussion about how team members can benefit at work from awareness of their own and other members' MBTI preferences.

CURTAIN CALL

In 1990, Consulting Psychologists Press, publisher of the Myers-Briggs Type Indicator, reported that more than two million people completed the instrument in that year alone. Since then, the MBTI's popularity has grown exponentially, making it one of the most widely used psychological instruments in the world.

The 16 MBTI personality type classifications derive from the work of Carl G. Jung, the Swiss-born psychiatrist who in 1923 declared his belief that behavioral differences arise from our very distinct preferences in people, tasks, and events. In the 1930s, the mother-daughter team of Katharine Briggs and Isabel Briggs Myers began developing a way to measure the preferences or types that Jung had distinguished. During World War II, Briggs and Myers promoted the MBTI as a way to help Americans find jobs appropriate to their skill levels.

To learn more about and purchase any of the MBTI instruments, we recommend that you contact Consulting Psychologists Press, Inc. (CPP; 3803 E. Bayshore Road, Palo Alto, CA 94303; 800-624-1763; www.mbti.com). The self-scored Form M published by CPP in 1998 includes the Characteristics Frequently Associated with Each Type.

MBTI is a registered trademark of Consulting Psychologists Press, Inc.

SCENE 17: THE KIDNEY EXERCISE

When values are clear decisions are easy.

—Roy Disney

AUTHORS' NOTES

The business challenges you face are seldom simple, but are rarely matters of life and death. Still, they are critical in their own context, and your own and your team's professional survival can be at stake. In the Kidney Exercise, many people with renal failure have been saved by the famous (but fictitious) kidney machine at General Hospital in Seattle. Unfortunately, only five people can use the machine at one time, which leaves many people without hope.

The Kidney Exercise puts you in the position of life-giver. However, you can't save everyone, consequently, you must relegate certain people to sure death. Mercy may be infinite, but the instruments of salvation are not.

Life-and-death decisions—and major business decisions—are not lightly made. To be wise and fair, they must take into account many concerned opinions. Values clash. Agreement is elusive. Emotions can run high. Without basic trust in each other's goodness and best intentions, disagreement can polarize discussion and shatter it into irreconcilable points of view. The Kidney Exercise will teach your team to clarify their values so that, in keeping with Roy Disney's words, decisions will become easy.

How can you avoid this destruction by default? By accepting that there are choices upon which *no one* can totally agree, and then proceeding from this point to seek consensus on resolutions that everyone can at least live with and support.

If someone's actual life isn't hanging in the balance, your vital business interests are.

PLOT

To learn a systematic process for making value-based decisions.

RUNNING TIME

One to one and one-half hours

KEY PLAYERS

- Natural Work Team Leaders

PROPS

- Kidney Exercise Background (Exhibit 17-1)
- Kidney Exercise Psychological Reports (Exhibit 17-2)
- Kidney Exercise Biographical Information (one per partici-pant) (Exhibit 17-3)
- Flip chart
- Kidney Exercise Observation Form (one per role-play ob-server) (Exhibit 17-4)
- Kidney Exercise Criteria Weight Worksheet Example (Ex-hibit 17-5)

DIRECTOR'S SCRIPT

LIGHTS, CAMERA ...

1. Distribute to all team members:
   - Kidney Exercise Background;
   - Psychological Reports;
   - Biographical Information.
2. Select seven to ten team members to participate in the role-play. The maximum number of role-players is ten. Groups with more than ten must designate the extra mem-bers as observers.
3. Explain that this exercise may cause some people to expe-rience deep emotions. State that any participants with loved ones suffering from kidney disease may observe rather than engage in the exercise.

4. For teams larger than ten, distribute Observation Sheets to the members designated as observers.

5. Instruct all team members to read the Background, Biographical, and Psychological sheets. Ask the team members to consider as individuals which one of the potential kidney machine users should be selected for the single vacancy that exists.

6. Allow 5 minutes for reading and consideration.

7. Ask the overall team to arrive at a consensus on which potential kidney machine user should be selected.

8. Define consensus in this exercise as "everyone being able to support the decision of the team."

9. Encourage all team members to freely defend, discuss, and modify their selections.

10. Discourage seeking resolution by means of a majority vote, which is the easy way out and avoids reaching true consensus.

11. Allow participants to record their ideas, thoughts, and comments on the flip chart.

12. Allow 15 minutes for consensus decision making.

13. If a consensus is not reached after 15 minutes, allow 5 minutes more.

14. Ask the group for its consensus on which potential kidney machine user is to be selected.

CUT!

15. Debrief the exercise by asking the entire team:
- Did you experience difficulty in reaching a consensus?
- If you did experience difficulty, what were the prime obstacles to consensus?
- What created these obstacles?

16. Invite the observers to comment on the team's:
- general functioning,

- issue resolution skills,
- communication techniques, and
- decision-making process.

LIGHTS, CAMERA (Take Two) ...

17. Distribute the Kidney Exercise Criteria Weight Worksheet Example to all team members.

18. Explain that this worksheet helps break complex problems into smaller components that are easier to evaluate. It thus facilitates making value-based decisions.

19. Show the team how the worksheet could be used to form a consensus on selecting a single kidney machine user. Present the following guidelines for decision making:

- The team must first determine the criteria for selecting a machine user.

- All team members must agree to abide by the results of the worksheet.

- The team determines the weight for each criterion. The sum of all criteria is 100 percent.

- For each criterion, the team must reach consensus on a potential machine user's ranking. Rankings range from 1 (lowest) to 3 (highest). In the worksheet example, only three potential users are ranked, but team members are free to rank all five.

- Potential machine users' total weight ranks are computed by multiplying rank by weight. The total weight ranks are then recorded on the Criteria Weight Worksheet.

CUT!

20. Debrief the Kidney Exercise with a focus on:

- mechanics,
- process, and
- outcome.

CURTAIN CALL

We hold our own lives and fortunes in our hands.

Sometimes we also holds others' lives and fortunes, too. When we do, we must fully, seriously, and collectively weigh all relevant factors, temper emotion with reason, but not ignore our hearts.

We're not all-powerful or all-seeing; we're only human. That's why it's such a challenge to make critical decisions. However, by consulting our personal and communal values, deliberating the merits of every case, and seeking good-faith consensus, we'll choose to do the right thing most of the time. And when we don't, we'll have done the best that we can.

EXHIBIT 17-1
KIDNEY EXERCISE BACKGROUND

The kidney machine at General Hospital in Seattle is the only hope for certain sufferers of acute renal failure. Unfortunately, only five people can use the machine at a time. These lucky ones can remain alive indefinitely, whereas all other sufferers, without the machine, cannot.

Currently, there are four patients on the machine. The question is who, among all candidates, will take the one available place? In other words, who will live and who will die?

So far, doctors have examined all waiting patients and reviewed their backgrounds, screening out those with other diseases and those for whom the machine would provide only temporary relief.

The doctors have submitted their short list of five to the hospital committee that will make the final choice for the single place.

You are a member of this committee. You know that each of the five patients has an equal chance of survival if allowed to use the machine.

The committee's decision must be unanimous. You may consider any criteria you wish.

Your only medical information is that people over forty seem to benefit least from the machine, although they are definitely helped.

Five peoples' lives are in the hands of you and your committee. We wish them well, and we wish the same to you.

EXHIBIT 17-2
KIDNEY EXERCISE PSYCHOLOGICAL REPORTS

HANDOUT

These patients were examined and evaluated in preadmission interviews, as per the following data:

Re: Patients for Kidney Machine

From: Hospital Psychological Staff

Re: ALFRED

Is presently distraught over his physical condition. Reports that it interferes with his work. Seems very committed to his job and seems truly on the verge of an important cancer discovery. Staff had trouble getting him to talk about his work in terms they could understand.

Family relations seem strained and have been for some time due to his commitment to his work. Staff believes he is a first-rate scientist and scholar who has contributed much and could contribute more to medical research. Staff also considers that he is mentally disturbed and will eventually need psychiatric help.

Re: BILL

Is strongly devoted to his family. Appears to be an excellent husband and father.

Occupational growth potential seems limited. Performed poorly in high school, though his teachers say he tried hard. No record of delinquency. Will probably not achieve his business goals, and thus will remain employed at a fixed rate of pay.

Wife trained as legal secretary, has good employment prospects, but agrees with Bill that she should be a full-time mother. Is thus not seeking a job.

Bill seems unaware of the serious implications of his illness.

Re: CORA

Is president of the local Hadassah organization. Preoccupied with her religion and her children. Her new interest in interior decoration may indicate a broadening of interests, or may be just to impress the staff interviewers.

Husband works long hours, is in good health, is loved and respected by his children. Mother lives with family, handles most of the childcare.

Cora seems resigned to her illness and the likely prospect of death.

Re: DAVID

Is a bright, nearly straight A student. Respected by most of his teachers and friends. Appears confused, however, about his future. Enlists in student causes and joins protest demonstrations in almost random fashion. Dean of Student affairs says he will "demonstrate for anything."

Father has invested much money, time, and emotion in David, hoping he will become a lawyer. The father–son relationship is strained. David seems only mildly concerned about his two sisters, though they care deeply about him. David's future father-in-law is a highly successful businessman, expects David to enter the family enterprise after graduating from college.

Is bitter, almost paranoid, about his illness.

Re: EDNA

Is self-contained, inner-directed. Her natural aggressiveness and combative tendencies militate against any sort of marital attachment.

Has superb work record. Her employers consider her indispensable. Is very effective in her church and charitable groups. Is highly regarded by all who know her though she seems to have few, if any, close friends.

Appears resigned to her death. In fact, indicates she would prefer that someone other than herself be given the last place on the machine. Her attitude seems sincere.

EXHIBIT 17-3
KIDNEY EXERCISE BIOGRAPHICAL INFORMATION

HANDOUT

ALFRED

White. Male. Age 42. Married 21 years. Son, 18, daughter, 15, both in high school. Employed as research physicist at University Medical School, at work on cancer immunization project. Current publications show he is on the verge of a significant medical breakthrough.

Memberships: county medical society; Rotary International; Boy Scouts (Leader for 10 years).

BILL

Black. Male. Age 27. Married 5 years. Daughter, 3. Wife 6 months pregnant. Employed as auto mechanic in local car dealership. Attending night school courses in rebuilding automatic transmissions. Plans to open auto transmission repair shop after completing trade school program.

No community activities.

CORA

White. Female. Age 30. Married 11 years. Sons, 10, 8, daughters, 7, 5, 4 months. High school graduate. Has always been self-employed. Husband also self-employed (owns, operates tavern/short order restaurant). Couple has just purchased local suburban home. Cora is designing the interior to determine for self if she has serious talent; will attend interior design school if she decides she does.

Memberships: Several religious organizations.

DAVID

White. Male. Age 19. Single but recently engaged, will marry this summer. Sophomore at large eastern university: philosophy and literature major. Belongs to several campus organizations. Outspoken critic of college's administration. Once briefly suspended for "agitation." Has published own poetry in New York area literary magazines. Plans to earn Ph.D. and become a college professor. Father self-employed (owns men's clothing store). Mother deceased. Two sisters, 15, 11.

EDNA

White. Female. Age 34. Openly gay, with same partner for five years. Business college graduate. Employed since graduation as executive secretary in large manufacturing company.

Membership: Local choral society (alto soloist in Christmas production of Handel's Messiah.) Very active in several church and charitable groups.

EXHIBIT 17-4
KIDNEY EXERCISE OBSERVATION FORM

How did your team function as the hospital committee?

Did each individual have an opportunity to express his or her point of view?

How were issues resolved?

Was there a clear leader?

Did emotions rule over logic?

How did your team communicate?

Was there more talking than listening?

Was everyone allowed to participate?

How were the tough decisions made?

Was a clear consensus reached?

Was the issue brought to a vote?

Additional comments:

EXHIBIT 17-4
KIDNEY EXERCISE CRITERIA WEIGHT WORKSHEET EXAMPLE

HANDOUT

OPTIONS

CRITERIA	WT	Alfred		Bill		Edna	
		Rank	WT Rank	Rank	WT Rank	Rank	WT Rank
Age	.25	1	.25	3	.75	2	.50
Children	.50	2	1.00	3	1.50	1	.50
Contribution	.20	3	.60	2	.40	1	.20
Marital Status	.05	2	.10	3	.15	1	.05
Total WT Rank			1.95		2.80		1.25

SCENE 18: BROKEN SQUARES EXERCISE

All the king's horses and all the king's men couldn't put Humpty together again.

—Nursery rhyme

AUTHORS' NOTES

To that rhyme we might add, "To make omelets, you have to break eggs." Don't break more eggs than you need, though, because it's very hard to reassemble the broken shell. (Not to mention replacing the white and the yolk.)

The Broken Squares exercise uses pieces of paper, not eggs; but assembling five squares may feel as challenging as reconstructing Humpty's shell.

Why is that? Because this is a team exercise and teams must cooperate to gain victory—which is easier said than done, especially when people feel that to win they must force others to lose. They don't consider the possibility of everyone winning together. Only nice people let others win, they insist, and nice people finish last.

We say, forget about being nice or not nice. Forget about finishing last—or first, for that matter. Forget that feeling victory's thrill means others must agonize in defeat.

From now on, win–lose scenarios are out. Win–win is in.

The consequences of failing to think in terms of win–win can reach catastrophic levels. Recently, Disney's reputation for building solid partnerships and win–win agreements was jolted by the widely-publicized win–lose Eisner-Katzenberg case.

By all accounts, Katzenberg had launched a self-promoting campaign to replace Disney's President, Frank Wells, who had been tragically killed in a helicopter crash on Easter weekend in 1994. Incredibly, rumor has it that Katzenberg made the demand on the day of Wells' funeral, undermining any chance for a peaceful win–win result. This maneuver marked the beginning of the end of a long-standing personal relationship between Eisner and Katzenberg.

Our belief is that both parties were at fault.

Katzenbergs' contract stated that at his employment termination, he would be paid a lump sum of z percent of the future income from all the projects he had put into production. He asked Disney for $250 million, a play that cemented Eisner's hurt and disgust over the whole mess and soured him on negotiating a win–win agreement.

On April 9, 1996, Katzenberg filed a suit that set in motion a dramatic three-year court battle terminating in an undisclosed settlement. Sources closely connected with the case claim Katzenberg walked away with a whopping $270 million. At his so-called victory celebration, he summed up his feelings in a gripping statement, "It's like being in an auto accident and the insurance company paid you off." After all was said and done, he admitted there was nothing that could ever erase the trauma of his divorce with Disney.

Is win-win wishful thinking? Un-American? Simply naïve? Try the Broken Squares exercise; you may be surprised at the attitudes and behaviors the exercise reveals. You may even laugh—at people quitting when they're frustrated, or when they're unbeatably ahead. Or at people abandoning their teams to start solo acts. Or at their breaking the "no talking" rule when it's to their advantage to do so, and obeying it when it's not.

You may be surprised most of all at what you learn about true team success, because it's what you always knew in your heart, until an overly competitive society drummed it out.

PLOT

To demonstrate the difficulties in communication between team members; to dramatize the problems departmental teams experience when working together to accomplish a common objective.

RUNNING TIME

One-half hour

KEY PLAYERS

- Any team that is growing and developing relationships with one another (8 participants minimum)

PROPS

- Broken Squares Template (designating 5 equal-sized squares, each divided into 3 sections) (Exhibit 18-1)
- Five business-size envelopes

DIRECTOR'S SCRIPT

LIGHTS ...

1. From the Broken Squares Template, cut out each of the 5 squares.
2. Cut each square into its 3 designated sections, making 15 sections.
3. From the overall 15 sections, select 3 sections that *do not* fit together to make a complete square. Place these 3 non-fitting sections into one of the envelopes.
4. Select 3 other non-fitting sections and put these in another envelope.
5. Fill the remaining 3 envelopes with 3 non-fitting sections each.

CAMERA ...

6. Divide the team into subteams of 4 to 5 members each. (The ideal subteam membership number is 5.)
7. Seat each subteam around a table.
8. Give one envelope to each of the subteam members. (If a team has only four people, give one person two envelopes.)
9. Ask team members to refrain from opening their envelopes until you tell them to begin.
10. Explain the exercise:

- On your cue, team members will open their envelopes.
- Team members will then assemble the broken square pieces into a whole square.
- Together, the pieces make five equal-size squares.

11. State the object of the exercise: to win by completing all the squares. Thus, the exercise will be complete and victory achieved when each individual has a completed square in front of him or her.

12. State the following rules:

- No talking during the exercise.
- No signaling or motioning to others.
- No grabbing or throwing pieces.
- Pieces are exchanged when they are offered and accepted, from team member to team member.
- Each team member may work only on his or her own square. (See Illustration 18-1.)

ACTION!

13. Tell the team members they may now begin. Remind them of the no-talking rule.

Illustration 18-1

14. Observe the teams closely while they are working.

15. If necessary, provide the following hints, in order, one at a time:

- Rather than looking at what someone else is able to do, look at what you yourself are able to do.
- Keep an open mind. Be aware that sometimes when you think you have it together, you don't.
- Be willing to sacrifice your personal stake in the game in order to be a winner in the end.
- Be courageous. Take risks. Have faith. Know that blind action is often better than no action at all.

16. If the team members complete the squares without the need for the hints, proceed directly to ...

CUT!

17. Debrief by asking: "Which team won?"

After some discussion, most teams will say, "We all won!" because each person has a completed square in front of him or her—precisely what you originally said would be required for victory to be achieved!

18. Ask if anyone broke the rules. Give assurance that no rule breakers should feel embarrassed, because most teams do break some rules.

19. Ask the team that completed its square first: "If you broke the rules in your own team, why didn't you break the rules and help the other teams after you had finished your own square?"

This team will usually respond, "Because we were competing with them to win."

20. Discuss the instinctive urge to compete, citing that:

- Since early childhood, we have been raised to compete.

- To succeed in our work, we must evolve from a competitive to a cooperative mode with our team members and other partners.

- In this exercise, subteams felt that they were in competition to win by being the first to complete the square; but in fact, it was never stated that the first subteam to complete its square would win.

21. Invite team members to consider their own behaviors. Ask if they experienced any of the following:

- an impulse to quit after completing their own square;

- frustration to the point of wanting to give up;

- an urge to hoard pieces;

- a desire to keep the big pieces and give away the small ones.

CURTAIN CALL

Mark and delete the following slogans from your mental hard drive (and don't send them to the recycle bin):

Winning isn't everything; it's the only thing.
The thrill of victory, the agony of defeat.
My way or the highway.
It's a dog-eat-dog world.
To the victor go the spoils.

Winner takes all.
Copy the following words of wisdom into your random access memory:

United we stand, divided we fall.
One for all and all for one.
There is no "I" in "Team."
The whole is greater than the sum of its parts.
Judge your success by what you had to give up in order to get it.

EXHIBIT 18-1

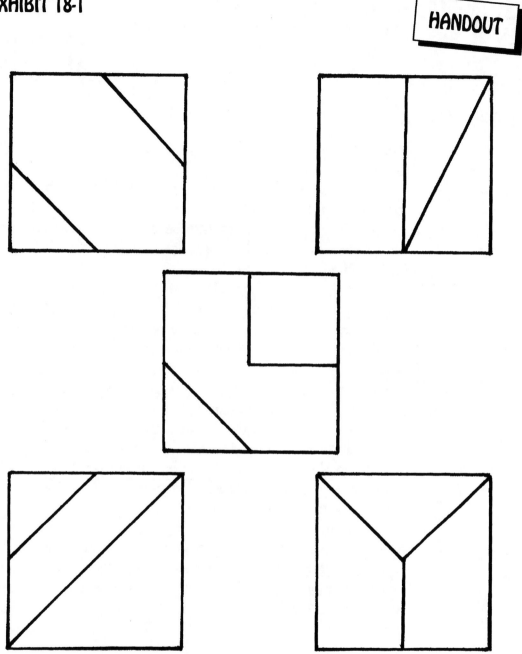

SCENE 19: BE HERE NOW EXERCISE

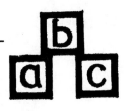

To be or not to be, that is the question.
—Shakespeare, *Hamlet*

AUTHORS' NOTES

We say: "To be here now or not to be here now, *that* is the question."

Why are *here* and *now* so important? Because they signal focus in both place and time.

Why is *focus* so important? Because place is limited and time is short and if effort is misdirected, diffused, or wasted, the job won't get done.

There's an old saying: "The pace of the leader will be the pace of the organization." Why is this true? Because followers watch the leader's step—not just its direction but its angle, its length, and even the print left by the shoe. The way the leader walks is how the followers walk, too. The result of Be Here Now leadership in the Disney culture is evidenced by their less than 30 percent turnover in the hourly ranks in an industry where over 100 percent turnover is the norm, and less than 6 percent turnover in their management ranks.

Remember this as you lead your own teams. You set the standard for committed, zeroed-in behavior. Your own focus keeps your team members' vision sharp.

Does this mean you're breeding copycats? No; emulators is a better word. Emulation is not dependency. Emulation is not submission to a master's will. Emulation is drawing direction, energy, and inspiration from a mentor, and using them to achieve total team success.

PLOT

To recognize the critical importance of focus and concentration in the achievement of any task.

RUNNING TIME

5–10 minutes

KEY PLAYERS

■ Natural Work Team Leaders

PROPS

■ One blank sheet of paper for every two participants

DIRECTOR'S SCRIPT

LIGHTS, CAMERA ...

1. Instruct each team member to select a partner.
2. Distribute one blank sheet of paper to each pair of partners.
3. Explain the exercise procedure:
   - One partner in each pair (Partner A) will tightly grasp the edges of the paper and face it at eye level toward the other partner (Partner B). The paper should be centered between the two partners.
   - While Partner A continues to hold the paper, Partner B will lean forward onto it with the palm of his or her hand.

ACTION!

4. Tell the partner pairs to begin the exercise. The paper should not break. (See Illustration 19-1.)
5. Observe and discuss:
   - Do the sheets of paper break?
   - Why or why not?
6. Ask the pairs to repeat the exercise, but this time with Partner B pressing the center of the paper with the tip of

Illustration 19-1

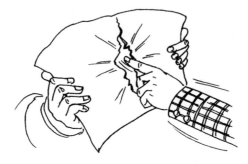

his or her index finger while Partner A continues to hold the paper. The paper should easily tear in two. (See Illustration 19-1.)

CUT!

7. Debrief by noting:

■ On the first try, Partner B's weight on the paper was distributed over a wide area. Diffused and lacking focus, it could not tear the paper. (The fact is, Partner B could have leaned against that paper all day without tearing it.)

■ When Partner B's weight was focused on the paper in one finger, the paper tore almost immediately.

CURTAIN CALL

Your team's goal is that little red dot in the center of the target. Line it up in your crosshairs, and then,

Ready ...

Aim ...

Fire!

Team Celebrations

In the 90s, bookstore shelves were overloaded with management books telling us how to reward successful teams and individual employees. Hand them candy bars, the books advised us; give them breaks from work, write them distinguished service citations, make them feel like "winners" in a race!

It was all about competition and commendations handed down from on high above.

Well, we say: How about employees celebrating their *own* successes, and in the process having a lot more fun?

A radical suggestion? Many strict old-time managers would think it is. We've met several over the years who are actually scared of fun. Inevitably, they pass their inhibitions down to their employees, who themselves then have a tough time loosening up.

But a new workplace paradigm is emerging, one that lets business be more like show business, which is an enjoyable enterprise as we all know. Instead of fixating on black-inked bottom-line results, teams now pool their talents to "perform" for customers, instead of just selling them a basket of goods.

This new paradigm does not ignore the bottom line; it just replaces classic black with multicolored ink, because magic sells these days, as indeed it always has. As this paradigm takes hold, the company "dreamers" are the real winners—and our hats are off to them as they pop their own champagne corks and toot their own horns for a change. As they sing karaoke, play laser tag, and climb through the Spider Web, they are actually spurring themselves toward even greater achievement (lest anyone think that having fun is just useless idling). Very gratifying, too, is how team members with little apparent affection for each other at work develop friendships when celebrating their common success.

We see team celebrations in a theatrical light. After the team members have performed for their audience of invited guests and taken their well-deserved bows, they repair to the cast party, where they sing and dance all night.

Act III: Dare

Courage is the main quality of leadership, in my opinion, no matter where it is exercised. Usually it implies some risk—especially in new undertakings. Courage to initiate something and to keep it going; pioneering and adventurous spirit to blaze new ways, often, in our land of opportunity.

—Walt Disney

SCENE 20: STAGES OF EXCELLENCE

If you design, build, operate, and maintain with quality, people will take pride in what they do.

—Dick Nunis, Retired Chairman of Walt Disney Attractions

AUTHORS' NOTES

"How can we do better?" is the question Walt Disney asked at every turn. But then complacency is unnatural to a perfectionist. He strove continually to improve the quality of his products. "Whenever I ride an attraction," he once said, "I'm thinking what's wrong with the thing and asking myself how it can be improved."

Good, better, best—it's a progression, a step-by-step ascent toward the shining ideal of excellence. The Stages of Excellence exercise will prepare you to lead your team on the trip.

Here's another progression: presumptions, observations, perceptions, conclusions, reality. Our exercise is a quick and cost-effective diagnostic to measure them all. Why bother? Because presumptions, perceptions and the rest will become reality, whatever you do. However, if you know where your team, department, and company are headed, you can make course corrections; you can avoid reality-by-default, and instead create the reality you want.

The diagnostic has two parts:

The Management Process section depicts management's approach to change, and its preparedness and ability to carry it out.

The Ongoing Measurement Technique appraises the organization's information gathering and measuring techniques. Is information used to create a "best show" customer or guest experience, or merely to affirm the status quo? Is employee input solicited and used in planning, or does management operate by command and control? Is cultural transformation pursued holistically or ad hoc?

The diagnostic can be undertaken by groups at various levels: leadership, middle management, and frontline workers alike. When all groups participate, their perceptions can be compared. When views are fairly similar, it means the organization has a clear, stable self-image and is well positioned for cultural transformation. When perceptions vary widely, caution is advised: Transformation cannot proceed until all groups agree on the current situation and are aligned toward a common goal.

PLOT

To use a diagnostic tool to determine potential areas of improvement in an organization.

RUNNING TIME

Half to full day; retreat setting

KEY PLAYERS

■   Leadership Team

PROPS

■   Stages of Excellence Description pages (one per team member) (Exhibit 20-1)
■   Stages of Excellence Summary Chart (one per team member) (Exhibit 20-2)
■   Storyboard materials (see Scene 30)

DIRECTOR'S SCRIPT

LIGHTS ...

1. Prior to the meeting, distribute to all team members the Stages of Excellence Description pages and the Stages of Excellence Summary Chart.

2. Ask each member to read and study the 12 categories and independently determine whether the organization is currently performing in stage I, II, or III.

CAMERA ...

3. At the start of the meeting, discuss:
- the Stages of Excellence Description categories,
- each member's assessment of the organization's current stage of performance, and
- the reasons behind each member's performance stage assessment.

4. Determine whether additional input from other leaders or employees would benefit the Leadership Team's analysis. If so, suspend the meeting until the additional information is assembled.

5. Analyze each category rated in Stage I.

6. Brainstorm or storyboard the barriers that are preventing the organization from moving to Stage II.

7. Repeat the analysis for Stage II categories.

8. Prioritize barriers by magnitude and by threat to the success of the organization.

9. Create action plans and assign responsibilities for accomplishing the agreed-upon goals.

CUT!

10. Reassemble at regular intervals to review the progress on the action plans and champion the results.

11. When implementation is well under way:
- Review areas for improvement in Stage III.
- Create additional action plans and assign responsibilities for accomplishing new goals.
- Begin Stage III implementation when resources are available.

CURTAIN CALL

We've said it already but we'll say it again because it's what Stages of Excellence is all about: Presumptions, Observations, Perceptions, Conclusions, Reality: Ignore the first four stages and you'll have to settle for whatever really happens.

Keep tabs on how everyone is viewing each other's work; then use your data to seek improvements, and you'll create the reality you want.

EXHIBIT 20-1
STAGES OF EXCELLENCE DESCRIPTION

Management Process

	Stages		
	I	**II**	**III**
■ Management Approach	• Management participation limited to informational meeting; employee inputs to improvement opportunities are not encouraged	• Managers participate through reviewing reports; limited resources and time available for quality and customer service improvements	• Top management relates quality and customer service improvement objects to the company's business plan • Managers and supervisors are active in quality and customer service improvements and work with departments to establish performance objectives
■ Adequacy of Information	• Few measurements exist and are only trend indicators or standards used to reward or reprimand	• Measures exist but not directly related to the business plan; department heads participate in setting measures and results are communicated to employees on an annual basis	• Performance plans are linked to the company's strategic direction; employees participate in establishing measures and results are communicated to them on a frequent basis
■ Ability to Change	• Procedures developed to handle every situation; company reacts defensively to change • Formal organization structure, changes occur when major problems are encountered and the old system will no longer function	• Teams are often formed to solve problems, then disbanded; company is generally looking for new ways of doing things	• Company is constantly experimenting with new approaches; employees interact with customers and suppliers to improve effectiveness and efficiency

153

EXHIBIT 20-1
STAGES OF EXCELLENCE DESCRIPTION (CONTINUED)

Ongoing Measurement Technique

<table>
<tr><th></th><th colspan="3">Stages</th></tr>
<tr><th></th><th>I</th><th>II</th><th>III</th></tr>
<tr>
<td>■ Production</td>
<td>• Tonnage mentality, long runs</td>
<td>• Economic order quantities; volume, low cost, and efficiency more important than quality and responsiveness
• Technology and science driven</td>
<td>• Focused factory, short production runs
• Customer and market driven</td>
</tr>
<tr>
<td>■ Defects</td>
<td>• Total cost</td>
<td>• Total cost
• Percentage</td>
<td>• Total cost
• Number per million</td>
</tr>
<tr>
<td>■ Training</td>
<td>• None</td>
<td>• Selective teams trained in problem-solving techniques</td>
<td>• All employees trained in problem-solving techniques
• Everyone in the organization understands the Dream, Believe, Dare and Do culture their first day on the job</td>
</tr>
</table>

EXHIBIT 20-1
STAGES OF EXCELLENCE DESCRIPTION (CONTINUED)

HANDOUT

Ongoing Measurement Technique (Cont'd)

	Stages		
	I	II	III
■ Marketing/Innovation	• React to market changes	• Lengthy market tests, analysis over intuition • Marketers spend 90% of their time in office • Central research and development as driver, big projects norm	• Quick data collection, small scale market tests, multifunctional marketing teams • Marketers spend 50% of their time in the field with customers • All activities are looking at innovative ideas to solve customer problems
■ Customer Service	• None	• New product ideas from marketing • Periodic, lengthy customer service surveys • Sales and marketing prime customer contact • Service people as mechanics, little or no customer service input	• New product ideas from sales, service, and customer focus groups • Continuous tracking of service • Line workers visit customers on regular basis • Service people trained as primary customer contact

155

EXHIBIT 20-1
STAGES OF EXCELLENCE DESCRIPTION (CONTINUED)

Ongoing Measurement Technique (Cont'd)

	Stages		
	I	**II**	**III**
■ Employee Participation	• None, people need tight controls	• Limited use of teams • Barriers between union and management • Capital more important than people	• Employee involvement in activities • More than 90% of employees participate in teams • Quality, service, and responsiveness are success keys through people more than capital
■ Rewards/Recognition	• None	• Traditional performance appraisals • One-to-one feedback	• Individual Development Plans • Ongoing one-to-one feedback and coaching
■ Organization	• Hierarchical, staff-centered	• Matrixed organization to solve coordination needs • Spans of control 1:10 at lower levels; 1:7 at higher levels	• "Business team," small group focus • Spans of control 1:75 at lower levels; 1:20 at top
■ Productivity	• None	• Output/employee	• Annual performance plan tracks improvements in effectiveness as well as efficiencies

EXHIBIT 20-2
STAGES OF EXCELLENCE SUMMARY CHART

Name _____ Company _____

Date _____

	I	II	III
■ Management Process			
• Management Approach			
• Adequacy of Information			
• Ability to Change			
■ Ongoing Measurement Techniques			
• Production			
• Defects			
• Training			
• Marketing/Innovation			
• Customer Service			
• Employee Participation			
• Rewards			
• Organization			
• Productivity			

STAGES OF EXCELLENCE
POTENTIAL IMPROVEMENT PROGRAMS

	I To II Breakthrough	II	II To III Breakthrough	III
Develop baseline quality and customer service measurements		✓		
Conduct competitive benchmark studies				✓
Develop and conduct a one day *Dream Retreat*® for all employees			✓	
Develop and begin an employee orientation program that occurs within the first two weeks of employment			✓	
Replace traditional Performance Appraisals with Individual Development Plans			✓	

HANDOUT

STAGES OF EXCELLENCE
POTENTIAL IMPROVEMENT PROGRAMS (CONTINUED)

	I To II Breakthrough	II	II To III Breakthrough	III
■ Begin use of statistical process controls	✓			
■ Customer Service Training				
• Team focus		✓		
• All employees			✓	
■ Preparation of company performance plans				
• Selected improvements		✓		
• Linked to strategic vision and drives budget			✓	
■ Establish employee participation teams				
• 10% of workforce		✓		
• 50% of workforce			✓	
• More than 90%				✓
■ Establish reward system linked to team results				
• Managers and above			✓	
• All employees				✓

	I To II Breakthrough	II	II To III Breakthrough	III
▪ Establish employee suggestion process	✓			
• 10 suggestions/worker/year		✓		
• 25 suggestions/worker/year			✓	
• 50 or more suggestions/worker/year				✓
• 80% or more suggestions implemented				
▪ Develop a communications plan to regularly inform employees of quality and customer service results		✓		
▪ Calculate the cost of nonquality and poor customer service		✓		
▪ Establish key vendor partnerships		✓		
• Key vendors identified	✓			
• Formal communication of expectations		✓		
• Vendor certification program			✓	
• Eliminates incoming inspection				

STAGES OF EXCELLENCE
TYPICAL RANGE OF BENEFITS

Major Improvement Category	Stage I to Stage II Breakthrough	Stage II to Stage III Breakthrough
■ Productivity improvements	10%–30%	40%–60%
■ Inventory reductions	15%–20%	60%–90%
■ Cycle time reductions	10%–15%	60%–90%
■ Scrap and rework reductions	5%–25%	60%–80%
■ Improved market share	Not Applicable	50%–70%

SCENE 21: PARADIGMS...
A BLUEPRINT FOR SUCCESS

The future is where our greatest leverage is.

—Joel Barker

AUTHORS' NOTES

From *The Business of Paradigms* to *The Power of Vision*, Joel Barker has cemented his international title, "the father of business paradigms." At the cornerstone of his exploration of future-defining bright ideas and groundbreaking innovations is, in Barker's words, the real definition of paradigms: any set of rules and regulations that do two things:

1. define, establish boundaries or create limits within which one must operate;

2. give you specific instructions on how to solve problems that exist within the boundaries or limits.

He adds: "rules can be explicit or implicit. It makes no difference. In the simplest form a paradigm defines 'the rules of the game.'"

What W. Edwards Deming did for quality, Barker did for paradigms. Reminiscent of the often hard-to-swallow, curmudgeonly Deming style, Barker says, "Only the simplest paradigms are of one rule. it is the simplistic interpretation of paradigms that causes grief again and again, because a department changes one rule and thinks it will create a new paradigm. It NEVER does. So ... it is the set of rules that makes a paradigm as it was for the Swiss watch makers." And like Deming, Barker is right on.

We see businesses every day where paradigms are not even questioned—that is, until industry rules are rewritten, or a new product line hits the market, or a new CEO comes in. When the status quo is disrupted like this, all bets are off and current paradigms are fair game. Unless these paradigms are revised to meet the new challenges, old strengths can become potentially fatal weaknesses. This can happen over a year's time or overnight. If it catches you napping, it will rudely jolt you awake. If you're awake but unwilling to swim with the tide, it will leave you far out at sea.

But, if you expect the unexpected and can fill your sails with—not fight—the new prevailing wind, you'll stay on course.

Swiss watchmakers should have heeded this advice. For much of the twentieth century they had the corner on the mechanical watch market.

When electronic quartz technology emerged in 1968 and promised a thousandfold increase in timekeeping accuracy, did they jump?

No, they discounted the revolutionary watchmaking paradigm—even though they had launched the revolution themselves by creating the world's first quartz watch!

Why did the Swiss hold back? Paradigm-lock. A quartz watch's single moving part, they declared, was inferior to their traditional chronometers' interworking gears and bearings. So disdainful were they of their own quartz technology that they didn't even patent it!

By the time they awoke to the folly of their intransigence, they had lost enormous ground in the market and faced a huge struggle to make it back up.

PLOT

To guide teams to define and challenge their existing paradigms and to develop new paradigms for future success.

RUNNING TIME

Two to four hours

KEY PLAYERS

- Team leaders

■ Team members

PROPS

■ Flip chart
■ Storyboard supplies (See Scene 30)

DIRECTOR'S SCRIPT

LIGHTS ...

1. Write the word Paradigms at the top of a flip chart page.

CAMERA ...

2. Assemble the players in a private and comfortable setting such as a conference room or retreat location.

3. State your definition of the word "Paradigm": A rule, custom, ritual, or pattern that dictates human behavior.

ACTION!

4. Ask: What are our team's paradigms? To stimulate responses, invite the participants to brainstorm or use the storyboard technique (see Scene 30).

5. On the flip chart, record the paradigms upon which participants agree.

6. Ask the participants to assess the effectiveness of their current paradigms.

7. Record participants' assessments on the flip chart. If you are using the storyboard technique, you may wish to record the assessments on index cards. The cards would then be posted on the flip chart beside the paradigms to which they refer.

8. On a separate flip chart page, post the question: What seems impossible for us to achieve but would greatly benefit our team if we could only figure out a way to do it?

9. Encourage the team to suggest more than one potential achievement.

10. Discuss and record the team's suggestions.

11. Ask: What is stopping us from achieving (insert one of the potential achievements)?

12. Encourage the team to brainstorm all conceivable barriers to achievement. Restrain participants from challenging each other's thoughts and suggestions during the brainstorming process.

13. Record all ideas on the flip chart, even those that are important to only a single participant.

Note: At this time, team members may become frustrated as they recognize the difficulty in overcoming old, outdated paradigms.

14. State that brainstorming obstacles to achievement is essential to eliminate outdated paradigms and to develop new ones.

15. Ask: What actions we can take to overcome the old paradigms?

16. Initiate team storyboarding to answer the question.

17. Collect the team's storyboarding cards and post them in columns under the header cards.

18. Use multiple-colored, self-adhesive dots to designate priority actions.

19. Determine who will be responsible for pursuing each action.

20. Challenge the team to form subteams to plan how to change or replace old, outdated paradigms.

21. On the flip chart, record the subteam members' names.

22. Solicit a volunteer to prepare a hard copy report of this session's essential results, including:

■ major questions and answers;

■ brainstorming and storyboarding ideas, suggestions, and thoughts.

Have the volunteer distribute copies of the report to all team members.

CUT!

23. Instruct the subteams to systematically report on their work to the entire team, preferably in a follow-up team meeting.

CURTAIN CALL

Question
How are outdated paradigms worth more than a pair o' dimes?

Answer
They're not.

SCENE 22: RESOLVING CONFLICT PEACEFULLY

At least we should try to get along together.
—Cinderella, *Cinderella*

AUTHORS' NOTES

Have you ever seen two bull elks charging each other, bashing skulls, locking horns, and thrashing around until one of them concedes defeat? That's one way to resolve conflicts, for animals in the wild.

Human beings need a more civilized way to work out issues. Walt Disney and his brother Roy often assumed conflicting positions when faced with key business decisions, but they managed to avoid any irreparable damage to their solid bond of trust and respect. Walt believed it was his job to dream up new ideas, and that Roy should figure out how to pay for them. As a leader, your job is to establish trusting relationships with your team members and help them avoid building destructive relationships that ultimately cause entire teams to fail.

PLOT

To learn a systematic process for resolving conflicts between team members.

RUNNING TIME

One to two hours

KEY PLAYERS

■ Any leader responsible for developing individual team members and teams as a group

PROPS

- Flip chart

DIRECTOR'S SCRIPT

LIGHTS ...

1. Review these five tips for conducting one-on-one conflict resolution sessions:

   - *Protect confidences.* Don't disclose personal information about others or comments they have made.

   - *Don't overreact.* Conflict between team members often dissipates without intervention. Determine whether you can be helpful in reducing or resolving the conflict.

   - *Don't expect people to tell the whole truth.* Team members often go to great lengths to avoid conflict. They may therefore be unwilling to disclose their true and complete feelings about others. Many people do not know how to define their feelings, and thus are truly unable to provide feedback. Don't push people too hard to share information; invite them to do so only in a safe environment.

   - *Don't expect to "fix" people.* Ultimately, people change their *own* behaviors, but only when they see the benefits of doing so.

   - *Know when the situation is bigger than you are.* If you have not been successful in formally or informally helping team members resolve their conflicts, seek assistance from a qualified individual. In cases when a team member has a long-term personal problem, encourage him or her to seek professional counseling, either through an Employee Assistance Program or from an outside source.

2. Review these three goals for one-on-one conflict resolution sessions:

- To gain background information on the problem;
- To gain the team member's commitment to seek a win–win solution for all involved parties;
- To gain the team member's commitment to participate in a joint conflict resolution session with all involved parties.

3. Review the two steps for conducting one-on-one conflict resolution sessions:

   - Meet separately with each party in a private location.
   - Do not give third-party feedback (e.g., "Linda said you don't show respect for her opinions during team meetings").

4. Review the three goals for conducting joint conflict resolution sessions:

   - To help establish or restore the relationship between the parties;
   - To gain both parties' commitment to change their behaviors;
   - To gain both parties' commitment to a follow-up session.

5. Review the steps for conducting joint conflict resolution sessions:

   - State the reason for the meeting. You may say something like: "I met with each of you individually to hear your personal views on your issues of concern. In those meetings, each of you committed to discuss the issues further to reach a solution. Today is our chance to exchange views and accomplish that goal."
   - Ask both team members to express what they wish to gain from this session. You may say something like: "I'd like to begin by hearing your own expectations for this meeting. What do each of you want to accomplish here today?"

- Clarify and record both team members' expectations on a flip chart.
- Set up ground rules such as:

    Each team member must make "I" statements when expressing how he or she was affected by the other person's behavior. For example, "I felt angry when you interrupted my report." As opposed to, "You made me furious when you interrupted my report.")

    Each team member must be allowed to finish his or her statements without being interrupted.

- If either team member breaks a ground rule or attacks the other team member, call a time out and state what you have just heard. For example, you might say, "Chris, that sounded like you were blaming Jackie for the problem. I'd like you to rephrase your comment using 'I' instead of 'you.' "
- When a team member makes a major point during the discussion, ask the other team member to repeat, or play back what he or she has just heard. Then allow the first team member to confirm the accuracy of the playback and, if necessary, to respond.
- Give the team members feedback on what you perceive to be their conflicting priorities. Then, ask them for feedback on your understanding of the situation. If they say you misunderstood the issue, ask for clarification.
- Invite the two parties to brainstorm solutions and ask their permission to record these on the flip chart.
- Gain consensus on the best solutions.
- Ask both team members to consider their original expectations for this meeting. Ask them if they agree that those expectations have been met. If the expectations have not been met, continue facilitating the discussion, or schedule another meeting at an appropriate time. If the expectations have been met, ask each team member to state the positive outcomes of the meeting. You

may also ask the team members to state the positive effects today's resolution may have on other team members.

■ Schedule a mutually convenient time for a follow-up meeting to check on how the team members' relationship is now working out.

CURTAIN CALL

Conflict is friction. Friction creates heat.

Don't be afraid of heat. Steel can't be forged, after all, until it's hot. It's cooled after it's fashioned into shape.

As a conflict-resolving leader, you're a blacksmith of sorts. When conflict arises, don't shun it. Use its heat to forge ahead.

SCENE 23: BEAM EXERCISE

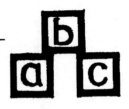

Giving up is for rookies.
—Phil, *Hercules*

AUTHORS' NOTES

Persistence pays off, or so we are told. How long should you persist, though, before giving up? Is simple trial and error the best approach? At some point, should you stop and consider new ways of achieving success? Walt Disney's first company went bankrupt, and the Disney Studios were on the verge of going belly up on more than one occasion. Through tenacious resourcefulness, Walt was able to create the leading company in family entertainment … in fact, he defined the entire industry.

The Beam Exercise requires not only persistence, but also mental and physical resourcefulness to succeed. Through this challenging problem-solving opportunity, people learn how failure can be turned into success … that is, if they think beyond the obvious. On the other hand, failure can snowball for those who can't or won't allow their creativity to run free.

PLOT

To help teams develop creative problem-solving skills.

RUNNING TIME

30–45 minutes

KEY PLAYERS

- Teams of at least five members

PROPS

- Two 4″ ×4″ boards, four feet long, notched and bolted together with a carriage bolt and wing nut (See Illustration 23-1.)
- Stopwatch or watch with second hand

DIRECTOR'S SCRIPT

LIGHTS ...

1. Prior to the team's arrival, assemble the beam.

Note:

- See Illustration 23-1 for recommended beam design.
- You can either notch the 4×4's with a saw or purchase two prenotched cedar mailbox posts.
- Use multiple beams for teams larger than 10.

CAMERA ...

2. Ask all team members to stand in a line on the beam.

Illustration 23-1

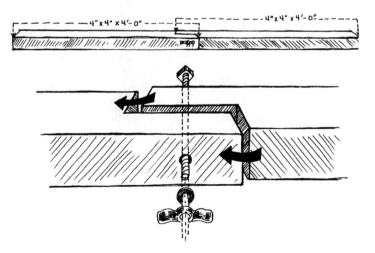

3. State the objective of the exercise: To change places with one another as quickly as possible without stepping off the beam.

4. Explain:

- The team will form a single line beside the beam and then step onto it.

- The team members on each end of the beam will change places with one another without leaving the beam or touching the ground. Continue this process until all members have changed places with their counterparts on the opposite end of the beam. (See Illustration 23-2.)

- Each time a team member touches the ground a defect will be charged against the team.

- When the team is ready and positioned on the beam, begin timing and counting defects.

- The exercise is complete when all team members have changed places.

Illustration 23-2

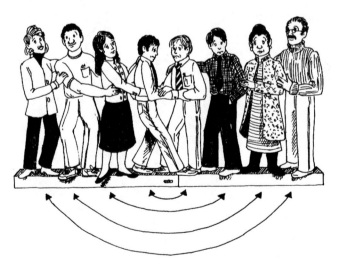

Illustration 23-3

Note: For your information but not to be revealed to the team: The key to success is disassembling the two beam sections and placing them parallel to each other, two inches apart, as opposed to leaving them joined end-to-end. (See Illustration 23-3.) With half the team standing on one section directly across from their counterparts on the other section, all team members can quickly and easily change places by joining hands, lifting one foot up, and stepping to the opposite beam. (This can be accomplished in a matter of seconds.)

5. Since safety is the number one priority, permit any participants with physical limitations to participate only in the planning activity.

6. Make sure team members understand the exercise procedure and objective.

7. Begin the exercise by instructing the team to begin planning strategy, which may include practicing changing places. Allow 5 to 10 minutes for strategizing and practicing.

ACTION!

8. Direct team members to take their starting positions on the beam.

9. Tell the team members to begin and start timing.

10. Count defects.

11. If the team has not achieved the objective within 10 minutes, tell them:

    - They are working too hard.

    - The exercise can be accomplished in much less than 10 minutes and with zero defects.

    - They should start thinking "outside the box" to expand the range of possible solutions.

    - They should intensify brainstorming within the team.

12. If the team starts looking for props to help achieve the objective (e.g., chairs or tables), praise them for their creative thinking. Then say, "However, the world record is less than 10 seconds with zero defects and without any props."

13. If within 30 minutes the team has not tried disassembling the beam sections and replacing them in parallel alignment, ask them: "Have you really studied the beam?" Then stare at the wing nut for a few seconds to give them the hint.

14. When the team has disassembled the beam and succeeded with the parallel alignment approach, stop timing and call a halt to the exercise.

CUT!

15. Debrief the exercise by asking:

    - What did you learn from this experience?

    - Why do we fail to see the barriers, real or perceived, that block us from achieving our goals?

    - How can we remember to think "outside the box"?

CURTAIN CALL

Albert Einstein said, "Problems cannot be solved at the same level of awareness that created them." This means that the kind of thinking that gets us into trouble won't get us out.

What will get us out? Not trial and error, which is not thinking at all, but merely knocking on doors of ever-diminishing possibility until our knuckles turn red. Not a reliance on the tried and true, which has been tried too often and in today's new circumstances is no longer true.

Only courage, wit, and calm resolve will stop us from banging our heads against brick walls, so that finally we can find the window through which the dawn breaks.

SCENE 24: BLIND WALK

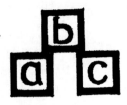

*I'm only brave when I have to be ... being brave
doesn't mean you go looking for trouble.*
—Mufasa, *The Lion King*

AUTHORS' NOTES

When we can't see, our ears perk up. We navigate by sound, by touch, and we smell much more keenly what's in the air. Many people who lose their sight claim they gain a heightened sense and appreciation of the world around them. Blind persons must be especially alert for hazards in their way, and often, they must be led by sighted people or seeing-eye dogs.

In the Blind Walk, people are thrust into the darkness and are challenged to overcome numerous obstacles. In the process, they gain an appreciation of the "holistic" world, the smells, the textures, and the temperature. They are forced to listen closely to their lender's directions and learn the power of negotiating an unknown course that tests their risk-taking tolerance along the way.

PLOT

To build trust between team members; to develop active listening skills.

RUNNING TIME

10–15 minutes

KEY PLAYERS

- Natural Work Team Leaders
- Natural Work Teams

PROPS

- Obstacle course, indoor or outdoor (You need not create a formal course. In most settings, a wide variety of natural obstacles will be found.)

- Bandannas or blindfolds (one per participant) (optional)

DIRECTOR'S SCRIPT

LIGHTS, CAMERA ...

1. Ask team members to pair off with partners.

2. Introduce the exercise by explaining:

   You are about to walk through an obstacle course. One person in each pair will lead the other person, who will be blindfolded. The sighted partners will be responsible for:

   - avoiding potentially hazardous situations;

   - describing the obstacles encountered;

   - confirming your "blind" partners' understanding of how to negotiate the obstacles;

   - assuring your "blind" partners that they will be protected from all dangers. (See Illustration 24-1.)

   Every team member will have the chance to be both the sighted leader and the "blind" follower. Safety is the number one priority.

3. Ask the pairs to decide who will initially be the leader and who will be the follower.

4. Instruct the sighted partners to hold their "blind" partners by the forearm.

5. Ask the pairs to form a line behind you.

6. Instruct the sighted partners to:

   - Follow you and maintain their positions in the line.

   - Maintain a safe distance between other pairs—approximately two yards.

   - Continue holding their "blind" partners' arms throughout the entire walk.

Illustration 24-1

- ■ Describe every obstacle before asking the "blind" partners to confront it.

ACTION!

7. Lead the team through the obstacle course.

Notes: For indoors: stairs, tables, and chairs are effective obstacles. For outdoors: tree branches, puddles, small streams, fences, and rocks work well. Use your imagination in creating obstacles, but put safety first.

8. After about 5 minutes, say that from now on the sighted partners must be silent: Only the "blind" partners may speak.

9. Continue the walk for several additional minutes, then halt.

10. Have all the partners change roles.

11. Restart the walk, taking a different route if possible.

CUT!

12. Debrief the exercise by asking:

- ■ Did you trust one another? Why or why not?
- ■ What happened to the trust level when I asked the sighted partner to remain silent?

CURTAIN CALL

Blindness has its ironic advantages: Sometimes it helps us perceive more distinctly the bonds that connect us as human beings. That perception is essential for team cooperation, especially in risky ventures where success depends on mutual trust.

SCENE 25: ALL ABOARD

If you're not living on the edge, you are taking up too much space.
—Lou Whitaker

AUTHORS' NOTES

An old college stunt was stuffing as many students as possible into a telephone booth. In a famous episode of the television series *M.A.S.H.*, the 4077th crammed an impossible number of staff members into a jeep.

In its own way, the All Aboard exercise emulates these rowdy, comical stunts, by packing team members into close quarters and letting them learn through experience that only trust, daring, and cooperation can bring success.

Disney's ability to bring cast members together in a spirit of daring, teamwork, and trust is evidenced by the frequently held even know as the Gong Show. Named after the popular television show dating back to the 1970s, the Gong Show is an opportunity for any cast member to present an idea to a team that includes the top-level Disney executives. This experience enhances the atmosphere of freedom—the freedom to take risks and venture into unchartered territory.

PLOT

To encourage goal setting, risk taking, and trust between team members.

RUNNING TIME

30–45 minutes

KEY PLAYERS

■ Teams of at least 6 members (although this exercise is more challenging with 12 to 15 team members)

PROPS

■ Nails or screws
■ Saw
■ Sandpaper
■ Stopwatch or watch with a second hand

Lumber for teams up to 24

■ 4"×4" lumber, at least 4' long
■ Three 2"×8" boards, each 2' long

Lumber for teams of 25 or more

■ 4"×4" lumber, at least 6'8" long
■ Five 2"×8" boards, each 3' long

DIRECTOR'S SCRIPT

LIGHTS ...

1. Build the platform in the following way:

■ Cut two 2' sections from the 4"×4" lumber.

■ Place the two sections parallel to one another, with the outside edges two feet apart.

■ Use nails or screws to attach the three 2"×8" boards (each 2' long) to the top of the two 4"×4" lumber sections, creating a 2'×2' platform.

Note: For teams of 25 or more, a 3'×3' platform can be built with the lumber indicated in the materials list using the same procedure.

■ Sand the edges to ensure safety in case of a fall.

CAMERA ...

2. Assemble the team.

3. Since safety is the number one priority, permit team members with physical limitations to participate only in the planning process.

4. State the objective of the exercise: To assemble all team members on the platform for 5 seconds without anyone touching the ground.

5. Explain:

- It is not required that everyone have both feet on the platform, as long as no feet are touching the ground.

- Any foot touching the ground is counted as a defect. (See Illustration 25-1.)

6. Strictly prohibit stacking team members like lumber in a woodpile, as this technique is extremely dangerous.

7. Tell the team to begin planning strategy. Encourage creative thinking and candid feedback on each other's ideas.

Illustration 25-1

8. Allow 10 minutes for strategizing.

9. Have the team choose one person to say "Go" to start the exercise.

ACTION!

10. Tell the person to say "Go." Begin timing the exercise.

11. When all team members are assembled on the platform, stop timing and call a halt. (See Illustration 25-2.)

12. Announce the elapsed time and the number of defects.

13. Challenge the team to try again, to improve their time and reduce the number of defects.

14. Repeat the exercise.

CUT!

15. Debrief the exercise by asking:

■ What did you learn from this experience?

Illustration 25-2

- Why did you allow yourselves to take risks during the exercise?
- What risks should we be taking in our work and with our team members?

CURTAIN CALL

Too many cooks spoil the broth, and too many sailors can sink the ship, but sometimes you just have to work with the number of colleagues you've got.

Remember another saying: The more the merrier.

And, there's safety in numbers.

SCENE 26: ISLAND CROSSING

When you get to the end of your rope, tie a knot and hang on.

Henry David Thoreau

AUTHORS' NOTES

No one actually hangs on for dear life in the Island Crossing exercise, but team members must coordinate their efforts to make it across "swampy water" to "dry land." Anyone trying to save just himself or herself jeopardizes the survival of the group.

We are always fascinated by the team dynamics that physical bridge-building ignites. Very often the most assertive team member grabs a board and enlists a group to get started building right away.

Simultaneously, a few less impulsive individuals gather to consider and debate solutions before trying them out.

In both groups, if success doesn't come quickly, the tone of discussion heats up as frustration sets in. Team members who get along well in the real workplace now often find themselves quite distinctly at odds.

We recall one team of engineers who invited their human resources representative to help them bridge the swamp. Actually, the engineers didn't want help, they just wanted to impress the representative with their own famous problem-solving skills. As they calculated and plotted their course, the human resources fellow quietly solved the problem on his own. The engineers didn't speak to him for the rest of the day. (Well, for the next ten minutes, at least.)

Interestingly, total failure to bridge the swamp often breaks the tension instead of bringing it to a peak. Team members realize that each person's viewpoint must be heard and respected because each person has an equal stake in success.

Disney management realizes that everyone's point of view is valuable. One of our favorite stories took place in 1994 when EPCOT greeter Mike Goames met Disney CEO Michael Eisner.

That was the day Eisner realized that the Innovations exhibit was not living up to its name. While walking through the exhibit, he was directed to Mike Goames by another greeter who commented that Mike was, "always thinking of ways to change things." Eisner approached Goames, solicited his feedback, and asked Goames to send written suggestions to him. The key here is that the CEO wasn't just making the rounds, shaking hands in an attempt to prove that he was just "one of the guys." No, indeed. They actually implemented Goames' ideas!

PLOT

To provide a challenging and fun teamwork experience utilizing planning and problem-solving skills.

RUNNING TIME

30–45 minutes

KEY PLAYERS

■ Natural work teams

PROPS

■ Two 4"×4"×8' boards
■ 11 cinder blocks
■ Stopwatch or watch with second hand
■ Tape measure

DIRECTOR'S SCRIPT

LIGHTS ...

1. Prearrange the cinder block islands as shown in Illustration 26-1.
2. Confirm proper distances between the islands.

Illustration 26-1

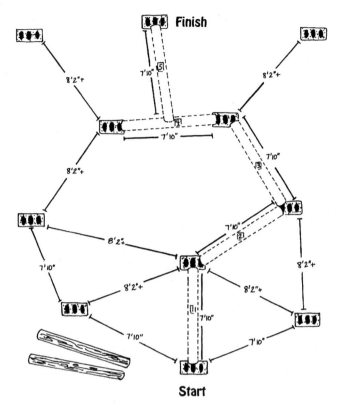

CAMERA ...

3. Assemble the team.

4. Describe the exercise terrain as follows:

The area is a swamp. The cinder blocks are islands in the swamp. The boards are bridges between the islands.

5. State the team's collective objective in the exercise: to move from one side of the swamp to the other as quickly as possible, using the bridges and the islands.

6. Warn the team that if anyone falls into the swamp, the entire team must return to the starting point.

7. For safety, prohibit jumping from island to island without using bridges.

8. Permit any team members with physical limitations to participate only in the planning phase of the exercise.

189

ACTION!

9. Signal the team to begin. Start timing the exercise.

10. Allow 20 minutes for the exercise.

11. If the team has not discovered the "solution" (See Illustration 26-2) within 20 minutes, suggest that they think outside the box or try a new paradigm.

12. When all team members have moved from one side of the swamp to the other, halt the exercise and stop timing. (See Illustration 26-3.)

13. Announce the elapsed time.

CUT!

14. Debrief the exercise by asking:

- How did you work together as a team?
- Did everyone contribute ideas for a solution?

Illustration 26-2

Illustration 26-3

- If everyone did not contribute ideas, why didn't they?
- Did some team members talk more than others?
- Did some communicate by asking questions while others simply stated their views?

Notes:

  - The so-called tell-assertive individuals normally do most of the talking, and may end up solving the problem without any input from the ask-assertive people.

  - The ask-assertives are typically reluctant to declare their views in a large group, but appreciate being asked for their opinions and ideas.

- Was there respect for all team members' communication styles?
- What is the importance of respecting all communication styles?

- How can we ensure that everyone is able to communicate in his or her own way?
- How can we ensure that problem-solving efforts are not dominated by just a few individuals?
- How can we tap the creative energy of every member of the team?

CURTAIN CALL

In the tale of the little boy who cried wolf, the boy is ignored because he has already talked too much. In the Island Crossing exercise, the risk is that some people will be ignored because they talk too little, or too softly, or not at all.

Remember the admonition: "If you're not part of the solution, you're part of the problem." People with good ideas who don't or can't express them are certainly not part of the solution. The challenge is to make them fully heard and contributing members of the problem-solving group.

SCENE 27: SPIDER WEB

The very things that held you down are going to carry you up.

—Timothy Mouse, *Dumbo*

AUTHORS' NOTES

This exercise, with its nightmarish aspect of being trapped and unable to escape, is actually one of the most entertaining and often hilarious to undertake.

Don't be surprised if one or two people step forth as leaders to guide the others through the web. Make sure the followers aren't so relieved to have help that they become passive and don't help in planning for a successful team result.

PLOT

To develop team communication and trust; to practice problem- solving and planning skills.

RUNNING TIME

30-45 minutes

KEY PLAYERS

■ Natural Work Teams Leaders

PROPS

■ Spider Web made out of rope or elastic cord
■ Two trees or posts, placed approximately 12 feet apart
■ Stopwatch or watch with second hand
■ Myers-Briggs Type Indicator list of types of participants (optional)

DIRECTOR'S SCRIPT

LIGHTS ...

1. Preassemble the Spider Web.

Notes:

- See Illustration 27-1 for recommended spider web design.
- Openings should be approximately 18″×18″.
- Premade spider webs may be purchased from a variety of outdoor adventure suppliers.

CAMERA ...

2. Assemble the team.

3. Explain the exercise procedure:

The team will try to pass each of its individual members through the openings, from one side of the web to the other, without touching any part of the web. Any time a team mem-

Illustration 27-1

ber touches the web, it will be counted as a defect. One team member must be a spotter while any given person is being passed through the web. Each web opening may be used only once. When there are more team members than openings, the team must use each opening at least once. When there are significantly fewer members than openings, the more difficult openings should be chosen for a greater challenge.

You will be timing the exercise.

4. State the objective of the exercise: to pass all team members through the web as quickly as possible without any defects.

5. State that anyone with a physical limitation may participate in the strategizing and spotting activities only.

Note: Do not press any team member on his or her reasons for limited participation.

6. For safety, ask team members to remove all jewelry, watches, and anything in their pockets that might cause injury during the exercise.

7. State that spotters are responsible for protecting the head, neck, and spine of a team member being passed through the web.

8. Tell the team that they can begin planning strategy, but they cannot practice passing members through the web.

ACTION!

9. Start the exercise. Begin timing when the first team member starts through an opening. (See Illustration 27-1.)

10. Continue timing and counting defects until all members are through the web. Halt the exercise.

11. Announce the number of defects. If there were no defects, congratulate the team. If there were defects, declare that it is possible to complete the exercise with zero defects.

12. Challenge the team to repeat the exercise and to aim for zero defects.

Note: Typically, teams without a clear and effective initial strategy learn from their mistakes and reduce their time and defects in the second attempt.

13. Tell the team to begin planning strategy for the second attempt. If team members have completed the Myers-Briggs Type Indicator and are aware of their respective types, provide these guidelines for this strategy planning session:

    ■ The E's (Extraversion preference) should remain silent while the I's (Introversion preference) present their ideas for reducing time and defects.

    ■ The E's may join the discussion after the I's have expressed their ideas.

    This procedure prevents the typically more vocal E's from dominating the session, and thus lets the "hidden" ideas of the I's come out.

    If the team has not completed the Myers-Briggs Type Indicator, do the following:

    ■ Ask if team members freely shared their ideas during the initial strategy planning session. Typically, the highly verbal team members will have dominated the first strategy planning discussion.

    ■ Ask all team members to contribute an idea during the second strategy planning session.

14. Suggest that the new strategy should specify the openings to be used, who will be passed through each opening, and the sequence of team members to be passed through the web.

15. Clarify the roles to be played during the exercise:

    ■ the person being passed;

    ■ the passers;

    ■ the receivers; and

- the spotter, whose role is to protect the person being passed, watch out for potential defects and direct the work of the passers.

16. Allow 5 to 10 minutes for planning strategy.

17. Start the second round of the exercise. Begin timing and counting defects.

18. Halt the exercise when all members are through the web.

19. Announce the number of defects.

20. Lead a round of applause for the team's effort.

21. If time permits, conduct a third exercise round. Typically, the results will be even better the third time.

CUT!

22. Debrief the experience by asking:

- How important is planning to the overall result of a project?
- How important was trust in this exercise?
- Do we have the same level of trust in the workplace as we did in this exercise? If not, why not?
- How did clarifying team members' roles help you perform in the exercise?
- How do you clarify roles in the workplace?
- Do you have an effective process for clarifying roles in the workplace? Why or why not?
- What factors contributed to your improvement in the second (third) round?

CURTAIN CALL

The Spider Web exercise is a key experiential challenge in our *Dream Retreat®*. While demonstrating how planning and communication get us through the tangled web of life, it shows how challenging (and fun) surviving in the jungle of work can be.

SCENE 28: ACID RIVER EXERCISE

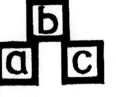

You don't have time to be timid—you must be bold, daring.

—Lumiere, *Beauty and the Beast*

AUTHORS' NOTES

Imagine yourself on a river—paddling a canoe, perhaps fishing, perhaps slipping over the side of the cause for a dip in the water.

Now imagine that the river is saturated with chemicals and that, like Cleveland's Cuyahoga River, it catches fire.

Imagine that instead of canoeing or swimming, you're suspended over that toxic soup, clinging to a rope.

In the Acid River exercise, that's exactly the position you and your fellow team members will be in.

In such a crisis situation, personal survival is a matter of individual strength and tenacity. Team survival, though, calls for strategy, coordination, risk-taking courage, and a commitment to common success. Adopting an approach of every person for himself or herself will leave some high and dry but others acid-burned to a crisp.

How does a team work together to save all its members? By choosing a leader, for a start.

PLOT

To encourage leadership, goal setting, risk taking, self-confidence, and trust within a team.

RUNNING TIME

One hour

KEY PLAYERS

- Teams of at least 5 members (although the exercise is more challenging with 10 or more)

PROPS

- A 2'×2' platform for most teams (a 3'×3' platform for teams of 10 or more)
- Strong rope long enough for swinging and knotted at one end
- Two 12' pieces of rope
- A rock or other marking device
- A stopwatch or watch with second hand

DIRECTOR'S SCRIPT

LIGHTS ...

1. Build a platform using the instructions in the All Aboard exercise. (See Scene 25.)

2. Secure the rope over a tree branch or interior ceiling beam.

3. Position the platform approximately 7' from the hanging rope.

4. Mark the starting point with the rock or other marking device, approximately 7' from the other side of the hanging rope, opposite the platform. The entire distance from starting point to platform should thus be approximately 14'.

5. Stake out the "river" edges with the two extra pieces of rope. The "river" edges should run parallel to the front edge of the platform. The hanging rope will be in the middle of the "river."

CAMERA ...

6. Since safety is the number one priority, state that participants with physical limitations may choose to participate only in the planning process.

7. Set up the exercise by establishing the elements of the exercise environment: the platform, the rope, the starting point, and the acid river.

8. State the goal of the exercise: for each participant to swing on the rope across the river and onto the platform, without getting "acid river burn." (See Illustration 28-1.)

9. Explain:

Everyone must remain on the platform without touching the ground until the last member swings onto the platform. (See Illustration 28-2.) Each time someone falls into the "river," everyone must return to the starting point. You will time the exercise.

ACTION!

10. Tell the team to begin planning strategy. Allow 10 minutes for strategizing. Encourage an open exchange of ideas and candid feedback on why various strategies might or might not work.

Illustration 28-1

Illustration 28-2

11. Have the team select one person to say "Go" to start each participant on his or her swing.

12. Tell the team to begin the exercise. Begin timing the exercise.

13. When appropriate, call an end to the exercise and mark the elapsed time.

14. Ask the team:

   ■ Did you select a leader for the exercise?

   ■ If so, what did the leader do? What part did leadership play in the ultimate result?

   ■ If there was no leader, how might a leader have helped?

15. If the team did not have a leader in the first round of the exercise, have them select a leader for the second round.

16. Permit additional strategizing, if desired. Allow 5 minutes for additional strategizing.

17. Begin the second round of the exercise. Begin timing.

18. At the end of the exercise, mark the elapsed time.

CUT!

19. Debrief by asking:

- What did you learn from this experience?
- How did having a leader influence the results?
- What were the leader's most important functions?
- Compare how you approached the exercise both with and without a leader, in terms of goal setting, risk taking, individual and team self-confidence, and trust within the team.
- What risks should we be taking as individuals and as teams in our real-world work?

CURTAIN CALL

Question
What inspires team members to accomplish challenging goals?

Answer
- Leadership
- Leadership
- Leadership

Question
What are the results of establishing strong trust bonds between team members?

Answer
- Optimal team performance
- Challenge one another to reach greater potential

SCENE 29: TRUST FALL

There's a great big hunk of world down there, with no fence around it.

—Tramp, *Lady and the Tramp*

AUTHORS' NOTES

Why would you trust someone with your life and not with a task at work?

The Trust Fall exercise asks team members to free-fall into their colleague's arms, and to trust that those arms will be there. After surviving this experience (which we can guarantee everyone will), people have a new willingness to rely on each other's advice and support in pursuing "good show" business results.

Of course, reliance can't be blind. It must be learned, practiced, relearned, and reinforced.

Sometimes, though, people take reckless plunges. Consider John, the 6'6", 300-pound manager who stood on the Trust Fall platform and, without waiting for his team members to assemble in position to catch him, toppled like an oak. He was so anxious to get his skydive over with that he leaped before he looked. Miraculously, enough team members lunged and grabbed him to stop his descent one inch above the floor. To this day, everyone still chuckles about the day "Big John" fell.

PLOT

To build self-confidence in individual team members and strengthen bonds within the team.

RUNNING TIME

45–60 minutes

KEY PLAYERS

■ Natural Work Teams with at least 9 team members

PROPS

■ A stable platform 3′ to 4′ high

DIRECTOR'S SCRIPT

LIGHTS ...

1. Preposition the platform.

CAMERA ...

2. Assemble the team.

3. Since safety is the number one priority, permit anyone with a physical limitation to be an observer. Do not press anyone to justify his or her reasons for limited participation.

4. State the objective of the exercise: to experience trust within a team environment.

5. Ask all team members to select partners.

6. Ask all partners to stand facing the same direction, with one member of each pair standing behind the other.

7. Explain the exercise procedure: In each pair, the partner standing in front will fall back. The other partner will catch the falling partner.

8. Demonstrate the proper catching procedure (see Illustration 29-1):

■ Start with feet shoulder-width apart.

■ Step back 6 to 10 inches with one foot.

■ Bend knees.

■ Raise arms to chest high with elbows slightly bent, fingers up and palms forward, 6 to 8 inches from the faller's back.

■ Concentrate solely on the faller.

■ When the faller falls back, use your palms to break the fall.

9. Ask the partners to assume their positions.

Illustration 29-1

10. Check each pair for proper stance.

11. Teach the following dialogue to be spoken by the partners before the faller falls:

> *Faller:*   *Catcher ready?*
>
> *Catcher:* *Ready.*
>
> *Faller:*   *Ready to fall?*
>
> *Catcher:* *Fall. (The catcher must now be ready to support the faller's weight.)*
>
> *Faller:*   *Falling.*

12. Tell the team to begin.

13. After each pair's first fall, have them try a few more. The distance between the partners may be progressively increased, as long as both partners feel safe.

14. Have fallers and catchers switch roles and repeat the exercise.

15. After the second round, lead the team to the platform for the real challenge.

Catchers

- Have the team members form two facing parallel lines, extending out from the platform below the faller.

- Have these team members assume the same catching position they used when catching their partners.

- Tell the team members to alter their positions by:

  - facing their palms toward the sky;

  - positioning their arms in an alternating fashion (do not allow participants to grasp arms or hands);

  - holding their heads slightly back (to avoid the faller falling in their faces).

Faller

- Ask for a volunteer faller.

- Have the faller remove any jewelry, watches, clothing articles, or other items that might cause injury in a fall.

- Ask the faller to stand on the platform.

- Back the faller to the edge of the platform, heels touching or just slightly over the platform edge.

- Instruct the faller to stand upright as straight as possible, hands at their side of the body or crossed tightly over the chest. (This prevents arms and elbows from swinging during the fall.)

- Instruct the faller to assume a rigid position when falling, and to fall straight back. (This ensures that the faller's weight is well-distributed over many catchers, not concentrated on the hands of just a few.)

16. State that the same faller–catcher dialogue will be used this time:

    Faller: *Catchers ready?*

    Catchers: *Ready.*

    Faller: *Ready to fall?*

Catchers:	Fall. *(The catchers must now be ready to support the faller's weight.)*
Faller:	Falling.

17. Stand on the platform with the faller.

18. Remind the faller to assume a rigid position when falling, and to fall straight back.

19. Keep one hand on the faller's shoulder until she or he says, "Falling."

20. If the catchers are not ready, do not let the faller fall.

21. When the catchers are ready, let the faller fall (See Illustration 29-2.)

22. Repeat the exercise, giving each team member a chance to fall.

CUT!

23. Debrief the exercise by asking:

Illustration 29-2

- How was your performance in this exercise determined by the way you communicated? By your training in how to perform your role? By your values as an individual and as a member of a team?

- Do you trust each other in the workplace as fully as you did with your physical safety here today? If not, why not?

- What did you learn from this exercise that might increase your trust of your team members on the job?

CURTAIN CALL

An amazing indication of the depth of employee trust at Disney is the fact that its ticket-takers in the Theme Parks have $500,000 in tickets and cash in their constant possession to hand out to guests who lose or forget their tickets or encounter some other problem that merits attention. That's an extraordinary sum of money to place at the discretion of employees, but Disney obviously trusts their well-trained cast members to use sound judgment.

What to Do When You Miss the Mark

Even if you follow the instructions in the *Fieldbook* User's Guide to the letter, you might not always get the results you expect.

Stay calm. It's not your fault. Anything from bad weather to a bad night's sleep to a saboteur in your midst can rock the ship.

Don't guess at what went wrong. Check this list of possibilities, which includes suggestions for getting the session back on track.

INSUFFICIENT PREPARATION

Did you "practice, practice, practice" as we advised you to do in Chapter 8 of *The Disney Way?*

Being underprepared leaves you wide open to justified criticism of how you are conducting the exercises. If you don't understand an exercise well enough to administer it, don't go ahead with it anyway and do a shoddy job. Try a different exercise, or work at this one until you've mastered it. For insurance, practice leading the exercise with a low-risk group of peers or family members before you engage your team.

If you are in the midst of an exercise that doesn't seem to be working, discuss the problem with the team. Ask them what they think is going wrong. Such a discussion can in itself be a valuable experience for all concerned. Express yourself candidly. Remember, team success depends on collective honesty and mutual trust. Always be honest about the result. Trust between you and the team is the most important ingredient in the success of the team.

MISTAKEN EXPECTATIONS

Be alert for signs of confusion or distraction in the team. The members might not clearly understand your role as facilitator, or the goal of the exercise, or how the whole experience will benefit them in the end.

Always present yourself as an active helper, not as a taskmaster with a whip or as a detached observer standing passively at the side. You are a facilitator whose duty is to help every team member have the safest, most educational, and most enjoyable experience he or she can.

Blank stares on team members' faces or off-the-subject chatting in the group could signal that the instructions have been confusing. If so, restate and clarify them right away. If some team members are finding the exercise too difficult—or even too easy—it's probably best to proceed. Matching an exercise's difficulty to the team's capabilities is best done before the session actually begins. A team member who is already personally familiar with this type of exercise can still benefit from doing it for the first time with this group.

DIFFICULT PEOPLE

It takes all kinds, even in the best companies. Most troublesome people aren't malicious, but some are too unruly to be positive contributors to the process. They might be loud, tactless, heedless of the others' feelings, or just plain rude. Their self-involved shenanigans waste everyone's time. The exasperated other team members will look to you to save them from these boorish assaults.

What should you do? Try avoiding the difficult person while focusing on the other team members. If this doesn't work, you can—in extreme cases—literally turn your back on the offender. A less radical act would be to break the team into subgroups and give a new assignment to alter the pace and format of the session. Changing course like this often works wonders, especially when boredom, fatigue, or stress were causing the obstreperous team member to act up. If a break in the routine doesn't work, you might need to take the difficult individual aside and discuss the matter one-on-one. Be firm but respectful. Choose your words carefully and maintain a measured tone of voice. Protect the person's dignity at all costs. Be open to the possibility that the attitude problem masks a frustrated urge to think in different ways. Be open to suggestions. The worst troublemakers sometimes have the brightest, most original ideas.

Another group of saboteurs (intentional or not) are the solemn, silent types. These people are especially unnerving to facilitators who need positive reinforcement from the group. These stone-faced team members may not feel invested in the exercise, or may just be having a bad day, or could be distracted by other events in their lives. Try asking each team member, "What's most important to you today?" and grant the quiet ones enough time to consider their answers before they speak. Naturally, your question can't seem like a set-up. You must show sincerity in your expression, body language, and tone of voice. If your passionate interest in everyone, including the quiet people, comes through, you have a chance of establishing mutual trust. Also, consider that individuals who are reticent when the whole team is present often open up in smaller groups.

THE CLOCK

Time marches on. Start all your sessions punctually, even if all team members have not arrived yet. (The odds are that some will always be late.)

In estimating the time required for any exercise, go beyond what you expect. Allow plenty of time between exercises, for stretching, pit stops, and so on. Don't allow interruptions once the session is under way. Designate a team member to be the timekeeper, when appropriate. If you find you're running late, ask team members to suggest what you should do. You shouldn't get into a time bind if your agenda is well laid out. Still, the best-laid plans go awry, so be ready to flex if they do. If all activities are completed early, don't improvise to fill the remaining time; just call a halt.

THE WEATHER

You can talk about it but you can't do anything about it. If the weather's bad and you planned an outdoor retreat, make the best of it. How? Consider rescheduling. Or, if "the show must go on," alter your agenda and select activities (like the All Aboard and Beam exercises) that can be undertaken indoors.

Trouble can be managed with forethought, resourcefulness, grace, and human concern. Don't forget your sense of humor. We're coming together to learn, but also to have fun.

Act IV: Do

An important secret of living: the giving and taking in the group, the development of the qualities and behaviors that will stand us in good stead through life in pursuits both personal and professional.

—Walt Disney

SCENE 30: STORYBOARD TECHNIQUE

The value of an idea lies in the using of it.
—Thomas Edison

AUTHORS' NOTES

What two things did Leonardo da Vinci and Walt Disney's mother have in common?

One, Walt Disney admired them both.

Two, they both used the storyboard technique. Leonardo sketched his ideas and pinned them to the walls before committing them to canvas. Walt's mother organized the family's activities on a bulletin board in the kitchen. Walt took note and began asking his artists to pin their drawings—pencil sketches and fully colored renderings alike—on boards. Walt then sequenced the boards, hung them on the walls, and thus beheld the stories spring to life.

Today, Disney employees use the storyboard to develop movie plot lines, design theme parks, solve business problems, and plan corporate strategy. Generating and juxtaposing ideas graphically, instead of just verbally, expands team members' perspective, sharpens their focus, and spurs them to see and feel and dream, not just to think.

In almost all of our consulting engagements, we start people storyboarding on day one. Its appeal is immediate—it's fun. Later, its long-term usefulness becomes clear.

Storyboarding is a very democratic process, engaging people at all levels and in all functions and benefiting all personality types:

- *Quiet and reserved people* need not speak until they are ready.
- *Assertive and talkative people* focus on putting pencil to paper, and thus don't dominate the discussion.

- *Visual people* revel in generating and arranging pictures that become stories in front of their eyes.
- *Detail-oriented people* can see how the smallest elements combine to create the big picture: Now they see the forest *and* the trees.

What's *your* story? The Storyboard Technique will help you find out.

PLOT

To visually display and organize a team's ideas, thoughts, and concerns.

RUNNING TIME

One hour to a full day, depending on the complexity of the ideas or concerns

KEY PLAYERS

- Any leader or team with responsibilities in project planning, problem solving, or decision making

PROPS

- Blank wall or board
- Drafting tape
- Masking tape or push pins
- 4×6 inch index cards
- One or two water soluble felt-tip markers in black and red
- One water soluble blue marker for each participant
- Self-adhesive 1/4-inch dots in red and blue (6 or more of each color for each participant)
- Storyboard example (one per participant) (Exhibit 30-1)

DIRECTOR'S SCRIPT

LIGHTS ...

1. Place 12 three-foot vertical strips of drafting tape (sticky side out) on the blank wall or board. The wall or board will be the storyboard. Anchor it with 24 one-inch strips of masking tape (or push pins, if on fabric). The tape strips will be the storyboard columns.

CAMERA ...

2. Distribute 4×6 inch cards to all team members.

3. State the goal of the exercise: to acquire the skill of visually displaying and organizing your team's ideas, thoughts, and concerns.

ACTION!

4. Invite the team to suggest storyboard topics or questions, and then to agree upon a single one for use in the exercise. Examples are: How might we adopt a Dream, Believe, Dare, and Do culture? Or, what are the barriers for producing a new product, instituting a new process, or providing legendary customer service?

5. Use a black marker to write the chosen topic or question on a 4×6 inch index card. This is the Topic Card. Post this card at the top of the storyboard.

6. Instruct team members to write personal responses to the topic or question on their 4×6 index cards, one idea per card. These are the Detail Cards. To assure anonymity, everyone should use a blue marker.

Team members should place completed cards face down for you to collect as they continue to write additional cards.

7. Allow 10 minutes for this activity.

8. While the team members are writing, read as many of the collected cards as possible. Select six cards that are the most distinctly different from the others, and place them on top of the stack.

9. When team members have completed their cards, read each card aloud, beginning at the top of the stack.

Note: Having placed the six most distinctly different cards on top, you will read these first. The wide array of these responses will provide a broad base upon which to launch "big picture" thinking. (Reading cards with similar responses could limit the range of creative thought.)

10. Ask team members to tell you where to post the cards on the storyboard. Encourage the clustering of similar cards in the same column.

11. Assure the team that all ideas are important and valuable. Inform them that once the cards are collected, the ideas belong to the group at large.

Note: Your role as director is to protect the individual team members and facilitate the storyboarding process.

12. Whenever 3 or 4 cards are in one column, ask the team to assign a name to the column.

13. Have a team member use a red marker to write the column name on a card, and place the card over the appropriate column. This is the Header Card.

14. Give team members red and blue dots.

Rule of thumb: For 12 columns or fewer, each team member receives two red dots and three blue dots. Increase the number of red and blue dots, by one each, for every 12 columns. Always give out one more blue dot than red.

15. Instruct team members to use their red dots to mark the Header Cards that they feel are the most important.

16. Instruct team members to use their blue dots to mark the Detail Cards they feel are most important.

CUT!

17. Debrief the exercise by asking these questions:

- Does the storyboard provide an overview of the question or topic?

- What are the most significant storyboard cards to be examined?

- Is there a need for an additional storyboard to clarify key issues?

18. Create an action plan to address the issues that received the most red and blue dots.

CURTAIN CALL

Question
When is a picture worth a thousand words?

Answer
At Disney, every day.

EXHIBIT 30-1

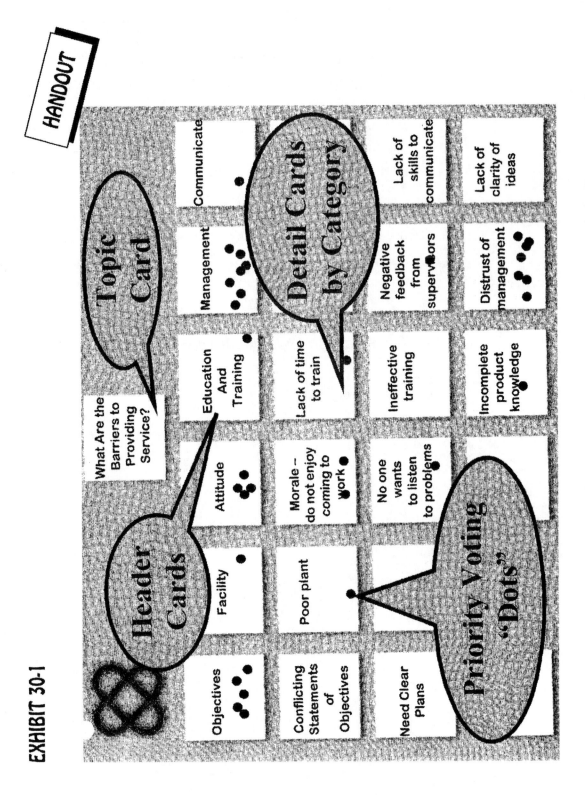

220

SCENE 31: PERSONAL DEVELOPMENT PLANNING

Sometimes the right path is not the easiest one.
—Grandmother Willow, *Pocahontas*

AUTHORS' NOTES

In the 1950s, human resource departments began adopting employee performance appraisals and using the results to determine compensation or managerial action. This highly subjective process was the standard until the early 1980s, when 360-degree feedback instruments were introduced. Not that 360-degree feedback was an overnight hit. Most management rejected being assessed by subordinates. Eventually, though, huge companies like Disney, AT&T, and General Motors embraced 360-degree feedback, creating a climate for the system to flourish nationwide.

Most of the managers we have interviewed over the years say they believe they are above-average performers. So why did American management reject 360-degree feedback at first? What were they afraid of? Did they secretly fear low ratings of their work?

In a 1994 *Fortune* magazine article, "360° Feedback Can Change Your Life," several executives expressed their initial reactions to feedback they had received from their staffs. Raychem CEO Robert Saldich was stunned that shortcomings he thought he had kept hidden were on full view to his top team. Kim Jeffery, CEO of Nestlè's U.S. Perrier operation said, "I thought I was seen as a regular guy. I didn't realize the impact of my words on people." Both of these men, though, took and used the feedback in the constructive spirit in which it was given. Instead of defending their current performance, they acted to eliminate weaknesses and build upon strengths.

Feedback on one's performance can be a blessing or a curse, depending on how it is framed and presented and on what purpose it serves. Traditional performance appraisals typically regard an employee's results over time, usually one year. These five factors comprise the typical performance appraisal that is still in use today:

1. Education—What was the employees' educational background before being hired for this job?
2. On-the-Job Training—How well was the employee trained by the company after being hired?
3. Effort—How hard does the employee work? How much does he or she care?
4. The Process—How much of the employee's success or failure is determined by factors outside his or her control?
5. The Measurement System—How much is the employee's performance rating dependent upon the evaluator's subjective view? (For example, one supervisor may rate an employee average in attendance for missing two days of work in a year. Another supervisor may call this attendance record excellent. Also, an employee's performance in the period immediately preceding the appraisal may be weighted more heavily than the performance over the rest of the year.)

So, these appraisals simply assume you can add the five factors together to arrive at a result. The employee is in a no-win situation. The only factor over which the employee has complete control is *effort*, and it is impossible to isolate and quantify the effect of effort on overall result. Further, we agree with Dr. W. Edwards Deming, the late father of the Total Quality movement, and with social scientist Kurt Lewin, who say that *process* is the prime influence on an employee's performance. In fact, Deming found that more than 85 percent of productivity problems in America are caused by process. Since employees can't control process, performance appraisals actually appraise surrounding circumstances, not the employees themselves!

Here's a real-life illustration of the point:

A team of automotive milling operations workers was rated "average" for "doing enough to get by." When their work then descended to "unacceptable," the human resources department diagnosed a departmentwide "attitude problem" and prescribed communications training to clear it up. The training failed; the workers' work did not improve. Some time later, the automotive company changed materials vendors, and the workers' performance levels rose almost immediately. What had been falsely assumed to be a personal communications issue was in fact a process problem beyond the worker's control.

A problem is that in judging employees as individuals, performance appraisals ignore team results. Not only does teamwork thereby suffer, but employees come to realize that high personal ratings (and consequent compensation boosts) come from pleasing not the customers but the boss. This self-interested attitude cripples group morale, and the resulting lackluster performance is a huge non-value-added overhead cost. It also leads to frustration and debilitating stress when appraisals aren't good. Dr. Deming didn't mince any words here when he said, "Performance appraisals leave people bitter, crushed, bruised, battered, despondent, dejected, feeling inferior, some even depressed, unfit for work for weeks after receipt of their rating. ... It is unfair, as it ascribes to the people in a group differences that may be caused totally by the system that they work in." In addition to dragging down productivity, this system exacts an intolerable human cost.

Personal development Planning is a proactive approach to understanding, channeling, and refining professional behaviors for personal growth. The 360-degree feedback tool helps determine the behaviors and actions that will raise performance to the maximum degree. *Human Resource Magazine* reported on how this approach works:

- It reveals the continuity of values throughout the organization.
- It bolsters support for team initiatives.

- It assigns accountability to all levels.
- It assesses developmental needs of employees.
- It identifies barriers to success.
- It avoids single-rater discrimination.

There are numerous multi-rater feedback instruments on the market. Our *Vision 360®* links the 360-degree review process with the Personal Development Planning process. By combining these two approaches into one self-contained instrument, *Vision 360®* allows users to administer their own Personal Development Plan with minimum administrative hassle. With input from leaders, coworkers, customers, and process partners, *Vision 360®* benefits most of all those who have prime responsibility for carrying out the Plan—the employees themselves. A demonstration of *Vision 360®* can be downloaded from our Web site at **www.Capojac.com.**

Vision 360® starts with a Behavioral Styles assessment. Of course, we all form distinct impressions of other people from the moment we meet. On the slightest evidence, we may decide that someone is animated, stern, or easygoing, and begin treating them accordingly. When we're correct in our assessment, a positive relationship can develop. When we're off the mark, communication can become strained right away. *Vision 360®* helps us accurately perceive our team members' behavioral styles, and so develop healthy, productive, and lasting relationships—and build a more successful team.

Behavior is often thought to be synonymous with personality. Behavior is the outward, observable manifestation of personality. Personality comprises the values and patterns of thought of an individual's core self.

In Vision 360® we classify behaviors by their relative measures of Assertiveness and Responsiveness, and have designated them Driver, Promoter, Supporter, and Analyzer. (These terms are further explained on page 3 of the Behavioral Styles Report contained within *Vision 360®*.) A behavioral label, of course, is not meant to pigeonhole anyone. It is intended as a departure point for a journey toward understanding and accepting that person more fully. Team members undertaking this journey will gain the most from their relationships with each other and with their customers and guests.

It's clear that developing individuals, not appraising them, must be the goal of every organization. We believe that Personal Development Planning is the best way to achieve this result.

PLOT

To increase team performance levels by replacing traditional performance appraisals with systematic, proactive Personal Development Plans based on 360-degree feedback.

RUNNING TIME

Two to four hours; twice a year.

PLAYERS

- Team leaders who are responsible for developing individuals and teams on an ongoing basis

PROPS

- *Vision 360®* self-contained feedback disk or appropriate 360-degree Personal Development Planning instrument
- Process Flow Diagram for Personal Development Planning (one for each participant) (Exhibit 31-1)
- *Vision 360®* Sample Personal Development Plan (one for each participant) (Exhibit 31-2)
- Flip chart for Behavioral Styles Exercise
- Markers

DIRECTOR'S SCRIPT

LIGHTS ...

1. Select a method for gathering multi-rater or 360-degree feedback, one that will promote an environment of commitment and trust.

   Note: 360-degree feedback instruments are available in a variety of forms. *Vision 360®*, a self-contained disk combining feedback and Personal Development Planning, is based on a similar process used by the Disney organization.

CAMERA ...

2. Meet with team members as a group to discuss the benefits of 360-degree feedback. The two central themes of this discussion should be:
   - parlaying individual performance goals into successful team results; and
   - using 360-degree feedback to provide well-defined, credible performance information to build and strengthen individual effectiveness and teamwork.

3. Assure the team members that:
   - Your own role is to ensure confidentiality.
   - The feedback will not cause status changes in either pay or job.
   - Resistance to any new process is natural, but 360-degree feedback is one of the best methods for setting realistic goals and facilitating personal growth.

4. Review the Process Flow Diagram with the team members.

5. Review the sample *Vision 360®* Personal Development Plan with the team members. Discuss the two parts:

Behavioral Styles

   - Knowledge of one's own behavioral style and an awareness of others' behavioral styles will aid in effective

226

communication with team members as well as with customers.

- The first 20 questions determine Behavioral Style.

Detail Report

- The report is divided into as many as 10 categories.
- Results are displayed in Gap Size and Gap Distribution.
- Each reviewer rates how often an employee should exhibit the behavior cited in each question, and how often the employee actually does exhibit the behavior. The gap is the difference between the desired behavior and the observed actual behavior.

ACTION!

6. Meet one-on-one with each team member to:

- Clarify his or her role on the team.
- Verify his or her understanding of the team's mission and the company's values.
- Discuss the work processes for which he or she is responsible.
- Solicit his or her views on the work environment.

Notes: Team leaders are charged with guiding their teams to make wise choices that lead to sound decisions.

Process and environmental improvements can entail policy changes that temporarily derail team members' efforts to achieve success. Team leaders must work with diligence and sensitivity to get these team members back on track.

7. Ask each team member to complete the self-review questions.

8. Assist each team member to select other individuals who should be invited to provide feedback on the team member's performance.

Notes:

- At least two individuals are required for feedback in the categories of Coworker, Process Partner, and Customer.

- The feedback instrument's questions are the same as those answered by the team member in his or her self-review.

- You, the exercise leader, will record your own perceptions of each team member's performance by answering the same feedback instrument questions.

9. Schedule a time to review each team member's proposed Personal Development Plan.

CUT!

10. At the scheduled times, review the Personal Development Plans by asking each team member to:

- State what he or she has learned about himself or herself from the 360-degree feedback.

- Propose development projects he or she would like to pursue in the next six months. Establish Behavioral Objective(s) and Checkpoints for these projects.

- Suggest ways to help achieve the stated Behavioral Objective(s). For example, if you both agree the team member needs to develop project-planning skills, he or she could:

a) Attend Project Planning in the Widget Industry seminar.

b) Be assigned as project leader.

The Checkpoints could be:

- Attending the seminar within the next six weeks.

- Leading a project that comes in on time and on budget by year-end.

    (The team member will not be faulted if a lack of money or time prevents attendance at a seminar.)

11. Help the team member compare his or her Self and Others Behavioral Styles Report pie charts. Explain that:

- The percentages indicate the perceived strengths of each style.

- These percentages may reflect either a well-defined dominant style or a blend of styles (if the percentages are more balanced).

- Our perceptions of ourselves often differ from others' perceptions of us.

- It is natural to feel misunderstood when the style perceptions of Self and Others are vastly different.

- Vastly different Self and Others style perceptions send a signal to become more aware of how our behaviors are perceived by others.

12. Ask:

- What is the value of learning about different behavioral styles?

Answer:

Knowledge and acceptance of our own and team members' styles is essential for developing long-term, win–win relationships with our colleagues.

Behaviors we consider "efficient" are not necessarily "effective" in all situations.

- Why is our method and manner of communicating with other team members so important?

Answer:

Because communication creates perception, and perception becomes reality.

13. Plan to work with each team leader twice a year on this activity.

Fear of the same old tired and demoralizing performance appraisal continues in every industry with few exceptions. Many employees assume that the 360-degree feedback process is simply a repackaging ploy. Not so. Invite your team members to experience the 360-degree feedback difference. Here are some of the keys to 360-degree feedback's success:

- It is not used for purposes of appraising and financially compensating work.
- It is kept absolutely confidential in every detail.
- It gives employees access to feedback and reinforces mutual trust and respect. In all cases, all parties' input contributes to the eventual Personal Development Plan.
- It generates guidelines more than strict procedures for achieving improved performance results. (That's because guidelines liberate creative energy and let each person use his or her own initiative to uphold organizational values while pursuing "good show" team results.)

EXHIBIT 31-1
PROCESS FLOW DIAGRAM
PERSONAL DEVELOPMENT PLAN

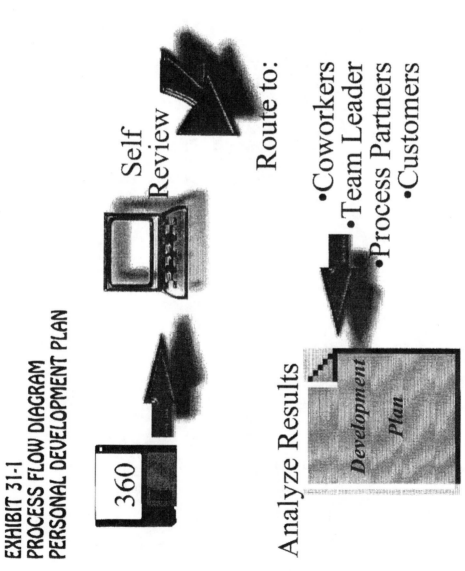

360

Self Review

Route to:
•Coworkers
•Team Leader
•Process Partners
•Customers

Analyze Results

Development Plan

231

Self

Driver: 80%

Analyzer: 20%

Others

1 Leader
3 Coworkers
1 Customer
2 Process Partners

Driver: 84%

Promoter: 8%

Analyzer: 8%

© 1997 Capodagli Jackson Consulting

Overview

Behavioral Styles - Development Plan

Studying human behavior is a discipline for most organizational leaders and a favorite pastime for many others. People of different styles are required to work together every day throughout the functions and positions in most organizations. Those who form the best partnerships are those who are willing to adapt their styles to meet the needs and expectations of others.

Behavior is often thought of as one's entire personality, but this assumption is inaccurate. Personality is holistic, or everything a person is including values, viewpoint, ideas and behavior. By observing other people's behavior, we have clues to their deeper personalities.

Three factors are central to an understanding of human behavior.

1. We are all creatures of habit.

People tend to react with observable and repetitive patterns of action. Therefore, most people have a style which is automatic and comfortable for them.

2. We are all judgmental.

Human nature dictates that people are opinionated about the world around them including others whom they encounter. Differences in style are often the cause of strained relationships, particularly when people fail to understand the styles of others. When people are willing to accept that differences are healthy, they are more likely to develop positive working relationships with others.

3. We are all adaptable to some degree.

Most people interact with others on a daily basis. Some relationships are easier than others due in part to behavioral style similarities. People of different styles may communicate well, but these relationships generally require more energy to develop and maintain. Being open to the viewpoints of others often is situational and mood related. On a "bad day," you may have difficulty communicating with almost anyone; conversely, on a "good day," you may relate in a natural and easy manner with those whom you might avoid on another day.

Social scientists have agreed on two measurable dimensions of behavior: Assertiveness and Responsiveness.

Assertiveness is defined as the degree to which we attempt to influence the thoughts and actions of others. The scale is shown as the horizontal axis on the following matrix from Ask (asserting oneself through questions) to Tell (asserting oneself through statements).

Responsiveness is defined as the degree to which we reveal our feelings to others. The scale is shown as the vertical axis on the following matrix from Control (guarding emotions) to Emote (displaying emotions).

All of us display behavior in all four of the quadrants of the matrix from time to time, but there is usually one style which is dominant for us, our "true" comfort zone.

Overview Continued

We use labels (Driver, Promoter, Supporter, Analyzer) for each quadrant as simply descriptive generalizations of each style. They should not be used to "pigeonhole" people. Remember, the value of understanding behavioral styles is really a better understanding and acceptance of others.

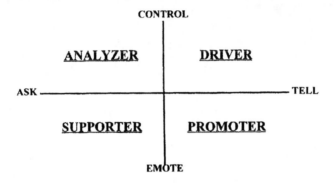

Each style is unique and positive in many ways. Organizations which build upon the best attributes of their people will likely be the ones who also develop long-term relationships with their customers. Here are the most outstanding benefits of each style:

Driver
  --Results oriented
  --Task focused
  --Calculated risk taker
  --Project and people director

Promoter
  --People focused
  --Idea generator
  --Motivational team player
  --Communications link

Supporter
  --Empathetic listener
  --Supportive team member
  --Strives for WIN/WIN in relationships
  --Loyal to leaders

Analyzer
  --Investigation oriented
  --Policy creator
  --Measurement oriented
  --Utilizes details for decision-making

Adapting across the quadrants (Supporter/Driver and Promoter/Analyzer) may require patience on the part of each style. For example, if a Driver supervisor begins coaching sessions with a Supporter employee by stating, "Today, you will be learning how to respond to a customer complaint," the Supporter may not vocalize his or her concerns. Since Supporter styles tend to develop rapport on a more personal tone, asking the question, "Do you feel that some feedback might help you in responding to customer complaints?" might actually motivate them to high performance.

Under pressure, people exhibit behaviors which signify that they are out of their comfort zone. Here are the tendencies of each style during these times of conflict:

Drivers
--Become autocratic
--FIGHT pattern exhibited

Promoters
--Attack
--FIGHT pattern exhibited

Supporters
--Acquiesce
--FLIGHT pattern exhibited

Analyzers
--Avoid
--FLIGHT pattern exhibited

What to Do with Your Feedback

Compare the results of your Self and Others pie charts. The percentages will help you to understand the apparent strength of each style. There may be a well-defined dominant reflected, or if your percentages are more balanced, your comfort zone is simply a greater blend of the styles. Often we perceive ourselves differently from the way others perceive us. When the percentages of Self and Others are vastly different, people often feel misunderstood. If your pie charts differ greatly, you might use the information to help you a.) develop an awareness that the perceptions of others may differ from your own and b.) develop a greater awareness of the behaviors which you display to others.

You may pose the question, "What's the value in knowing about different styles?" or "Does it really matter how I word my statements or question to my coworkers?" The answer is "Only if you are concerned about developing long-term, win-win relationships with them." Effective leaders must be able to use appropriate degrees of assertiveness and responsiveness in order to guide their staff members through a healthy development process.

© 1997 Capodagli Jackson Consulting

235

HANDOUT

Gap Size

Category:
Respect

Category Ave		Gap Size 0 1 2 3 4
	Self .34	
	Others .34	

How often does this person... **Gap Size** **Gap Distribution**

1. treat coworkers at all levels as equal in importance

	Gap Size	Gap Distribution (0 1 2 3 4)
Self	1	1
1 Leader	0	1
3 Coworkers	0	3
2 Process Prtnrs.	1	1 (at 0), 1 (at 2)
1 Customer	NA	

2. respect the dignity and potential of others

	Gap Size	Gap Distribution (0 1 2 3 4)
Self	0	1
1 Leader	0	1
3 Coworkers	0	3
2 Process Prtnrs.	.5	1 (at 0), 1 (at 1)
1 Customer	NA	

3. treat others in accordance with the desired treatment of self

	Gap Size	Gap Distribution (0 1 2 3 4)
Self	0	1
1 Leader	0	1
3 Coworkers	.34	2 (at 0), 1 (at 1)
2 Process Prtnrs.	1	1 (at 0), 1 (at 2)
1 Customer	NA	

GAP DISTRIBUTION - the distribution of answers selected for each question
GAP SIZE - the difference between the observed behavior and the desired behavior

© 1997 Capodagli Jackson Consulting

EXHIBIT 31-2 (CONTINUED)
PERSONAL DEVELOPMENT PLAN
DETAIL REPORT

Gap Size

Category:
Partnerships

Category Ave		0	1	2	3	4
Self	.26					
Others	.21					

How often does this person...   **Gap Size**   **Gap Distribution**

1. develop and maintain positive relationships with process partners

	Gap Size						Gap Distribution				
		0	1	2	3	4	0	1	2	3	4
Self	0						1				
1 Leader	0						1				
3 Coworkers	.34						2	1			
2 Process Prtnrs.	.5						1	1			
1 Customer	NA										

2. review key processes with partners on a regular basis to gain their feedback

	Gap Size						Gap Distribution				
		0	1	2	3	4	0	1	2	3	4
Self	0						1				
1 Leader	0						1				
3 Coworkers	.34						2	1			
2 Process Prtnrs.	0						2				
1 Customer	NA										

3. establish measurable criteria that describes the desired level of quality

	Gap Size						Gap Distribution				
		0	1	2	3	4	0	1	2	3	4
Self	1							1			
1 Leader	0						1				
3 Coworkers	0						3				
2 Process Prtnrs.	.5						1	1			
1 Customer	NA										

4. communicate to process partners measurable criteria that describes the desired level of quality

	Gap Size						Gap Distribution				
		0	1	2	3	4	0	1	2	3	4
Self	0						1				
1 Leader	0						1				
3 Coworkers	0						3				
2 Process Prtnrs.	.5						1	1			
1 Customer	NA										

GAP DISTRIBUTION - the distribution of answers selected for each question
GAP SIZE - the difference between the observed behavior and the desired behavior

© 1997 Capodagli Jackson Consulting

EXHIBIT 31-2 (CONTINUED)
PERSONAL DEVELOPMENT PLAN
DETAIL REPORT

HANDOUT

Gap Size

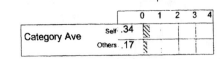

Category:			0	1	2	3	4
Leadership	Category Ave	Self .34					
		Others .17					

How often does this person...   Gap Size   Gap Distribution

1. demonstrate the behaviors of an effective leader

	Gap Size 0 1 2 3 4	Gap Distribution 0 1 2 3 4
Self	0	1
1 Leader	0	1
3 Coworkers	0	3
2 Process Prtnrs.	.5	1 1
1 Customer	NA	

2. demonstrate coaching and counseling behaviors as appropriate to the situation

	Gap Size 0 1 2 3 4	Gap Distribution 0 1 2 3 4
Self	1	1
1 Leader	0	1
3 Coworkers	0	3
2 Process Prtnrs.	.5	1 1
1 Customer	NA	

3. support coworkers through challenging projects and assignments

	Gap Size 0 1 2 3 4	Gap Distribution 0 1 2 3 4
Self	0	1
1 Leader	0	1
3 Coworkers	0	3
2 Process Prtnrs.	.5	1 1
1 Customer	NA	

GAP DISTRIBUTION - the distribution of answers selected for each question
GAP SIZE - the difference between the observed behavior and the desired behavior

EXHIBIT 31-2 (CONTINUED)
PERSONAL DEVELOPMENT PLAN
DETAIL REPORT

Gap Size

Category:
Innovation

Category Ave		0	1	2	3	4
	Self	.6				
	Others	.34				

How often does this person...   Gap Size   Gap Distribution

1. display an openness to new ways of doing things

	Gap Size 0 1 2 3 4	Gap Distribution 0 1 2 3 4
Self	0	1
1 Leader	0	1
3 Coworkers	0	3
2 Process Prtnrs.	.5	1 1
1 Customer	NA	

2. invite customers to share ideas to improve your products and services

	Gap Size 0 1 2 3 4	Gap Distribution 0 1 2 3 4
Self	1	1
1 Leader	0	1
3 Coworkers	0	3
2 Process Prtnrs.	1	1 1
1 Customer	NA	

3. encourage individuals to explore creative ideas with process partners

	Gap Size 0 1 2 3 4	Gap Distribution 0 1 2 3 4
Self	1	1
1 Leader	0	1
3 Coworkers	0	3
2 Process Prtnrs.	1.5	1 1
1 Customer	NA	

4. reward innovative ideas of your staff members

	Gap Size 0 1 2 3 4	Gap Distribution 0 1 2 3 4
Self	1	1
1 Leader	0	1
3 Coworkers	0	3
2 Process Prtnrs.	1	1 1
1 Customer	NA	

GAP DISTRIBUTION - the distribution of answers selected for each question
GAP SIZE - the difference between the observed behavior and the desired behavior

© 1997 Capodagli Jackson Consulting

239

EXHIBIT 31-2 (CONTINUED)
PERSONAL DEVELOPMENT PLAN
DETAIL REPORT

Category:
Innovation Continued

How often does this person...   Gap Size   Gap Distribution

		Gap Size					Gap Distribution				
		0	1	2	3	4	0	1	2	3	4
5. celebrate worthy ideas even when they fail	Self	0					1				
	1 Leader	0					1				
	3 Coworkers	0					3				
	2 Process Prtnrs.	1					1		1		
	1 Customer	NA									

GAP DISTRIBUTION - the distribution of answers selected for each question
GAP SIZE - the difference between the observed behavior and the desired behavior

© 1997 Capodagli Jackson Consulting

EXHIBIT 31-2 (CONTINUED)
PERSONAL DEVELOPMENT PLAN
DETAIL REPORT

Category:
Values

Gap Size

		0	1	2	3	4
Category Ave	Self	1	▨			
	Others	.84	▨			

How often does this person...

Gap Size   Gap Distribution

1. understand the values of the organization

	Gap Size 0 1 2 3 4	Gap Distribution 0 1 2 3 4
Self	1	1
1 Leader	0	1
3 Coworkers	.34	2 1
2 Process Prtnrs.	2	2
1 Customer	NA	

2. demonstrate behavior consistent with the values of the organization

	Gap Size 0 1 2 3 4	Gap Distribution 0 1 2 3 4
Self	1	1
1 Leader	0	1
3 Coworkers	.34	2 1
2 Process Prtnrs.	1.5	1 1
1 Customer	NA	

3. align business decisions with the values of the organization

	Gap Size 0 1 2 3 4	Gap Distribution 0 1 2 3 4
Self	1	1
1 Leader	0	1
3 Coworkers	0	3
2 Process Prtnrs.	2	2
1 Customer	NA	

4. champion the alignment between the values of coworkers and the organization

	Gap Size 0 1 2 3 4	Gap Distribution 0 1 2 3 4
Self	1	1
1 Leader	0	1
3 Coworkers	1	1 1 1
2 Process Prtnrs.	2	2
1 Customer	NA	

GAP DISTRIBUTION - the distribution of answers selected for each question
GAP SIZE - the difference between the observed behavior and the desired behavior

© 1997 Capodagli Jackson Consulting

241

EXHIBIT 31-2 (CONTINUED)
PERSONAL DEVELOPMENT PLAN
DETAIL REPORT

HANDOUT

Gap Size

Category:
Customer Focus

Category Ave		Gap Size (0 1 2 3 4)
	Self	1.34
	Others	.45

How often does this person...   Gap Size   Gap Distribution

1. demonstrate a belief in quality in all aspects of work

	Gap Size	Gap Distribution
Self	3	1
1 Leader	0	1
3 Coworkers	0	3
2 Process Prtnrs.	1.5	1 1
1 Customer	NA	

2. develop positive relationships with key customers

	Gap Size	Gap Distribution
Self	2	1
1 Leader	0	1
3 Coworkers	.34	2 1
2 Process Prtnrs.	1.5	1 1
1 Customer	NA	

3. meet customer needs in a timely fashion

	Gap Size	Gap Distribution
Self	1	1
1 Leader	0	1
3 Coworkers	.34	2 1
2 Process Prtnrs.	1.5	1 1
1 Customer	NA	

4. communicate the importance of customer-focused values to coworkers

	Gap Size	Gap Distribution
Self	1	1
1 Leader	0	1
3 Coworkers	.67	1 2
2 Process Prtnrs.	.5	1 1
1 Customer	NA	

GAP DISTRIBUTION - the distribution of answers selected for each question
GAP SIZE - the difference between the observed behavior and the desired behavior

© 1997 Capodagli Jackson Consulting

EXHIBIT 31-2 (CONTINUED)
PERSONAL DEVELOPMENT PLAN
DETAIL REPORT

HANDOUT

Category:

Customer Focus Continued

How often does this person...   Gap Size   Gap Distribution

		0 1 2 3 4	0 1 2 3 4
5. explain decisions to coworkers in terms of customer impact	Self	1	1
	1 Leader	0	1
	3 Coworkers	.34	2 1
	2 Process Prtnrs.	0	2
	1 Customer	NA	

		0 1 2 3 4	0 1 2 3 4
6. promote ownership of customer complaints by all front-line coworkers	Self	0	1
	1 Leader	0	1
	3 Coworkers	.34	2 1
	2 Process Prtnrs.	0	2
	1 Customer	NA	

GAP DISTRIBUTION - the distribution of answers selected for each question
GAP SIZE - the difference between the observed behavior and the desired behavior

© 1997 Capodagli Jackson Consulting

EXHIBIT 31-2 (CONTINUED)
PERSONAL DEVELOPMENT PLAN
DETAIL REPORT

Gap Size

Category:
Communication

Category Ave		Gap Size 0 1 2 3 4
	Self .2	
	Others .67	

How often does this person...

Gap Size / **Gap Distribution**

1. listen openly to all inputs from others prior to decision making

	Gap Size	Gap Distribution 0 1 2 3 4
Self	0	1
1 Leader	0	1
3 Coworkers	1	1 1 1
2 Process Prtnrs.	.5	1 1
1 Customer	NA	

2. communicate to coworkers the importance of sharing knowledge and ideas throughout the organization

	Gap Size	Gap Distribution 0 1 2 3 4
Self	0	1
1 Leader	0	1
3 Coworkers	1	1 1 1
2 Process Prtnrs.	.5	1 1
1 Customer	NA	

3. explain ideas and suggestions in a clear and concise manner

	Gap Size	Gap Distribution 0 1 2 3 4
Self	1	1
1 Leader	0	1
3 Coworkers	0	3
2 Process Prtnrs.	2	1 1
1 Customer	NA	

4. communicate appropriate organizational information to coworkers

	Gap Size	Gap Distribution 0 1 2 3 4
Self	0	1
1 Leader	0	1
3 Coworkers	.34	2 1
2 Process Prtnrs.	2	1 1
1 Customer	NA	

GAP DISTRIBUTION - the distribution of answers selected for each question
GAP SIZE - the difference between the observed behavior and the desired behavior

© 1997 Capodagli Jackson Consulting

EXHIBIT 31-2 (CONTINUED)
PERSONAL DEVELOPMENT PLAN
DETAIL REPORT

HANDOUT

Category:
Communication Continued

How often does this person...   **Gap Size**   **Gap Distribution**

5. communicate performance feedback to coworkers on an informal basis		Gap Size							Gap Distribution 0	1	2	3	4
			0	1	2	3	4						
	Self	0							1				
	1 Leader	0							1				
	3 Coworkers	.67							1	2			
	2 Process Prtnrs.	.5							1	1			
	1 Customer	NA											

EXHIBIT 31-2 (CONTINUED)
PERSONAL DEVELOPMENT PLAN
DETAIL REPORT

HANDOUT

Gap Size

Category:
Speed

Category Ave		0	1	2	3	4
	Self: 1.2	▨				
	Others: .3	▨				

How often does this person...   Gap Size   Gap Distribution

1. champion the empowerment of coworkers to act without asking permission

	Gap Size	Gap Distribution
Self	0	1
1 Leader	0	1
3 Coworkers	.67 ▨	1 2
2 Process Prtnrs.	0	2
1 Customer	NA	

2. champion the elimination of non-value-added activities

	Gap Size	Gap Distribution
Self	1 ▨	1
1 Leader	0	1
3 Coworkers	.67 ▨	1 2
2 Process Prtnrs.	.5 ▨	1 1
1 Customer	NA	

3. identify customer needs, problems and ideas as input to new products and services

	Gap Size	Gap Distribution
Self	1 ▨	1
1 Leader	0	1
3 Coworkers	.34 ▨	2 1
2 Process Prtnrs.	0	2
1 Customer	NA	

4. assist in guiding new projects through the organization

	Gap Size	Gap Distribution
Self	2 ▨▨	1
1 Leader	0	1
3 Coworkers	0	3
2 Process Prtnrs.	0	2
1 Customer	NA	

GAP DISTRIBUTION - the distribution of answers selected for each question
GAP SIZE - the difference between the observed behavior and the desired behavior

© 1997 Capodagli Jackson Consulting

246

EXHIBIT 31-2 (CONTINUED)
PERSONAL DEVELOPMENT PLAN
DETAIL REPORT

Category:

Speed Continued

How often does this person...   Gap Size   Gap Distribution

		Gap Size	0	1	2	3	4		0	1	2	3	4
5. deliver projects within the specified time and budgetary guidelines	Self	2									1		
	1 Leader	0							1				
	3 Coworkers	.34							2	1			
	2 Process Prtnrs.	1								2			
	1 Customer	NA											

EXHIBIT 31-2 (CONTINUED)
PERSONAL DEVELOPMENT PLAN
DETAIL REPORT

Gap Size

Category:
Teamwork

Category Ave		Gap Size
Self	1	
Others	.39	

How often does this person... Gap Size Gap Distribution

1. encourage effective meeting management

	Gap Size	Gap Distribution
Self	1	1
1 Leader	0	1
3 Coworkers	0	3
2 Process Prtnrs.	1	2
1 Customer	NA	

2. demonstrate an understanding of team objectives and roles

	Gap Size	Gap Distribution
Self	1	1
1 Leader	0	1
3 Coworkers	.34	2 1
2 Process Prtnrs.	.5	1 1
1 Customer	NA	

3. communicate team objectives and roles to coworkers

	Gap Size	Gap Distribution
Self	1	1
1 Leader	0	1
3 Coworkers	.67	1 2
2 Process Prtnrs.	.5	1 1
1 Customer	NA	

4. champion project-planning efforts with coworkers

	Gap Size	Gap Distribution
Self	1	1
1 Leader	0	1
3 Coworkers	.34	2 1
2 Process Prtnrs.	.5	1 1
1 Customer	NA	

GAP DISTRIBUTION - the distribution of answers selected for each question
GAP SIZE - the difference between the observed behavior and the desired behavior

EXHIBIT 31-2 (CONTINUED)
PERSONAL DEVELOPMENT PLAN
DETAIL REPORT

Category:
Teamwork Continued

How often does this person...   Gap Size   Gap Distribution

5. support issue resolution between coworkers

	Gap Size	0	1	2	3	4	Gap Dist 0	1	2	3	4
Self	1		▨					1			
1 Leader	0						1				
3 Coworkers	.34	▨					2	1			
2 Process Prtnrs.	1		▨					2			
1 Customer	NA										

6. reward and celebrate team accomplishments

	Gap Size	0	1	2	3	4	Gap Dist 0	1	2	3	4
Self	1		▨					1			
1 Leader	0						1				
3 Coworkers	0						3				
2 Process Prtnrs.	1		▨					2			
1 Customer	NA										

GAP DISTRIBUTION - the distribution of answers selected for each question
GAP SIZE - the difference between the observed behavior and the desired behavior

EXHIBIT 31-2 (CONTINUED)
PERSONAL DEVELOPMENT PLAN
DETAIL REPORT

HANDOUT

Gap Size

Category:
Continuous Learning

Category Ave	Gap Size (0 1 2 3 4)
Self	0
Others	.6

How often does this person...   **Gap Size**   **Gap Distribution**

1. demonstrate the desire to explore new areas of expertise

	Gap Size	Gap Distribution (0 1 2 3 4)
Self	0	1
1 Leader	0	1
3 Coworkers	1	1 1 1
2 Process Prtnrs.	1	2
1 Customer	NA	

2. participate in networking and benchmarking with other organizations

	Gap Size	Gap Distribution (0 1 2 3 4)
Self	0	1
1 Leader	0	1
3 Coworkers	1	1 1 1
2 Process Prtnrs.	.5	1 1
1 Customer	NA	

3. evaluate the education and training needs of coworkers

	Gap Size	Gap Distribution (0 1 2 3 4)
Self	0	1
1 Leader	0	1
3 Coworkers	.34	2 1
2 Process Prtnrs.	.5	1 1
1 Customer	NA	

4. champion cross-training efforts for the best team results

	Gap Size	Gap Distribution (0 1 2 3 4)
Self	0	1
1 Leader	0	1
3 Coworkers	.67	1 2
2 Process Prtnrs.	1	2
1 Customer	NA	

GAP DISTRIBUTION - the distribution of answers selected for each question
GAP SIZE - the difference between the observed behavior and the desired behavior

© 1997 Capodagli Jackson Consulting

EXHIBIT 31-2 (CONTINUED)
PERSONAL DEVELOPMENT PLAN
DETAIL REPORT

Category:

Continuous Learning Continued

How often does this person...   Gap Size   Gap Distribution

			0	1	2	3	4	0	1	2	3	4
5. encourage coworkers to participate in networking and benchmarking with other organizations	Self	0						1				
	1 Leader	0						1				
	3 Coworkers	.34						2	1			
	2 Process Prtnrs.	1							2			
	1 Customer	NA										

GAP DISTRIBUTION - the distribution of answers selected for each question
GAP SIZE - the difference between the observed behavior and the desired behavior

EXHIBIT 31-2 (CONTINUED)
PERSONAL DEVELOPMENT PLAN
DETAIL REPORT

Gap Size

Category:
Details

Category Ave		0	1	2	3	4
	Self 1		▨			
	Others .46		▨			

How often does this person...   Gap Size   Gap Distribution

1. identify inconsistencies and defects in your products and services

	Gap Size	0	1	2	3	4		Gap Dist 0	1	2	3	4
Self	1		▨						1			
1 Leader	0							1				
3 Coworkers	1		▨					1	1	1		
2 Process Prtnrs.	0							2				
1 Customer	NA											

2. participate in continuous improvement efforts

	Gap Size	0	1	2	3	4		Gap Dist 0	1	2	3	4
Self	1		▨						1			
1 Leader	0							1				
3 Coworkers	1.34		▨					1		2		
2 Process Prtnrs.	0							2				
1 Customer	NA											

3. challenge coworkers to maintain accurate project details

	Gap Size	0	1	2	3	4		Gap Dist 0	1	2	3	4
Self	1		▨						1			
1 Leader	0							1				
3 Coworkers	.67		▨					1	2			
2 Process Prtnrs.	.5		▨					1	1			
1 Customer	NA											

4. champion continuous improvement efforts with coworkers

	Gap Size	0	1	2	3	4		Gap Dist 0	1	2	3	4
Self	1		▨						1			
1 Leader	0							1				
3 Coworkers	0							3				
2 Process Prtnrs.	.5		▨					1	1			
1 Customer	NA											

GAP DISTRIBUTION - the distribution of answers selected for each question
GAP SIZE - the difference between the observed behavior and the desired behavior

© 1997 Capodagli Jackson Consulting

EXHIBIT 31-2 (CONTINUED)
PERSONAL DEVELOPMENT PLAN
DETAIL REPORT

HANDOUT

Gap Size

Category:
*Problem
Solv./Decis. Making*

		Gap Size 0 1 2 3 4
Category Ave	Self .67	
	Others .39	

How often does this person...   **Gap Size**   **Gap Distribution**

1. consider all possible solutions before making a decision		Gap Size 0 1 2 3 4	Gap Distribution 0 1 2 3 4
	Self	1	1
	1 Leader	0	1
	3 Coworkers	.67	2 1
	2 Process Prtnrs.	0	2
	1 Customer	NA	

2. gain input from staff members prior to making decisions that will affect them		Gap Size 0 1 2 3 4	Gap Distribution 0 1 2 3 4
	Self	1	1
	1 Leader	0	1
	3 Coworkers	.67	2 1
	2 Process Prtnrs.	.5	1 1
	1 Customer	NA	

3. champion a cross-functional approach to solving problems which affect multiple areas		Gap Size 0 1 2 3 4	Gap Distribution 0 1 2 3 4
	Self	0	1
	1 Leader	0	1
	3 Coworkers	.34	2 1
	2 Process Prtnrs.	.5	1 1
	1 Customer	NA	

GAP DISTRIBUTION - the distribution of answers selected for each question
GAP SIZE - the difference between the observed behavior and the desired behavior

© 1997 Capodagli Jackson Consulting

253

EXHIBIT 31-2 (CONTINUED)
PERSONAL DEVELOPMENT PLAN
OBJECTIVE-SETTING WORKSHEET

Working Copy 4/26/00

Behaviors	Urgency of Improvement		Review Date
1. Respect			
2. Partnerships			
3. Leadership			
4. Innovation			
5. Values			
6. Customer Focus			
7. Communication			
8. Speed			
9. Teamwork			
10. Continuous Learning			
11. Details			
12. Problem Solving/Decision Making			

Critical = Gap of 2.5 or more
Moderate = Gap of 1.5 - 2.49
Low = Gap of .75 - 1.49
No Action = Gap of 0 - .74

© 1997 Capodagli Jackson Consulting

EXHIBIT 31-2 (CONTINUED)
PERSONAL DEVELOPMENT PLAN
OBJECTIVE-SETTING WORKSHEET

Working Copy 4/26/00

Behavioral Objective(s)	Measures	Corresponding Value	Results	*Rating EE ME BE

Overall:

*EE=Exceeded Expectations   ME=Met or Generally Met Expectations   BE=Below Expectations

© 1997 Capodagli Jackson Consulting

Personal Development Planning
Behavioral Styles Follow-Up Exercise

PLOT

To develop understanding and communication among team members.

RUNNING TIME

One hour

KEY PLAYERS

- Team leaders who are responsible for developing individuals and teams on an ongoing basis

PROPS

- Flip chart
- Markers
- Personal Development Planning Diagram
- Four tables, labeled Driver, Promoter, Supporter, and Analyzer

DIRECTOR'S SCRIPT

LIGHTS ...

1. Assemble the team in a workshop environment.

CAMERA ...

2. Explain the three factors that are central to an understanding of human behavior (see *Vision 360®* Sample Personal Development Plan):
   - We are all creatures of habit.
   - We are all judgmental.
   - We are all adaptable to some degree.

3. State that social scientists have agreed on two measurable dimensions of behavior, Assertiveness and Responsiveness.

ACTION!

4. Write, "Assertiveness is the degree to which we attempt to influence the thoughts and actions of others" at the top of the flip chart.

5. Draw a horizontal line, with arrows on each end, in the center of the flip chart page.

6. Write Ask next to the left-hand arrow. Explain that Ask means to assert oneself through questions.

7. Write Tell next to the right-hand arrow. Explain that Tell means to assert oneself through statements.

8. Write, "Responsiveness has been defined as the degree to which we reveal our feelings to others" at the bottom of the flip chart.

9. Draw a vertical line through the center of the horizontal line, with arrows on each end, forming a Behavioral Styles Matrix.

10. Write Control above the top arrow. Explain that Control means to guard one's emotions.

11. Write Emote below the bottom arrow. Explain that Emote means to display emotions.

Note: Tell the team members that we move through all the styles depending on the situation, but we all have a basic comfort zone, one that has been uniquely ours since we were very young.

12. Ask: Have any of you who have small children taken them to the grocery store and watched their behavior when they see candy? Some just grab the candy. Some ask for the candy.

13. Have the team members move to one of the four tables that corresponds to their Behavioral Styles.

Note: Don't be concerned if you have a low number or no team members in a particular style.

14. Ask each group to draw the Behavioral Style Matrix of their own style on a flip chart page.

15. Have each group choose three famous people and come to a consensus on the Behavioral Style of each individual. When they have decided, they will place a dot, along with their names, on the specific point of the matrix that depicts each individual. Ask them to make their decisions based on the two scales, one at a time, and record their clues to each individual's style on a piece of paper. These clues should include examples of tone, volume, and pacing of voice and body language.

16. Allow 10 minutes for each table to decide on three individuals.

17. Allow 20 minutes for groups to answer these questions on separate flip chart pages:

- List the behaviors that you agree represent your style.
- List the behaviors that you agree represent the style that is the opposite of yours. (Opposite is diagonal on the Behavioral Style Matrix.)
- How do you expect others to behave to meet your comfort zone?
- What about your style is potentially beneficial to your team?
- What phrase, picture, or slogan best represents your style?

18. After 20 minutes, invite each group to present its findings, one at a time. Ask the groups to hold the last question until the end of their presentation. During their presentations, post their responses on the wall.

CUT!

19. Debrief with the following questions:

- What did you learn from listening to the thoughts and feelings of the four style groups?
- How can we use this information in our team?

SCENE 32: PERFORMANCE LEARNING CYCLE

You know your path, now follow it.
—Grandmother Willow, *Pocahontas*

AUTHORS' NOTES

Disney's orientation program, Traditions, is the first step in the path of each and every cast member, but the true learning begins when cast members begin acting their roles in "the whole show." The Disney culture is in sharp contrast to so many organizations that employ the method we call, "spray and pray." They spray the training on, and pray that it sticks!

The performance cycle is not difficult to learn, and it will produce results. It does, however, require a disciplined approach to training. You decide which approach, Spray and Pray or the Performance Learning Cycle, should be your training strategy.

PLOT

To provide a systematic approach to skills training for employees at all levels; to provide a long-standing model for individual development.

RUNNING TIME

Unlimited

KEY PLAYERS

- Team leaders
- Department heads
- Training professionals

PROPS

■ Performance Learning Cycle (Exhibit 32-1)

DIRECTOR'S SCRIPT

LIGHTS, CAMERA ...

1. Assemble the team.

ACTION!

2. Present the four phases of the Performance Learning Cycle:

Training

■ As work team leader, address the following questions:

■ What training are we currently providing and to whom?

■ What are the training needs of each employee?

■ Have I instituted a 360-degree feedback and individual development planning process within my team?

■ Are we getting the results we need to be competitive?

■ Include each and every employee in some form of training. Training only a certain individual or group leaves other individuals and groups untrained in new skills, and workplace dysfunction is the result.

■ Review the five essential elements for conducting effective training sessions:

■ *Plan.*—Before you launch skills training, determine the specific expected result. Anticipate employees' questions, problems, or barriers, and predetermine how you will respond.

■ *Be fair and consistent.*—Expect peak performance from every employee, no matter how much prior training he or she may have had. A leader has no use for bias, prejudice, or favoritism.

■ *Be decisive.*—Be clear about your training expectations. Always show your absolute commitment to successful results.

- *Gain feedback.*—Do not take silence for understanding or approval. Whenever possible, have employees confirm in their own words what they have just heard you say.
- *Follow up.*—Assign a specific, focused work experience to continue helping employees do their very best work after their training is through.

Focused Experiences

- Supplement theoretical training with hands-on practice to ensure a "best show" experience for your guests.
- Schedule one-on-one follow-up sessions to discuss issues, strengthen trust, and ensure ongoing success.

Results

- Monitor and measure employees' ongoing performance. If you are dissatisfied with an employee's progress, ask yourself:
- Why did the results not meet my expectations?
- Did I do everything within my power to ensure the employee's success?
- Does any part of the training need to be repeated?
- What additional training and coaching should I provide?
- What barriers remain and how can I help to remove them?
- What next steps should be taken?

Recognition

- Sustain and enhance employee performance by commending superior work.
- Recognize outstanding performance (individual and team) at appropriate times and in appropriate ways such as:
- distinguished service pins (individual or team)
- achievement citations (individual or team)

- personal words of commendation (individual or team)
- monetary bonuses (individual or team)
- restaurant dinners (team)
- informal office parties (team)

Note: The Disney organization incorporates many of these celebrations in their cast member recognition process.

CURTAIN CALL

Question
Does learning take place in the classroom?

Answer
No. True learning happens when new skills are applied in a work experience. Seeing tangible results and receiving recognition will transform these new skills into habits.

If You Perceive It, You Believe It!

A newspaper editor once fired a young stringer named Walt Disney for a lack of good ideas.

Who do you think really lacked ideas, the editor or Walt?

Perceptions are subjective and situational, of course, and maybe Walt just wasn't suited for newspaper work. Still, you can bet that a few years later that paper would have loved to have Walt back. With his creative exuberance and entrepreneurial bent, he wouldn't have been happy, though. His destiny was to create a world of magic and make the world his guests.

Walt didn't collapse under early rejection, but plenty of people do. They wilt when they're not appreciated, not realizing that the problem is often in the minds of their managers, not in their own work. Some managers' problem is assuming the worst about their employees instead of the best. Their dim expectations inevitably produce dim results. It's the kind of self-fulfilling prophecy that Robert K. Merton documented at Columbia University in 1948: the syndrome of expectations unilaterally influencing behavior. Of course, the syndrome has its positive side, the Pygmalion Effect, in which high expectations breed success. Dr. Robert Rosenthal of Harvard conducted over 400 experiments to test this phenomenon. In one, rats were randomly labeled "maze dull" or "maze bright," and given to an assistant to run through a complex maze. The rats labeled and thus perceived as "bright" performed better every time through. The "dull" rats did poorly.

In another experiment, an elementary schoolteacher was given the names of certain students who were "intellectual bloomers." In fact, these children were chosen at random, and were intellectually no different from anyone else, except as their teacher now perceived them. By the end of the semester, these ostensible "intellectual bloomers" had performed significantly better than the rest of the class.

Experiments don't furnish all the proof of the Pygmalion effect; real life supports it, too. At one vocational training center, five men were identified to the welding instructor as having special aptitude for the work, even though in reality they did not. In test scores, absenteeism, and learning rate, these five men performed better in the class than their fellow students—who themselves picked these five as the men with whom they most wanted to work!

For every "chosen" employee, though, there are many more who are relegated by negative presumption to the "maze dull" heap. A good leader can and **must** prevent this tragic waste. How? By honestly and fairly assessing each employee's potential and giving it every chance to be fulfilled. When it is not fulfilled, the reasons for underachievement must be found out.

Typical reasons for lackluster performance are:

- little experience in the job;
- unfamiliarity with procedures, tools, equipment, etc.;
- insufficient or inappropriate materials;
- ignorance of what is expected;
- lack of direction and supportive feedback;
- physical or mental limitations;
- insufficient training (including none at all).

Some people, of course, just don't want to perform well. They are in the small minority and can be handled by human resources professionals, case by case.

The Disney organization expects the world of its cast members, and fulfills its expectations by thoroughly preparing them to do their best. Every organization without a skills and values training program should take note and repeat daily:

Helping Employees Fulfill Their Potential Is Job One.

All leaders must realize, however, that each employee learns and develops at a different rate. Instruction that overwhelms or confuses can nip unrealized potential in the bud. Training that is well-designed and well-administered helps it bloom forth.

EXHIBIT 32-1

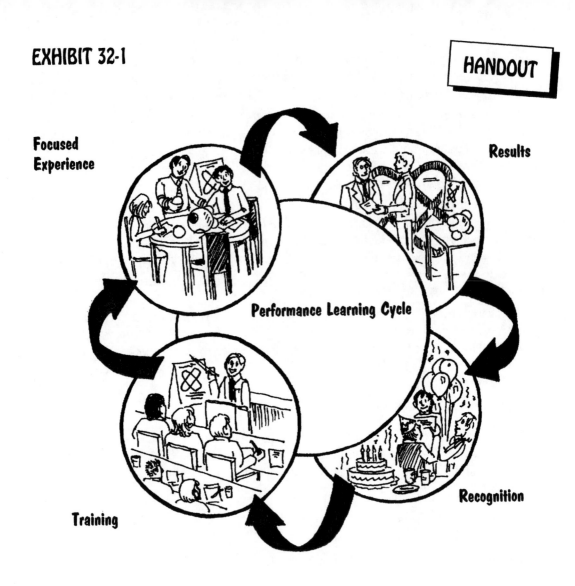

Focused
Experience

Results

Performance Learning Cycle

Training

Recognition

SCENE 33: Q24 LEADERSHIP ASSESSMENT

The dreams that they build now become your heritage.
—Walt Disney

AUTHORS' NOTES

The George Washingtons and Abraham Lincolns of this world only come around every century or so, but there are plenty of truly fine leaders in between, one being the creator of the most famous mouse in the world, Walt Disney! They are the ones whose own self-confident approach to life creates an environment in which their followers, too, can succeed.

In business, these leaders wear many hats: commander, diplomat, counselor, mediator, mentor—the list goes on and on. It's not enough to marshal a group of people, point them toward the horizon, and cry "March!" True leaders must teach, orient, guide, support, and rally the troops to move in step and with coordinated determination toward the goal. To be fully effective, leaders can't just hand out orders; they must be proactive in their approach. Also, they must be comfortable "turning the lens around" to regularly assess themselves. Only leaders who are not too proud or complacent to improve their personal performance can provide their followers with the feedback, knowledge, and motivation to perform great deeds of their own.

PLOT

To provide a method for assessing leadership style; to encourage leaders to assess their strengths and weaknesses in the spirit of continuous improvement; to provide input to regular development planning efforts.

RUNNING TIME

One to two hours

KEY PLAYERS

- Natural Work Team Leaders
- Any leader who is responsible for developing employees or team members

PROPS

- Q24 Leadership Assessment (Exhibit 33-1)
- Q24 Leadership Assessment Scoring (Exhibit 33-2)
- Q24 Leadership Assessment Results (Exhibit 33-3)
- Q24 Leadership Assessment Role Definitions (Exhibit 33-4)
- Q24 Leadership Assessment Skills (Exhibit 33-5)
- Q24 Leadership Assessment Tips (Exhibit 33-6)

DIRECTOR'S SCRIPT

LIGHTS ...

1. Choose a quiet location for the exercise.

CAMERA ...

2. Carefully read and answer each multiple-choice question on the Q24 Leadership Assessment. Answer by circling A, B, C, or D.

3. When you have answered all 24 questions, turn to the Q24 Leadership Assessment Scoring sheet. This sheet's numbered boxes correspond to the 24 questions you have just answered.

4. In each scoring sheet box, circle the letter (plus its associated number) of your answer to that question.

5. Add the circled numbers in each vertical column. Add the circled numbers in boxes 1, 5, 9,13, 17, and 21; then add boxes 2 through 22, and so forth.

6. In the Totals section at the bottom, record the sums of each column's numbers.

7. Turn to the Q24 Leadership Assessment Results sheet.

8. In the first column, labeled Investigator at the bottom, circle the number corresponding to your numeric sum for Investigator on the scoring sheet.

9. Do likewise for the columns labeled Appraiser, Advisor, and Mentor.

CUT!

10. Note which of the four columns contains the highest number. This indicates your prime Leadership style.

11. For a fuller understanding of your Leadership style and how you might develop new skills in these areas, refer to:

   ■ Q24 Leadership Assessment Role Definitions;

   ■ Q24 Leadership Assessment Skills;

   ■ Q24 Leadership Assessment Tips.

Note: Consider both the positive and potentially negative effects of your assessed style in your specific work environment. Consider modifying certain of your style elements and prioritizing your goals accordingly to achieve best results.

CURTAIN CALL

Lee Iacocca was fond of saying, "Lead, follow, or get out of the way."

We say, "Lead, and help others to be creative, courageous, and spirited followers so your whole team can move forward."

EXHIBIT 33-1
Q24 LEADERSHIP ASSESSMENT

The Q24 Leadership Assessment is highly effective in identifying areas in which to concentrate efforts for personal growth. The Assessment results are valuable input for your annual or biannual development plans.

Answer each question by circling A, B, C, or D.

1. One of your employees consistently meets expectations but does not take initiative in developing new skills or demonstrating enthusiasm for his current work. Your most appropriate action is:
   A. Invite him to discuss his feelings and views about his job and future goals.
   B. Ask him to consider what factors have positively or negatively affected his job performance.
   C. Assume that he is in a rut, and ask him if he would like to talk about it.
   D. Tell him that the company only wants top performers, and that they expect continuous improvement from all employees.

2. One of your employees, a below-average performer, has asked your permission to be your backup when you are absent. Your most appropriate action is:
   A. Tell her that she must consistently exceed customers' expectations before she can be given a leadership role.
   B. Meet with her to identify skills of hers that need improving, and how they might be developed.
   C. Suggest that she solicit commentary on her work from upper management and her peers.
   D. Describe to her the essential elements of your job, and ask if she feels prepared to handle them.

3. Your team performs with minimum resources and personnel. A top-rated member wishes to acquire skills beyond those required for her job. You are concerned that spending time learning new skills might make her unable to meet all her responsibilities on the team. Your most appropriate action is:
   A. Tell her you would like to let her do more challenging work, but with your limited resources and team personnel you can't afford her spending time on anything but her current assignments.
   B. Have her wait and see if organizational changes affect her career goals. Schedule a follow-up meeting to discuss next steps in case they do.
   C. Suggest that perhaps a schedule could be developed to coordinate her needs with those of the work group.
   D. Tell her that you'll have to check with other members of the work group to determine how this will affect their work.

4. One of your employees has decided to go back to school to finish his degree. He is interested in two schools, both within driving distance of his home and work. He would like your counsel on this issue. Your most appropriate action is:

A. Ask him to determine which curriculum would best fit his work schedule.

B. Tell him to choose the school that has the best academic reputation.

C. Tell him that both schools are probably fine, but that you are concerned that his school and work schedules may conflict.

D. Discuss with him how each school's curriculum might promote his short- and long-term career goals.

5. You have observed an employee failing to execute a technical procedure he was trained to perform several months ago. Your most appropriate action is:

A. Determine his specific technical deficiency by asking him to recall what he remembers from his training.

B. Tell him you would like to review his training with him before he performs the technical procedure again.

C. Remind him that his training was comprehensive, and assure him that you have faith in him to do the job properly.

D. Document his performance and provide feedback during a structured review session.

6. Two of your employees have been undergoing on-the-job skills training. One of them is doing well and recently began working on his own. The other one says he is not ready to go solo. Your most appropriate action with the hesitant employee is:

A. Tell him that you expect him at least to try to work on his own.

B. Ask him to define which aspects of the job are giving him the greatest problems, then jointly determine how to improve his skills.

C. Invite the more skilled employee to give him some appreciative and constructive feedback.

D. Ask the employee if he feels he'll be able to master and apply the skill sometime in the future.

7. One of your employees has expressed the desire to become a work group leader if the opportunity arises. Your most appropriate action is:

A. Give her a list of leadership courses that are offered in the local areas.

B. Tell her she should consider leadership as a long-term goal.

C. Ask her to relate her long-term goals to those of the organization.

D. Ask her to consider how she might increase her visibility within the organization.

8. One of your employees has expressed a wish for job training in an area where a few of her coworkers are already proficient. Your most appropriate action is:

A. Select the best trainer from among her coworkers; then observe at least one training session until you feel learning is taking place.

B. Tell her you will select a trainer for her, and that you will confirm she is comfortable with the training after it begins.

C. Tell her you will have to consider whether training another person in this area is worthwhile.

D. Suggest that you jointly select an appropriate teacher from within the workgroup, and arrange a convenient training schedule.

9. You have received feedback from a customer who was upset that one of your employees was "short" with him when providing customer service. Your most appropriate action is:

A. Ask the employee to give his own account of the customer encounter, and to explain what he thinks ideal customer service should be.

B. Arrange to observe the employee in a few customer situations, and a subsequent meeting to provide feedback on his performance.

C. Call a meeting of all your employees to affirm the importance of excellent customer service.

D. Tell the employee that among the company's core values is friendly, informative customer service.

10. You often ask your employees to assist you with administrative projects. One employee with poor attention to detail has volunteered to help you as often as she can. Your most appropriate action is:

A. Tell her that her work is not up to standard, and she should improve it before she works again with you.

B. Provide specific examples of her performance deficiencies and ask her to discuss with you how she can improve.

C. Point out to her details she missed on her last project with you, and suggest that she get feedback on her work from that project's "customers."

D. Tell her that you will be glad to give her small projects that you know she can handle.

11. One of your employees thinks your team members are not working well together. He suggests that some social activities might relax the tension that has developed, and thus reinspire the members to cooperate as a group. Your most appropriate action is:

A. State that you are mainly concerned with each person's individual performance.

B. Invite him to share his ideas for social activities with the group.

C. Ask him to cite the specific problem issues and to propose specific solutions for each.

D. Suggest that social activities are not the only ways to break down barriers at work.

12. One of your employees wants to forge closer working relationships with two other departments whose work is linked to yours. You have heard that those departments would like closer relationships, too. Your most appropriate action is:

A. Arrange to meet with the supervisors of those other two departments to discuss mutual goals.

B. Ask your work group to identify opportunities for working more effectively with other departments.

C. Arrange to meet with the members of the two other departments to discuss mutual goals.

D. Invite the employee to ask all interested parties if they wish to meet to discuss mutual goals.

13. One of your employees is an above-average performer who rarely engages coworkers to discuss joint projects. Your most appropriate action is:

A. Praise her for her superior work, then ask her how she thinks she and her coworkers might perform more effectively as a team.

B. Encourage her to help you achieve your prime goal: to achieve optimum team results.

C. Explain to her that her coworkers are as much her partners as customers are. Encourage her to work proactively to promote the interests of each.

D. Remind her that she is a member of a team, and that she should work with more team spirit.

14. One of your employees, an inconsistent performer, is always making negative comments about company management. You feel that if she spent more time working and less time complaining, her performance would improve. Your most appropriate action is:

A. Tell her it is inappropriate and counterproductive to create a negative atmosphere in the workplace.

B. Express disappointment that she has not channeled her negative feelings in a more appropriate way. Schedule a meeting to discuss how these feelings might be hindering her performance.

C. Point out that her negative comments are hurting team morale. Arrange a meeting to discuss her frustrations.

D. Ask her if she would be willing to express her feelings to you in private.

15. One of your employees has told you he is upset with himself for not completing the college degree he began pursuing 10 years ago. You have always been happy with this person's performance and his eagerness to learn new skills. Your most appropriate action is:

A. Share your views on how college helps and hinders people, depending on who they are and the jobs they are in.

B. Tell him that a college degree may not benefit him at this stage of his career.

C. Suggest that a degree might indeed broaden his range of opportunities.

D. Listen to his concerns, and suggest that he see a career counselor.

16. One of your strongest performers says he is on the verge of burnout because he spends every waking hour thinking about his job. He suggests that involving himself in community activities might clear his mind and restore a sense of balance in his life. Your most appropriate action is:

A. Give him a list of community activities from which he might choose.

B. Suggest he contact a global organization such as United Way, as well as researching local options.

C. Suggest that he interview with representatives of various community organizations.

D. Encourage him to set personal goals for achievement spanning the next three months to a year.

17. Members of your work group have recently attended an in-service on a newly installed piece of equipment. One of these recent trainees, however, has not been using the new equipment in her work. Your most appropriate action is:

A. Ask her if she understands how to use the new equipment, and if she is aware of its benefits.

B. Offer to observe her work and provide feedback on her performance.

C. Explain to her the benefits of using the equipment, and assure her that once she starts using it she will feel more comfortable.

D. Tell her to begin using the equipment on the next appropriate application.

18. You have an exceptional performer who is experiencing job burnout. He has volunteered to train a few of his inexperienced coworkers on some new software that might help them in their work. Your most appropriate action is:

A. Inform him that tutorials and help-line consultants can help his coworkers learn the new software.

B. Ask him to demonstrate his proficiency with the software. Give him feedback on his skills and, if warranted, arrange for him to train his coworkers.

C. Arrange to meet with the entire work group to learn their training needs.

D. Ask the work group how they feel about being trained by a fellow group member.

19. One of your exceptional employees would like an opportunity to change work groups to broaden her horizons. Your most appropriate action is:

A. Tell her you don't think the company is encouraging transfers at this time.

B. Tell her that she should be creating new challenges in her existing work group.

C. Ask her how changing groups would specifically make her work more rewarding. Provide feedback on her comments.

D. Tell her you will find out if management will approve a transfer at this time.

20. An average-performing employee of yours wants to learn a new skill. His inflated ego, however, prevents him from taking advice from his peers. You have a hunch, though, that he might be able to learn from one particular coworker who is the most capable of the group. Your most appropriate action is:

A. Tell him you want him to train with this very capable coworker, and that only by setting aside his ego will he learn the new skill.

B. Explain that all group members must learn from each other in order to succeed as a unit.

C. Tell him that group members are required to learn from each other in any job in any industry today.

D. Encourage him to let this coworker be his trainer. Arrange a meeting with both of them to discuss the training.

21. Your work group has told you they don't know what the company expects of them anymore. Now you are meeting with them to explain the company's expectations as you perceive them to be. Your most appropriate action is:

   A. Ask each group member to assess his or her performance, skills, and educational or training goals.

   B. Arrange to meet monthly with each group member to review his or her goals and accomplishments.

   C. Encourage each group member to set a new learning goal each month.

   D. Arrange to meet regularly with each group member to discuss learning expectations and opportunities.

22. One of your employees spends too much time chatting with customers and coworkers, and his performance is slipping as a result. One customer has complained that this employee is "too chatty." Your most appropriate action is:

   A. Explain to the employee that he should only talk to customers about how their needs can be met.

   B. Tell the employee that a customer has called him too talkative. Say that you feel he talks too much in the workplace. Ask how much conversation with customers he thinks is appropriate.

   C. Invite the employee to seek feedback from his coworkers about his behavior.

   D. Tell the employee that you have observed his behavior, and that you advise him to communicate only relevant information to the customer.

23. One of your employees consistently performs at high levels but does not communicate well with management. In fact, when she and your boss are together they barely exchange a word. Your most appropriate action is:

   A. Request that she talk with management whenever possible.

   B. Explain that conversing with management is the best way to raise her own visibility within the organization.

   C. Tell her to feel free about asking management about company business matters.

   D. Invite her to talk with management in your presence so you can give her feedback on her communication style.

24. One of your underachieving group members blames his poor performance on being overworked. You perceive that he strongly wishes to improve. Your most appropriate action is:

   A. Review with the employee the prime aspects of his job. Ask him to rate his performance in each.

   B. Ask the employee to observe and try to learn from the top performers in his group.

   C. Tell the employee that all workers in his position have similar duties, and you don't feel he is being overworked.

   D. Arrange to observe the employee during some customer interactions so you can give him feedback and suggest ways for him to improve.

EXHIBIT 33-2
Q24 LEADERSHIP ASSESSMENT SCORING

HANDOUT

Name _____

1	2	3	4
a=4 b=3 c=2 d=1	a=1 b=4 c=3 d=2	a=2 b=1 c=4 d=3	a=3 b=2 c=1 d=4
5	**6**	**7**	**8**
a=4 b=3 c=2 d=1	a=1 b=4 c=3 d=2	a=2 b=1 c=4 d=3	a=3 b=2 c=1 d=4
9	**10**	**11**	**12**
a=4 b=3 c=2 d=1	a=1 b=4 c=3 d=2	a=2 b=1 c=4 d=3	a=3 b=2 c=1 d=4
13	**14**	**15**	**16**
a=4 b=3 c=2 d=1	a=1 b=4 c=3 d=2	a=2 b=1 c=4 d=3	a=3 b=2 c=1 d=4
17	**18**	**19**	**20**
a=4 b=3 c=2 d=1	a=1 b=4 c=3 d=2	a=2 b=1 c=4 d=3	a=3 b=2 c=1 d=4
21	**22**	**23**	**24**
a=4 b=3 c=2 d=1	a=1 b=4 c=3 d=2	a=2 b=1 c=4 d=3	a=3 b=2 c=1 d=4

Totals			
Investigator	*Appraiser*	*Advisor*	*Mentor*

EXHIBIT 33-3
Q24 LEADERSHIP ASSESSMENT RESULTS

HANDOUT

Name _____

	Investigator	Appraiser	Advisor	Mentor
Very High	24	24	24	24
	___	___	___	___
	___	___	___	___
	20	20	20	20
High	___	___	___	___
Average	17	17	17	17
	___	___	___	___
	15	15	15	15
Low	___	___	___	___
Very Low	12	12	12	12
	___	___	___	___
	___	___	___	___
	___	___	___	___
	___	___	___	___
	___	___	___	___
	6	6	6	6

EXHIBIT 33-4
Q24 LEADERSHIP ASSESSMENT RESULTS

HANDOUT

Here are the basic role definitions for the four leadership styles:

Investigator
- Analyzes talents.
- Explores interests.
- Discovers individual values.

Appraiser
- Provides detailed feedback.
- Communicates strengths.
- Examines development planning needs.

Advisor
- Imparts knowledge.
- Communicates goals.
- Provides career planning options.

Mentor
- Presents various learning opportunities.
- Provides candid feedback.
- Suggests action plans for development.

EXHIBIT 33-5
Q24 LEADERSHIP ASSESSMENT SKILLS

Investigator
- Establishes impressions based on data.
- Listens attentively; asks probing questions without being directive.

Appraiser
- Shares personal experiences during coaching.
- Provides appropriate examples of superior performance.

Advisor
- Provides resources for personal development.
- Monitors progress and provides follow-up feedback to ensure goals are met.

Mentor
- Gains consensus on performance goals.
- Focuses on proactive positive change, not reasons for failure.

EXHIBIT 33-6
Q24 LEADERSHIP ASSESSMENT TIPS

HANDOUT

Investigator
- Limits the time spent analyzing individual development.
- Offers proactive suggestions for performance goals.

Appraiser
- Specifies goals and consequent results.
- Limits detail in performance goal descriptions.

Advisor
- Develops employees for long-term performance improvement and growth.
- Promises only what can be delivered.

Mentor
- Emphasizes professional over personal counseling.
- Teaches employees to build strong business networks to aid in business research.

SCENE 34: NATURAL WORK TEAM LEADER CHECKLIST

Leadership means a group, large or small, which is willing to entrust such authority to a man or a woman—in judgment, wisdom, personal appeal, and proven competence.

—Walt Disney

AUTHORS' NOTES

A singles tennis player doesn't have to worry about teamwork. Neither does a boxer or a golfer. But imagine a World Series–winning baseball team without an all-for-one work ethic, or a Super Bowl winner or NBA championship team.

Even the most cohesive, tightly-knit teams experience internal stresses that can turn a winning streak into a slump. Coaches and managers are primarily responsible for refocusing and reenergizing on-the-field play. Facilitation skills of the coaches and managers are essential to any long-term team success.

The same happens in business, where Natural Work Teams confront productivity-threatening problems and conflicts every day.

We define Natural Work Teams as units within departments, comprised of team members and a leader, working together on a daily, ongoing basis, and serving:

- internal partners;
- process partners (team members from other Natural Work Teams); and
- external customers.

At their best, Natural Work Teams meet their quotas and deadlines but also produce breakthrough improvements in products and services, and even transform cultures from their roots up. Such Work Teams are living proof that the sum can be greater than its parts.

A Team Leader's facilitation skills are of particular help in the areas of:

- problem solving,
- planning,
- decision making, and
- conflict resolution.

In all cases, a team leader:

- Is unbiased and objective during the meetings.
- Always demonstrates respect for the members.
- Always protects the team process.
- Creates a climate in which people feel free to express their points of view.
- Believes in and promotes the principle of win–win.

Are you a potential Natural Work Team Leader or Facilitator? You're off to a great start with this checklist. Many team facilitators live by this one!

PLOT

To provide team leaders with a tool to evaluate their own behaviors.

RUNNING TIME

15–30 minutes

KEY PLAYERS

- Natural Work Team Leaders
- Team Leaders (cross-functional, planning, and any other type of team)

PROPS

- Natural Work Team Leader Checklist (Exhibit 34-1)
- *Vision 360®* or other development planning tools (optional)

DIRECTOR'S SCRIPT

LIGHTS ...

1. Remove yourself from all distraction.

CAMERA ...

2. On the Natural Work Team Leader Checklist, place a checkmark in the column that you honestly feel represents your behavior for each item.

   Note: Usually, your first thought will be the most accurate.

3. Circle and prioritize the items in the Needs Improvement column.

ACTION!

4. Create an action plan for improvement.

   Note: You may wish to refer to the Personal Development Planning Exercise (see Scene 31) to record actions taken toward improvement in the most critical areas.

5. Repeat the Checklist exercise on a quarterly basis to check your progress and to plan to work on additional areas of development.

CURTAIN CALL

No Natural Work Team is such a perfectly synchronous, self-regulating, and self-sustaining perpetual motion machine that it can't use occasional recalibrating, retuning, and recharging from its leader or facilitator.

EXHIBIT 34-1
NATURAL WORK TEAM LEADER CHECKLIST

HANDOUT

Here is the best way to prepare to conduct that upcoming meeting!

	Do Well	Needs Improvement	No Perceived Need
1. Begin and end on time.	___	___	___
2. Bring past meeting's minutes and current meeting's agenda.	___	___	___
3. Work with team members to establish structure and direction.	___	___	___
4. Refocus, the discussion when necessary (Clarify by asking questions, confirm understanding, etc.)	___	___	___
5. Keep team members focused on how best to serve customers.	___	___	___
6. Revisit ground rules as needed.	___	___	___
7. Provide training and/or training resources to the team as needed.	___	___	___
8. Encourage the team to evaluate processes not personalities.	___	___	___
9. Don't flaunt your expertise. Give advice only when appropriate.	___	___	___
10. Use appropriate tools and techniques to spur thought and discussion. (e.g. Storyboarding, skills assessment, etc.)	___	___	___
11. Encourage frank expression of concerns.	___	___	___
12. Cite members for positive behaviors, breakthroughs and successes when appropriate.	___	___	___
13. Urge team to appreciate, develop and fully utilize members' talents and skills.	___	___	___
14. Conclude the discussion by reviewing key points and next steps.	___	___	___
15. Arrange for minutes to be filed at a central location where they are accessible to all team members.	___	___	___
16. Provide feedback on both positive and negative behaviors during the meeting.	___	___	___
17. Confirm understanding of your feedback.	___	___	___
18. Determine actions for improving behavior.	___	___	___
19. Offer assistance in pursuing these actions.	___	___	___
20. Discuss and determine agenda for a subsequent meeting.	___	___	___
21. Offer to mediate any future conflicts between members, assuming all vested parties' consent.	___	___	___
22. Take a "temperature check" of members' feelings about the meeting. (e.g. "How did it go?" "What did we do well?" "How can we improve?")	___	___	___
23. Close the meeting.			

SCENE 35: TEAM EFFECTIVENESS SURVEY

Share and share alike.
—Happy, *Snow White and the Seven Dwarfs*

AUTHORS' NOTES

What does the word "team" conjure for you?
World Series–winning baseball players mobbing the pitcher on the mound? Surgeons working together to transplant a heart? Maybe four yoked oxen pulling a plow?

In all cases, the collective job can't be done without each individual team member's contribution. Walt Disney knew that. He realized that every single cast member—onstage and backstage—was essential in making sure that the "whole show" was a "good show" for every guest.

As consultants, we're most gratified when individual efforts create an overall team effort that is even greater than the sum of its parts. The breakthrough results—from the creation of new product lines to the revamping of outmoded processes to the development of new systems—always bolster the bottom line while solidifying partnerships with customers old and new. These high-powered, well-meshed teams feel like businesses unto themselves, responsible for their own development and balance sheet health. On their own, they break old paradigms, present flawless cases to management, and think long-term. Periodically, they take internal "temperature checks" to see how well they are functioning, what improvements they could make, and what barriers they could knock down to clear the way for continued success.

PLOT

To provide a tool for teams to examine the most critical and essential areas of their existence.

RUNNING TIME

30 minutes

KEY PLAYERS

- Natural Work Team Leaders and teams
- Departmental Team Leaders and teams

PROPS

- Team Effectiveness Survey (one per team member) (Exhibit 35-1)
- Team Effectiveness Survey Scoring Sheet (Exhibit 35-2)
- Team Effectiveness Survey Summary Graph Sample (Exhibit 35-3)

DIRECTOR'S NOTES

LIGHTS, CAMERA ...

1. Assemble the teams and team leaders in a quiet location.
2. Distribute copies of the Team Effectiveness Survey to all team members and team leaders.

ACTION!

3. Have all members and leaders complete the survey.
4. Collect the surveys and tally the responses.
5. On the Scoring Sheet, record the team members' tallies in the boxes under Compiled Responses. Record the team leaders' tallies in the right-hand column.
6. On a Team Effectiveness Survey Summary Graph, plot the team members' responses by category. The sample depicts the scores from two consecutive years and clearly indicates the team's progress. You may wish to create a graph with a separate bar for the team leader's results.

7. Share the results with the team members and team leaders.

8. Create a plan to address specific areas where improvement is desired.

CURTAIN CALL

There is an irony to success. Just when teams feel they've mastered a situation, they should stop, take stock, and consider changing focus, planning new activities, and even moving members in and out.

Why rock the boat when the sailing is the smoothest? To stir the waters so that complacency, like algae on a millpond, does not set in.

EXHIBIT 35-1
TEAM EFFECTIVENESS SURVEY

TEAM NAME_____ DATE _____

TEAM LEADER _____

TEAM FACILITATOR (if applicable) _____

Reviewed by _____

INSTRUCTIONS

This survey promotes the development of healthy, productive teams by helping leaders and members assess their own efforts toward achieving that goal.

Each question is followed by two diametrically opposed responses. Circle the number that indicates where your own response falls within the range of those two poles. Consider the way you feel *most of the time*.

Answer questions regarding team members in terms of the members' *typical* behavior.

A. Team Identity

1. Do members have a sense of team identity?

   No, members have little   (1) (2) (3) (4) (5) (6) (7)   Yes, members are very
   or no sense of themselves   aware of themselves as
   as a team.   a team.

2. Are members of the team clearly designated?

   No, it is unclear who is   (1) (2) (3) (4) (5) (6) (7)   Yes, it is very clear
   a member of the team   who the team members
   and who is not.   are.

3. Do team members appear to be actively committed to team activities?

   No, most members do not   (1) (2) (3) (4) (5) (6) (7)   Yes, most members
   care what happens   are very concerned
   within the team.   about the team
                                                                activities.

286

EXHIBIT 35-1
TEAM EFFECTIVENESS SURVEY (CONTINUED)

B. Team Goals

4. How clear are the goals of the team?

> None of the members has   (1) (2) (3) (4) (5) (6) (7)   All the members
> a clear idea of the team's   clearly understand
> goals.   the team's goals and
> how they relate to
> the overall success of
> the organization.

5. Do all team members agree on the goals of the team?

> No, some members'   (1) (2) (3) (4) (5) (6) (7)   Yes, everyone agrees
> goals differ from   on the goals of the team.
> those of the team.

C. Team Roles

6. Is each team member's role clearly defined and understood?

> No, there is much   (1) (2) (3) (4) (5) (6) (7)   Yes, each member
> confusion about who   knows exactly what
> is supposed to do what.   he or she is supposed
> to do.

D. Member Participation

7. Do all team members speak and participate equally?

> No.   (1) (2) (3) (4) (5) (6) (7)   Yes.

8. To whom do most people direct their comments?

> Most members direct their   (1) (2) (3) (4) (5) (6) (7)   All members seem to
> comments to one person   be talking to each
> or a few people.   other.

9. Is attention paid to all members' opinions and points of view?

> No, some members'   (1) (2) (3) (4) (5) (6) (7)   Yes, all members'
> inputs are ignored.   inputs are heard
> and respected.

EXHIBIT 35-1
TEAM EFFECTIVENESS SURVEY (CONTINUED)

HANDOUT

E. Openness of Communication

10. How openly do team members express their feelings?

Team members generally keep their feelings to themselves.　　(1) (2) (3) (4) (5) (6) (7)　　Team members express their feelings freely.

11. How supportive are team members toward each other?

Members are not supportive.　　(1) (2) (3) (4) (5) (6) (7)　　Members are very supportive.

12. Are team members willing to confront each other on key issues?

No, team members do not confront each other.　　(1) (2) (3) (4) (5) (6) (7)　　Yes, team members are very confrontational.

13. How well do members receive constructive comments?

Poorly. People seem threatened by constructive comments and react defensively.　　(1) (2) (3) (4) (5) (6) (7)　　Very well. People accept, appreciate, and make use of constructive comments.

F. Problem Solving

14. Does the team define problems before starting to work on them?

No, the team jumps into problem solving without clearly defining what the problem is.　　(1) (2) (3) (4) (5) (6) (7)　　Yes, the team clearly defines the nature and scope of the problem before starting work.

15. Does the team generate multiple solutions?

No, the team usually adopts the first solution and ceases looking for others.　　(1) (2) (3) (4) (5) (6) (7)　　Yes, the team considers a range of solutions before taking action.

288

EXHIBIT 35-1
TEAM EFFECTIVENESS SURVEY (CONTINUED)

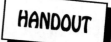
HANDOUT

G. Conflict

16. How often does personal conflict arise between team members?

Very often. (1) (2) (3) (4) (5) (6) (7) Very seldom.
Conflict is
almost always
over issues.

17. Are conflicting opinions openly expressed?

No. Conflicts are (1) (2) (3) (4) (5) (6) (7) Yes. Conflict is
usually suppressed aboveboard.
and the real issues The real issues
are not addressed. are addressed.

H. Leadership

18. Are leadership roles and functions clear?

No. It is not clear (1) (2) (3) (4) (5) (6) (7) Yes, leadership roles and
who is in charge of functions are clear.
doing what.

19. Are leadership responsibilities shared?

No. One person performs (1) (2) (3) (4) (5) (6) (7) Yes. All persons
all leadership functions. have opportunities
to perform
leadership functions.

20. How would you characterize the style of the team leader?

Very directive. (1) (2) (3) (4) (5) (6) (7) Very participative.

21. How effectively does the leader perform directive functions (e.g., setting goals, assigning responsibilities, etc.)?

Not effectively. (1) (2) (3) (4) (5) (6) (7) Very effectively.

22. How effectively does the leader perform supportive functions (e.g, encouraging team members, providing resources, etc.)?

Not effectively. (1) (2) (3) (4) (5) (6) (7) Very effectively.

EXHIBIT 35-1
TEAM EFFECTIVENESS SURVEY (CONTINUED)

I. Decision Making

23. Does the team make decisions when they need to be made?

No, important questions   (1) (2) (3) (4) (5) (6) (7)   Yes, the team always
are often not answered   makes timely
and issues are not   decisions.
resolved.

24. How much do team members participate in decision making?

Very little. A few people   (1) (2) (3) (4) (5) (6) (7)   A great deal. The
make the decisions and   whole team is
others are not involved.   involved in making
most decisions.

25. How are decisions usually made? (Circle one.)

1. By indecision.
2. By the team leaders' boss.
3. By the team leader.
4. By a subteam on behalf of the team.
5. By secret ballot.
6. By open voting.
7. By consensus.

J. Overall Team Effectiveness

26. How would you rate the group's effectiveness in the following areas?

	Ineffective	Effective
1. Problem solving.	(1) (2) (3) (4) (5) (6) (7)	
2. Decision making.	(1) (2) (3) (4) (5) (6) (7)	
3. Getting the work done.	(1) (2) (3) (4) (5) (6) (7)	
4. Making use of members' skills, abilities, resources.	(1) (2) (3) (4) (5) (6) (7)	
5. Meeting individual needs.	(1) (2) (3) (4) (5) (6) (7)	

27. How would you rate your team experience?

One of the worst   (1) (2) (3) (4) (5) (6) (7)   One of the best
I have ever had.   I have ever had.

EXHIBIT 35-2
TEAM EFFECTIVENESS SURVEY SCORING SHEET

TEAM NAME_____ DATE _____

TEAM LEADER _____

TEAM FACILITATOR (if applicable) _____

Prepared by _____

		Compiled Responses							Team
		1	2	3	4	5	6	7	Leader
A.	**Team Identity**								
1.	Do members have a sense of team identity?								
2.	Are members of the team clearly designated?								
3.	Do team members appear to be actively committed to team activities?								
B.	**Team Goals**								
4.	How clear are the goals of the team?								
5.	Do all team members agree on the goals of the team?								
C.	**Team Roles**								
6.	Is each team member's role clearly defined and understood?								
D.	**Member Participation**								
7.	Do all team members speak and participate equally?								
8.	To whom do most people direct their comments?								
9.	Is attention paid to all members' opinions and points of view?								
E.	**Openness of Communication**								
10.	How openly do team members express their feelings?								
11.	How supportive are team members toward each other?								
12.	Are team members willing to confront each other on key issues?								
13.	How well do members receive constructive comments?								
F.	**Problem Solving**								
14.	Does the team define problems before starting to work on them?								
15.	Does the team generate multiple solutions?								
G.	**Conflict**								
16.	How often does personal conflict arise between team members?								
17.	Are conflicting opinions openly expressed?								

EXHIBIT 35-2
TEAM EFFECTIVENESS SURVEY SCORING
SHEET (CONTINUED)

HANDOUT

		Compiled Responses							Team
		1	2	3	4	5	6	7	Leader
H.	**Leadership**								
18.	Are leadership roles and functions clear?								
19.	Are leadership responsibilities shared?								
20.	How would you characterize the style of the team leader?								
21.	How effectively does the leader perform directive functions?								
22.	How effectively does the leader perform supportive functions?								
I.	**Decision Making**								
23.	Does the team make decisions when they need to be made?								
24.	How much do team members participate in decision making?								
25.	How are decisions usually made? (choose one)								
	1. By indecision.								
	2. By the team leaders' boss.								
	3. By the team leader.								
	4. By a subteam on behalf of the team.								
	5. By secret ballot.								
	6. By open voting.								
	7. By consensus.								
J.	**Overall Team Effectiveness**								
26.	How would you rate the group's effectiveness in the following areas?								
	1. Problem solving.								
	2. Decision making.								
	3. Getting the work done.								
	4. Making use of members' skills, abilities, resources.								
	5. Meeting individual needs.								
27.	How would you rate your team experience?								

EXHIBIT 35-3
TEAM EFFECTIVENESS SURVEY SUMMARY GRAPH SAMPLE

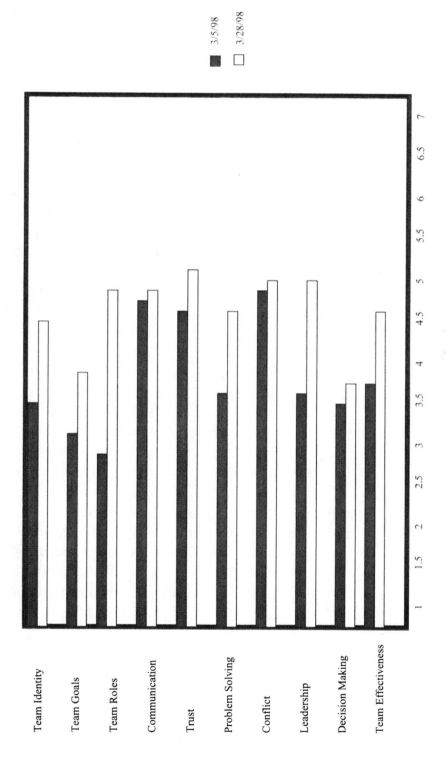

■ 3/5/98
□ 3/28/98

Team Identity
Team Goals
Team Roles
Communication
Trust
Problem Solving
Conflict
Leadership
Decision Making
Team Effectiveness

1   1.5   2   2.5   3   3.5   4   4.5   5   5.5   6   6.5   7

SCENE 36: THE BEAD FACTORY

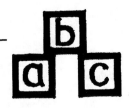

Can't be too careful, you know.
—Jiminy Cricket, *Pinocchio*

AUTHORS' NOTES

Often, it's hard to know who is most responsible for failure and success—the leader who choreographs the projects and processes, or the team members who perform the steps. When performance breaks down and productivity suffers, are employees necessarily to blame? Are team leaders the only other responsible parties? Shouldn't upper management sometimes be held accountable? And what about circumstantial factors—the workplace equivalents of poor lighting, insufficient rehearsal, and a slippery stage?

The sad fact is that in too many American companies, the frontline employees take the heat for poor results, due to careless, but well-intentioned leadership. They are subjected to ineffective processes and tools, resulting in negative performance appraisal reports. "Guilty until proven innocent" seems to be the operating judicial code. That's tragic, because employees are all too often the victims, not the perpetrators, of workplace dysfunction. They're battered by forces beyond their control.

All of this becomes painfully clear in the Bead Factory exercise, which was conducted by Dr. Edwards Deming from the early 1980s until his death in 1993. The exercise puts participants into departmental team members' shoes so they can experience the demoralizing effects of stern, outmoded performance evaluation paradigms. Despite the frustrations that can arise during the session, it's revelatory, enlightening, and fun.

PLOT

To experience the importance of reviewing the process rather than the workers.

RUNNING TIME

30–45 minutes

KEY PLAYERS

- Process Improvement Team Leaders
- Natural Work Team Leaders

PROPS

- One container with minimum dimensions of 12" long x 9" wide x 5" deep (see Illustration 36-1)
- At least 200 marbles or plastic craft beads (80 percent should be white and 20 percent should be red)
- One paddle with handle having 25 indentations in which marbles or beads can rest (see Illustration 36-1)
- 2 flip charts
- 3 one-dollar bills

Illustration 36-1

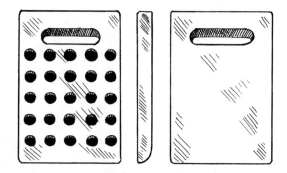

- Table
- Bead, Inc. Daily Individual Production Report template (Exhibit 36-1)
- Bead, Inc. Daily Defect Percentage Graph template (Exhibit 36-2)

DIRECTOR'S SCRIPT

LIGHTS ...

1. Post the Bead, Inc. Daily Individual Production Report template and the Bead, Inc. Daily Defect Percentage Graph template on respective flip charts.
2. Pour the beads into the container.
3. Place the container and the paddle on a table.

CAMERA ...

4. Select volunteers for the following roles at Bead, Inc.:
   - Willing Workers (4)
   - First-line supervisor (1)
   - Inspector (1)
   - Accountant (1)
   - Statistician (1)
5. Explain that the team is employed by Bead, Inc. You are the owner of Bead, Inc. The factory produces white beads.
6. Ask the first-line supervisor and inspector to join you at the front table for training.

First-line Supervisor's and Inspector's Instructions

7. Explain to the first-line supervisor that each worker must come in turn to the table and do the following:

Workers' Instructions

- Pick up the container, shake it for 5 seconds, then place it back on the table.
- Pick up the paddle with one hand.

- Grasp the edge of the container with the other hand and tilt it at a 45-degree angle.
- Dip the paddle into the container and lift, so the beads will rest on the indentations.
- Show the paddle to the inspector, who will count the white beads in the indentations and announce the count to the other participants. (See Illustration 36-2.)

The above will constitute one shift. After all four workers have worked one shift, the workday is done.

8. Ask the first-line supervisor to start training the four workers to do the work detailed above. Each worker may have one practice dip.

9. As the owner, affirm that you want only white beads.

10. Praise workers who, in their practice dip, get almost all white beads. Say, "That's really good for just a training attempt. I know you'll only get better when you start real production."

Illustration 36-2

11. Ask the accountant and statistician to stand by the flip charts.

Accountant's Instructions

12. Tell the accountant that he or she will be responsible for maintaining individual production records.

13. Tell the accountant to record the workers' names on the Bead, Inc. Daily Individual Production Report.

14. Inform the accountant that after each worker completes a shift, the inspector will announce the number of white beads the worker produced. The accountant should then:

- Immediately record this number for this worker on the appropriate day.
- At the end of every day, add all the workers' production numbers, record the sum as the day's Total, and announce the total aloud.

Statistician's Instructions

15. Inform the statistician that he or she will compute and record the Daily Defect Percentage. Defects are red beads.

16. State that the optimal daily production is 100 white beads.

17. Explain that if the accountant announces "100" at the end of the day, the statistician should compute the percent of defects, in this case 0%, and record a dot at "0" on the Bead, Inc. Daily Defect Percentage Graph. However, if the accountant announces "87" at the end of the day, the statistician should record a dot at "13" (because 13 red beads out of 100 white beads is 13% red beads).

18. Tell the entire Bead Factory team that in your experience, chanting a slogan every morning increases productivity.

19. Lead the workers in chanting: "Zero defects is our goal! Zero defects is our goal! Zero defects is our goal!"

20. Tell the team that you have just received an order for 400 white beads to be shipped four days from today.

21. Ask the workers if they feel able to produce 400 white beads in four days. If anyone says it will be impossible to produce 400 beads in four days without defects, remind the workers that they just chanted, "Zero defects is our goal!"

ACTION!

22. Begin the first day's production.

23. At the end of the first day, ask the supervisor for the daily white-bead production figures. The odds are that white-bead production will be less than 100.

24. Ask the supervisor to repeat the goal to you: "Zero defects!"

25. Suggest to the supervisor that the workers may need additional on-the-job training.

26. Have the supervisor invite the best worker to conduct a training session for the other workers.

27. During this training session, make sure all workers follow the procedures being taught by their fellow "star" worker.

28. Start the second day by having all four workers chant the slogan "Zero defects is our goal!"

29. Begin the second day's production.

30. At the end of the second day, discuss the results with the supervisor.

- If production increased, declare that the extra training helped, as you knew it would.
- If production decreased, blame the supervisor. Say, "Management must make sure that workers are really serious about producing a quality product."

31. Tell the supervisor to hire an additional inspector.

32. Invite the new inspector to the front of the room.

33. Tell the original inspector:

- You do not feel he or she has done a bad job.
- An additional inspector will make a statement to the workers.

New Inspector's Instructions

34. Tell the two inspectors that:

- Each of them will make his or her own independent inspection.

- Then the original inspector will say, "Ready, set, report." This inspector will then loudly announce his or her count of the beads produced by each worker.

- The new inspector will then loudly announce his or her own count of the beads produced by each worker.

- If there is any discrepancy, the supervisor will make a personal inspection to reconcile the counts.

35. Assemble the four workers to chant the slogan, "Zero defects is our goal!"

36. Begin production for the third day.

37. At the end of third day, review the results with the supervisor.

38. Assemble the workers and tell them you believe in rewarding good performance.

39. Reward the top producer with $2 and the second producer with $1.

Note: Rewards can be based on total production to date, or just the current day's production.

40. Tell the third and fourth ranked workers that you cannot tolerate their poor performance, and they are dismissed.

41. Tell the remaining workers (the top and second ranked producers) that they will have to work double shifts to make up for the staff reductions. They will consequently have to produce twice as much.

42. Assemble the two remaining workers to chant: "Zero defects is our goal!"

43. Begin production for the fourth day.

44. Have the accountant add the total production for all four days.

CUT!

45. Thank all participants and debrief the exercise by asking them: If you experienced these production problems in a real business, what would you do? Responses may include:

- Ship short.
- Schedule overtime.
- Miss the deadline.
- Ship defects and replace them with good pieces if and when possible.

46. Ask the group to identify areas of Bead Inc. production process waste. These factors should be identified:

- Needless inspection by inspectors; workers could inspect their own work.
- Needless accounting and charting activities; workers could do the charting and accounting themselves.
- Overblown management hierarchy.
- The presence of red beads in the container; they should be eliminated before actual production starts.
- The ergonomically inefficient paddle.

47. Ask the group: Was the reward system fair?

48. Discuss the fact that most reward systems are based on results over which workers have little or no control. For example, in Bead, Inc., we rewarded and punished workers based on results they could not control.

49. Explain that results are a function of the following factors:

- workers' education;
- workers' on-the-job-training;
- workers' own effort;

- The design, capabilities, and inefficiencies of the process. (Many processes have the equivalent of too many red beads.)

50. State that the only factor a worker can control is his or her own effort. Unfortunately, effort is impossible to isolate, quantify, and reward as a contributing factor in achieving results.

51. Discuss the use and benefit of the Bead, Inc. Daily Defect Percentage Report. Make the following points:

- By collecting enough data, one can predict a range of defect percentage.

- The upper control limit indicates the best expected results.

- The lower control limit indicates the worst expected results.

- Any result between the upper and lower control limits is considered to be under control. (This does not imply a judgment of good or bad, simply an expected result.)

- Control limits typically lessen when improvement efforts are begun.

CURTAIN CALL

The Problem
Employees are reprimanded for poor results over which they have little, if any, control.

The Consequences
Employee demoralization. Productivity decline.

The Solutions
- Attack the process, not the people.
- Use data to determine process capability and eliminate individual performance measures.
- Help companies abolish counterproductive and demoralizing reward systems in which employees are pitted against one another.

- Consider replacing performance appraisals with development plans focused on future success rather than past performance.
- Replace individual rewards with team rewards for those who proactively improve their processes.

EXHIBIT 36-1
BEAD, INC. DAILY INDIVIDUAL PRODUCTION REPORT

HANDOUT

NAME	Day 1	Day 2	Day 3	Day 4	TOTAL
TOTAL					

EXHIBIT 36-2
BEAD, INC. DAILY DEFECT PERCENTAGE GRAPH

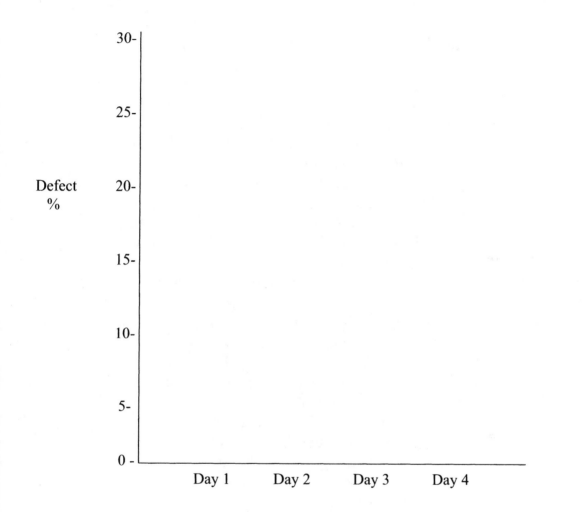

SCENE 37: TARGET GAME

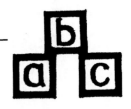

Just do your best.
—Flora, *Sleeping Beauty*

AUTHORS' NOTES

Remember playing "Pin the Tail on the Donkey" when you were a kid? Remember the howls of laughter (or the deathly silence) as you wandered blindly around the room? And bumped into furniture? And then pinned the tail on the oil painting of the birthday girl's maiden aunt?

No one gave you directions because they couldn't; those were the rules.

You'd think American companies had the same rules, for all the orientation they give their new hires. Sometimes they dump a policy manual in a new person's lap, but have you ever tried reading one of those fat volumes? You need a law degree. Lifting one is like pumping iron. When in-person advice is actually given, it's usually, "There's the supply closet," followed by, "We know you'll do your best to be a productive member of the team!" The new hire's "Trainee" badge should really say, "Untrained," with smaller print below reading: "Don't ask me any questions; I'm still trying to figure out what to do."

Not all companies are this delinquent, though. Some nail training and orientation on the head.

Here's Worthington Steel's policy manual: "Treat your customers, coworkers, and suppliers the way you want to be treated." One sentence, that's right.

Nordstrom says: "Use good judgment in all situations. There will be no other rules."

Disney teaches new cast members to call customers "guests," and to treat them as visitors in their own homes.

How well do you prepare your employees? Do you send new hires in the right direction with a sure step? If you don't, you should. The Target Game will help make sure you do.

PLOT

To demonstrate the problems that are caused by failure to provide appropriate direction and feedback for new team members.

RUNNING TIME

15–20 minutes

KEY PLAYERS

- Team leaders and team members with opportunities to help new employees with focused, constructive feedback

PROPS

- Target with Velcro surface
- 3 Velcro balls
- Blindfold

DIRECTOR'S SCRIPT

LIGHTS, CAMERA ...

1. Ask for two volunteers.
2. Select one of the volunteers to be blindfolded for the exercise. Assign the other volunteer to be his or her assistant.
3. Give the blindfold to the assistant.
4. Say that you will soon be asking the participant and the assistant to leave the room. Say that while they are out, the assistant should blindfold the other participant. Both persons will then await your invitation to reenter the room.
5. Ask the two volunteers to leave the room.
6. When they are out, tape the target to the front wall at approximately eye level.
7. Explain the first phase of the exercise to the team by saying:

We are about to welcome a new hire to our team.

When this new hire [the blindfolded volunteer; use his or her first name] enters the room, give a round of applause.

I will act as the new hire's manager.

I will give the new hire three balls and state that the three "tasks" must be completed this week.

I will then leave the new hire alone with you, the team.

Do *not* give the new hire any feedback. In fact, be absolutely silent, no matter what the new hire says or does.

8. Explain the second phase of the exercise. Tell the team that you will reassign the tasks. This time, though, tell the team to give the new hire strictly *negative* feedback, for example:

   ■ "Why don't you try something?"
   ■ "Don't just stand there."
   ■ "Where's your motivation?"
   ■ "Time's running out."

9. Explain the third phase of the exercise. Ask the team for a volunteer to be the new hire's coach. Instruct the coach to give specific, helpful feedback to help the new hire complete his or her tasks.

10. Call the two volunteers back into the room.

11. Ask the assistant (use his or her first name throughout) to escort the new hire (use his or her first name throughout) to the front of the room.

12. Introduce yourself to the new hire as the manager.

13. Place the three balls in the new hire's hand.

14. Assign the new hire the tasks. Say the tasks must be completed this week.

15. Say to the new hire: "We only hire winners at our company and I'm sure you'll be on target with everything you do."

16. Assure the new hire that he or she has a great team of people to guide her with feedback on her performance.

17. Say that you will be out of the office until the end of the week but will check the new hire's progress when you get back.

18. Wish the new hire and the team good luck, and "leave" the room.

19. After 2 minutes, "return" to the room. Tell the new hire to keep his or her blindfold on.

20. Ask the new hire to describe what happened this week while you were "away."

21. If the balls are not on the target, tell the new hire you are disappointed in his or her failure to perform as expected, especially since you assured the team that he or she was a real winner. (See Illustration 37-1.)

22. Ask the new hire why he or she failed to perform as you expected. Likely responses are:

- "I was left in the dark."
- "I had no clue about what to do."
- "I was given no direction."

Illustration 37-1

- "The team gave me no feedback at all."

23. Reassign tasks to the new hire and assure him or her that feedback will be available.

24. "Leave" the new hire alone with the team.

25. After 2 minutes, "return" to the room.

26. Ask the still-blindfolded new hire what happened this time.

27. If the balls are not on the target, give your own feedback on the new hire's repeated failure to perform.

28. Ask the new hire: "What would help you to be on target with these three tasks?" The typical responses to this question are "Some direction" and "Coaching."

29. Introduce the new hire to his to her new coach.

30. Ask the new hire to once again try to perform the tasks. (See Illustration 37-2.) This time, do not pretend to "leave" the room.

31. When the new hire is finally "on target" with his or her three tasks, ask him or her to remove the blindfold and remain standing with you at the front of the room.

Illustration 37-2

32. Lead a round of applause for the coach, who may now return to his or her seat.

33. Ask the new hire: "Which made you less comfortable, receiving negative feedback or receiving no feedback at all?"

Note: Many people prefer negative feedback to no feedback at all, because it shows they are not working totally alone.

34. Thank the new hire for being such a good sport, and permit him or her to be seated.

CUT!

35. Debrief the exercise with the entire team by asking:

- Does this exercise represent what often happens to new hires in our company?

- In your experience, do new hires who receive little or no helpful feedback feel abandoned? Do they fall into despair? Do they perform well?

- How can we help new hires feel that they are valued members of our work teams? How can we guide them to perform to their fullest potential?

CURTAIN CALL

Effective orientation does the following:

- Tells new hires exactly what is expected of them.
- Trains them in essential procedures.
- Gives them leeway to tap their own creative energies and exercise free will.
- Lays out rewards for both individual and team successes, large and small.
- Makes work an ongoing pleasure instead of a daily grind.

SCENE 38: ONE-TO-ONE FEEDBACK EXERCISE

You helped me. Now I will help you.
—Quasimodo, *Hunchback of Notre Dame*

AUTHORS' NOTES

Criticism can be hard to take. It can be even harder to give—constructively, that is. Anyone can chide or chastise. But how many can deliver substantive, measured, focused feedback that ultimately builds up its recipients instead of tearing them down?

We customarily ask our conference and *Dream Retreat®* participants: "Would you be more effective if you received more feedback?"

Their invariable answer is: "Yes!"

So why is constructive feedback so rarely given?

Because people are afraid of sounding insincere. They think they'll be resented or not trusted. They worry that the recipient will one day take revenge. They feel that giving feedback isn't safe, for either party.

Relax. Our One-to-One Feedback exercise takes the danger out of feedback and removes its sting. In place of adversarial tension, we instill mutual trust and concern. We show how launching criticism by saying, "The trouble with your work is ... " makes the recipient defend against, not openly receive, the suggestions that come next. Better to introduce feedback with words like "What I appreciate about your work ... ," as this establishes your positive view of the other person and your confidence in his or her ultimate success. Then you can proceed to suggest how the other person could be more effective in his or her work.

Of course, you must believe in your initial complimentary remarks. Flattery will get you nowhere when it's forced or false.

Other than being easier for its recipient to swallow, why is balanced, considerate feedback better than a purely negative critique? What are its bottom-line positive results?

Our two-word answer: higher productivity. Boosting team members' confidence while coaching their performance motivates and enables them to perform better as individuals and as members of the team.

British statesman Benjamin Disraeli said in the nineteenth century, "It is easier to be critical than correct." At the start of the twenty first century, we say, "It is better to criticize correctly."

With the One-to-One Feedback exercise, you will do exactly that.

PLOT

To give employees the opportunity to give and receive brief and spontaneous feedback.

RUNNING TIME

15–50 minutes, depending on team size

KEY PARTICIPANTS

- Any leader or team member with opportunities to improve colleagues' performance through constructive feedback

PROPS

- Stopwatch or a watch with a second hand

DIRECTOR'S SCRIPT

LIGHTS, CAMERA ...

1. Instruct each team member to select a partner.
2. Ask each pair of partners to sit facing one another in chairs, without tables between them.
3. Ask all participants: "How many of you feel you would be more effective if you received more feedback?" In most situations, all participants will raise their hands.

4. Introduce Round 1 of the exercise by saying:

> Participants will now have the opportunity to practice giving feedback in a safe environment.

> One partner in each pair will have 30 seconds to say to the other partner:

> "What I appreciate about you is . . . ," completing the statement in an appropriate and truthful way.

> The same partner will then have another 30 seconds to say:

> "I feel you would be more effective if you. . . . ," completing the statement appropriately and truthfully.

> During the 30 seconds, the partner giving feedback should attempt to provide a continuous flow of feedback.

> State that you will be timing the exercise.

5. Ask each pair of partners to decide who will be the speaker and who will be the listener in Round 1.

ACTION!

6. Start Round 1. Checking the stopwatch, allow 30 seconds for each statement.

7. Ask each pair to change roles for Round 2.

8. Repeat the process for Round 2.

9. Have all participants pair up with new partners.

10. Repeat the process for Round 3.

11. Continue having participants change partners, and repeat the process until every participant has paired with every other participant.

CUT!

12. Debrief by asking the following questions:

- Who is responsible for giving feedback?
  The typical response is, "Everyone."

- In this exercise, which type of feedback was more difficult to give?

- ■ "Good show" (appreciative feedback, e.g., "What I appreciate about you is ... ")
- ■ "Bad show" (constructive feedback, e.g., "I feel you would be more effective if you ... ")

- ■ Is there a difference between giving feedback to someone you know well and giving it to someone you have just met? What about when you are receiving feedback?
- ■ How did you feel about receiving feedback in this exercise?
- ■ If you feel you would be more effective with frequent, candid feedback, why do we so often fail to give this kind of feedback to others?
- ■ Raise your hand if you learned something new about yourself in this exercise. [Promise that you will not ask anyone to share his or her personal experiences.]

13. Inform the participants that:

- ■ Many studies show that candid feedback can raise a person's performance by 25 to 30 percent.
- ■ It is common to judge people quickly by their behaviors, often in less than a minute.
- ■ The One-to-One technique has been proven to enable people who are only slightly acquainted to learn a great deal about each other (and themselves).

14. Challenge the participants to practice giving and receiving feedback that:

- ■ is sincere, caring, and humane;
- ■ is substantive (Don't just "schmooze.");
- ■ specifies the individual's particular contribution to a "good show" or "bad show" result;
- ■ takes the immediate environment into account (e.g., "Bad show," constructive feedback, is best given in private.);
- ■ does not send a mixed message, by sliding a "dig" into the compliment or by sugarcoating a "bad show" response.

CURTAIN CALL

This exercise teaches one-to-one "feedback," not one-to-one "criticism." Criticism connotes judgment. Feed + back clearly means nourishing *food* for thought, and improved performance and results.

SCENE 39: PROCESS EVALUATION

A single grain of rice can tip the scale.
—The Emperor, *Mulan*

AUTHORS' NOTES

There's a saying: "God is in the details." It means that if you train your thought, care, and attention on the little things, the big things will take care of themselves.

We think Thoreau could live with that approach because it's not detail-obsessed; it doesn't fritter anything away. Instead, it values details as the intricately integrated elements, that create the wider, more coherent view.

Think of the dots in a newspaper photograph. When you view them up close they're just random inkspots. When you draw back, they lose their individuality and blend into a clear picture.

Or consider that high-definition television (HDTV) produces a finer picture by using more lines, not fewer, and that more pixels create a sharper image on a computer screen.

Process Evaluation entails scrutiny of myriad tiny details. Does that put you off? Does a long-term commitment scare you—up to six months if the job is especially complex?

Well, consider the benefits of Process Evaluation:

- It helps streamline key business processes.
- It confirms when performance is on target.
- It reveals when performance is falling short and thus suggests corrective efforts to achieve desired outcomes.
- It promotes a "good show" for cast and customers or guests.
- It bolsters financial results.

Sound worthwhile? Consider also that if you can't conduct formal benchmarking for every key process in your organization, a Process Evaluation Team (PET) study for these processes will put each of their elements into sharp relief. If you do then decide to benchmark a specific process, a PET study can make the benchmarking more productive and less time-consuming. It's wise to get your own business in shape before you go out to learn from the "best of the best."

As is true in benchmarking, Process Evaluation takes a real commitment from management and a dedicated team of people who are willing to get into minutia. Depending on the complexity of the process, the study can take up to six months to complete. This accounts for a team of 7 to 10 members spending about one day a week on PET activities. Obviously, if you can afford to assign a team full-time responsibility for the PET, it will be completed in less than six months.

We have seen the quickest and best results when the entire team can spend one day each week on PET activities. This means the members are removed from their daily work areas and operate within the four walls of a designated planning center. Some teams actually go off-site and rent meeting space for a day. We recommend that teams choose a day of the week that works best for them and stick to it; structure greatly contributes to members' commitment to the process and encourages team camaraderie.

PLOT

To organize a thorough evaluation of a business process.

RUNNING TIME

One to two hours to organize the evaluation. (The actual evaluation will require a considerable investment of time.)

KEY PLAYERS

- Leadership Team
- Process Evaluation Team (PET) leaders

PROPS

- Process Evaluation Team (PET) Workflow Diagram (Exhibit 39-1)
- Process Evaluation Team (PET) Planning Agenda (Exhibit 39-2)
- Cast Experience Data
- Guest Experience Data
- Benchmark Study for process (if completed)
- Storyboard Materials (see Scene 30)
- Process Evaluation Team Workbook (Exhibit 39-3)
- Process Evaluation Team Workbook Example (Exhibit 39-4)
- Process Evaluation Team Sample Schedule (Exhibit 39-5)
- Process Evaluation Team Checklist (Exhibit 39-6)
- Process Evaluation Workflow Diagram Standard Symbols (Exhibit 39-7)
- Process Evaluation "Going to Work" Workflow Diagram Overview (Exhibit 39-8)
- Process Evaluation "Going to Work" Workflow Diagram "Get up and Dress" Subprocess Detail (Exhibit 39-9)

DIRECTOR'S SCRIPT

LIGHTS ...

1. Predistribute the Process Evaluation Team Workflow Diagram and the Agenda for PET Planning to all members of the Leadership Team.

CAMERA ...

2. Assemble the Leadership Team.
3. Discuss the Workflow Diagram and review the Agenda.
4. Storyboard all key business processes. Using the prioritization technique, place self-adhesive dots on the three processes that might be most improved through Process

Evaluation. Take care in selecting processes that will enhance the guest or cast experience.

Note: If the key business processes have previously been identified, omit storyboarding, but ask the team to prioritize the processes.

5. Select the team leaders for Process Evaluation, one per process. Select team leaders who have proven leadership skills and will directly benefit from the improvements in the process.
6. Discuss the preliminary budget considerations for each process.
7. Give each of the selected PET leaders a copy of the key business process storyboard.
8. Assemble the Leadership Team and the PET leaders.
9. Give each Leadership Team member and PET leader a copy of the PET Workbook and the PET Workbook Example.

ACTION!

10. Begin organizing the evaluation by reviewing and discussing the Process Evaluation Workbook, with attention to the following:

Process Evaluation Overview
Review the four phases of the PET Method:
- Critical Success Factors
- Process Analysis
- Improvement Planning
- Implementation

General Team Information
- PET leaders will select their own PET members to assist in the evaluation. Selection criteria will include hands-on ex-

320

perience with the process to be analyzed, and a high stake in revamping the process.

Note: This is not the place for upper management intervention. Only those who have the most to gain or lose from the revamped process should become involved.

- A member of the Leadership Team should be assigned the role of PET Champion. The PET Champion's duties are to:
- Remove any barriers the team may face (ranging from insufficient time to difficulty in obtaining information from uncooperative departments).
- Act as a "sounding board" for team ideas.
- Play devil's advocate to spur, redirect, or reenergize team efforts as needed. (The PET Champion will not, however, approve or reject team recommendations.)
- The PET leaders will prepare mission statements. (See Scene 6.)

Driving Forces Analysis

Note: This activity typically generates great enthusiasm, because most team members have not given prior thought to these important process elements.

There are the nine Driving Forces:

- Outputs—Your final goods or services.
- Suppliers—The providers of the elements you need to produce your output.
- Technology—How you accept and utilize new and innovative tools and systems.
- Production—How your skills and capabilities influence your output.
- Support—How much assistance you need to deliver your output.
- Distribution—How you get your product or service to your customers.

321

- Resources—The time, personnel, systems, and materials needed to produce your products or services and to improve the process.

- Return—The potential Return on Investment (ROI).

- Experience—How process improvements will create happiness in your customers or cast.

Each Driving Force should be ranked according to its effect on the overall process. For example: Rank Production *High* if your production costs have been escalating. Rank Production *Low* if production costs have dropped.

Customers—Outputs—Subprocesses—Inputs—Suppliers
These are subprocesses to the overall process.

Customer Problem Analysis
The PET leaders determine and note the relative importance of customers' problems, needs, and dreams.

- Customers' problems, needs, and dreams may be product related or service related.

- Each problem, need, and dream is given a relative percentage of importance that is calculated from guest data. The total of all the percentages is 100 percent.

- Customer Experience data shows how well the company resolves problems and fulfills needs and dreams. The company is rated as either Consistently Exceeding, Meeting but Seldom Exceeding, or Seldom Meeting customers' expectations. For a sense of overall customer satisfaction, do the following:
  - ✓ In cases of Consistently Exceeds, multiply the element's Relative Importance percentage figure by 1. Enter the resulting figure under Consistently Exceeds for that element.
  - ✓ In cases of Meets but Seldom Exceeds, multiply the element's Relative Importance by 1/2, and enter the result under Meets but Seldom Exceeds.

✓ In cases of Seldom Meets, multiply the element's Relative Importance by 0 and enter this result under Seldom Meets.

✓ Add the figures in the respective Customer Experience Ranking columns.

Add the column sums and enter the resulting sum in the box immediately to the right of Customer Experience Totals.

Notes:

Of course, the level of accuracy will be dictated by the quality of customer or guest data.

Even an element of low relative importance may be worth pursuing.

Customer Experience Rankings for timely delivery can be misleading. Some customers may not rank timely delivery as a high priority, but will quickly switch to your competitor if you fail to deliver on time.

Process Workflow Diagram Tracking

The process workflow is one of the most important tools used in Process Evaluation. It can also be one of the most difficult to prepare and to document accurately.

Pairing up team members to document the workflow of a subprocess drastically cuts the time required to document the entire process. Use the Tracking Form to monitor the progress of this task.

Note: The team will choose the Process Evaluation Workflow Diagram Standard Symbols. Refer to the "Going to Work" Workflow Diagram Overview and "Going to Work" Workflow Diagram—"Get up and Dress" Subprocess Detail.

Cost Analysis

This is the step most often overlooked by PETs, whose errors of omission are often due to uncooperative accounting departments.

The PET must obtain from the accounting department:

- Total direct labor wage figures. (Specific individual payroll data are not required.)
- Overhead figures on anything within a department that adds value to the process outputs. (These numbers help the PET estimate every department's cost-per-output.)

Problem-Solving Information

Entered here are data regarding problems and barriers that threaten:

- the customer experience;
- the cast (employee) experience; or
- the financial results.

Relevant information is entered in these areas:

- *Problem Statement*—The effect of this problem. The gap between the existing situation and the ideal situation. The measurement process used.
- *Customer Experience Impact*—How this problem affects the customer.
- *Cast Experience Impact*—How this problem affects the cast member (employee).
- *Financial Results Impact*—The anticipated costs and benefits associated with solving this problem.
- *Six Steps to Problem Solving*—A sequence of actions to correct the situation.
- *Information Needed*—Supplemental input that may be needed to complete the problem-solving steps.

Performance Plan

Relevant performance information is entered in these areas:

- *Ideal Process Workflow*—Typically, an attachment to the Performance Plan.
- *Recommendation Overview*—A list of what needs to be done to produce the Ideal Workflow.

- *Performance Indicators*—The three or four factors of prime importance in achieving the desired Customer Experience, Cast Experience, and Financial Results.
- *Cost-Benefit Overview*—The resources allocated to produce the Ideal Workflow, plus the benefits gained from achieving that goal.

CUT!

11. Dispatch the teams to conduct the actual process evaluation. Schedule a meeting at the completion of the Improvement Planning phase for the team to deliver its final report and recommendations to the Leadership Team.

12. At the subsequent meeting, have the teams' PET Champion act as a critical evaluator during a dry run presentation.

Insist on a clear, accurate, and compelling PET report to the Leadership Team that "makes them an offer they can't refuse."

CURTAIN CALL

After their initial presentation to the Leadership team, we recommend that the PET continue meeting one hour per month for 12 months to review the status of the Performance Indicators. Then, every 18 to 24 months, a new team can be formed to conduct a follow-up Process Evaluation study.

EXHIBIT 39-1
PROCESS EVALUATION TEAM (PET) WORKFLOW DIAGRAM

HANDOUT

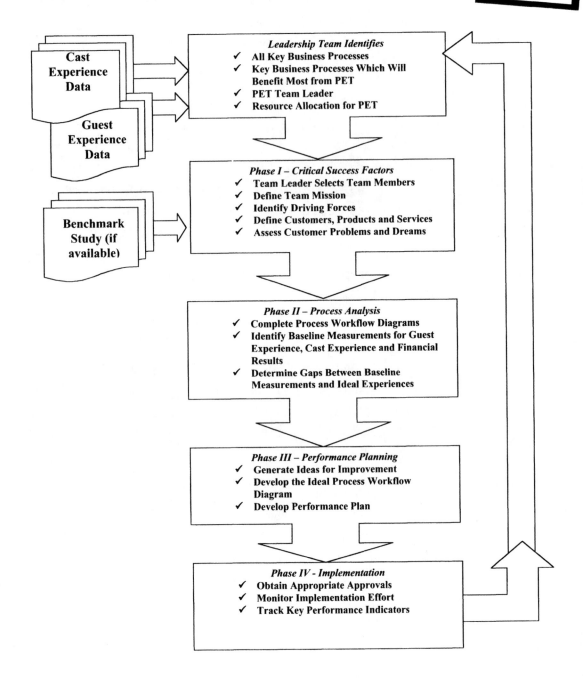

Cast Experience Data

Guest Experience Data

Benchmark Study (if available)

Leadership Team Identifies
- ✓ All Key Business Processes
- ✓ Key Business Processes Which Will Benefit Most from PET
- ✓ PET Team Leader
- ✓ Resource Allocation for PET

Phase I – Critical Success Factors
- ✓ Team Leader Selects Team Members
- ✓ Define Team Mission
- ✓ Identify Driving Forces
- ✓ Define Customers, Products and Services
- ✓ Assess Customer Problems and Dreams

Phase II – Process Analysis
- ✓ Complete Process Workflow Diagrams
- ✓ Identify Baseline Measurements for Guest Experience, Cast Experience and Financial Results
- ✓ Determine Gaps Between Baseline Measurements and Ideal Experiences

Phase III – Performance Planning
- ✓ Generate Ideas for Improvement
- ✓ Develop the Ideal Process Workflow Diagram
- ✓ Develop Performance Plan

Phase IV - Implementation
- ✓ Obtain Appropriate Approvals
- ✓ Monitor Implementation Effort
- ✓ Track Key Performance Indicators

EXHIBIT 39-2
PROCESS EVALUATION TEAM PLANNING AGENDA

HANDOUT

I. Review PET Workflow Diagram

II. Storyboard All Key Business Processes

III. Select Processes that Will Benefit from PET Study

IV. Select PET Team Leader

V. Prepare Preliminary Budget for PET Study

HANDOUT

EXHIBIT 39-3
PROCESS EVALUATION TEAM WORKBOOK

Name of Process _____

Date _____

Team _____

EXHIBIT 39-3 (CONTINUED)
PROCESS EVALUATION TEAM WORKBOOK
PROCESS EVALUATION OVERVIEW

PHASE	STEPS
CRITICAL SUCCESS FACTORS	1. Define Team Mission 2. Determine Process Purpose 3. Identify Driving Forces 4. Define Customers & Outputs 5. Determine Customer Needs
PROCESS ANALYSIS	6. Flowchart Major Processes 7. Identify Baseline Measurements 8. Determine Gaps between Customer Needs and Process Capabilities
IMPROVEMENT PLANNING	9. Generate Ideas for Improvement 10. Develop Ideal Process Flowchart 11. Develop Performance Plan
IMPLEMENTATION	12. Obtain Appropriate Approvals 13. Monitor and Evaluate Implementation Efforts 14. Track Key Performance Indicators

EXHIBIT 39-3 (CONTINUED)
PROCESS EVALUATION TEAM WORKBOOK
GENERAL TEAM INFORMATION

PROCESS NAME		TEAM MEMBERS	PHONE/MAIL
PROCESS PURPOSE			

TEAM CHAMPION	TEAM MISSION
TEAM LEADER	

330

HANDOUT

EXHIBIT 39-3 (CONTINUED)
PROCESS EVALUATION TEAM WORKBOOK
DRIVING FORCES ANALYSIS

DRIVING FORCE	COMMENTS	EFFECT ON PROCESS		
		HI	MID	LOW
OUTPUTS				
SUPPLIERS				
TECHNOLOGY				
PRODUCTION				
SUPPORT				
DISTRIBUTION				
RESOURCES				
RETURN				
EXPERIENCE				

EXHIBIT 39-3 (CONTINUED)
PROCESS EVALUATION TEAM WORKBOOK
CUSTOMERS—OUTPUTS—SUBPROCESSES—INPUTS—SUPPLIERS

CUSTOMERS	OUTPUTS	SUB-PROCESSES	INPUTS	SUPPLIERS

EXHIBIT 39-3 (CONTINUED)
PROCESS EVALUATION TEAM WORKBOOK
CUSTOMER PROBLEM ANALYSIS

Process:
Output:

Customer Problems/Dreams	Relative Importance	Customer Experience Ranking		
		Consistently Exceeds	Meets but Seldom Exceeds	Seldom Meets
Product-Related				
Service-Related				
Customer Experience Totals				

333

EXHIBIT 39-3 (CONTINUED)
PROCESS EVALUATION TEAM WORKBOOK
PROCESS WORKFLOW DIAGRAM TRACKING

Process

	START	COMPLETED	COMMENTS
SUBPROCESS			
ASSIGNED TO			
SUBPROCESS			
ASSIGNED TO			
SUBPROCESS			
ASSIGNED TO			
SUBPROCESS			
ASSIGNED TO			
SUBPROCESS			
ASSIGNED TO			

EXHIBIT 39-3 (CONTINUED)
PROCESS EVALUATION TEAM WORKBOOK
COST ANALYSIS

SUBPROCESS	COST	QUALITY (defects/million)	CYCLE TIME PER	COMMENTS
TOTALS				

335

EXHIBIT 39-3 (CONTINUED)
PROCESS EVALUATION TEAM WORKBOOK
PROBLEM-SOLVING INFORMATION

DATE _____

TEAM _____

TARGET DATE FOR
   SOLUTION _____

PROBLEM STATEMENT (effect, gap, measurable, pain)

INFORMATION NEEDED

STEPS

1. Identify

2. Analysis

3. Generate Possible Solutions

4. Select Solution

5. Implement

6. Evaluate

CUSTOMER EXPERIENCE IMPACT

CAST EXPERIENCE IMPACT

FINANCIAL RESULTS IMPACT

SOLUTION IMPLEMENTED

RESULTS

EXHIBIT 39-3 (CONTINUED)
PROCESS EVALUATION TEAM WORKBOOK
PERFORMANCE PLAN

PROCESS

IDEAL PROCESS WORKFLOW OVERVIEW	RECOMMENDATION OVERVIEW	PERFORMANCE INDICATORS
		COST-BENEFIT OVERVIEW

337

EXHIBIT 39-4
PROCESS EVALUATION TEAM WORKBOOK EXAMPLE

Name of Process _Purchase Requisition_

Date _3/21_

Team Name _Purchase Requisition Team_

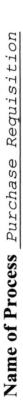

EXHIBIT 39-4 (CONTINUED)
PROCESS EVALUATION TEAM WORKBOOK EXAMPLE
PROCESS EVALUATION OVERVIEW

PHASE	STEPS
CRITICAL SUCCESS FACTORS	1. Define Team Mission 2. Determine Process Purpose 3. Identify Driving Forces 4. Define Customers & Outputs 5. Determine Customer Needs
PROCESS ANALYSIS	6. Flowchart Major Processes 7. Identify Baseline Measurements 8. Determine Gaps between Customer Needs and Process Capabilities
IMPROVEMENT PLANNING	9. Generate Ideas for Improvement 10. Develop Ideal Process Flowchart 11. Develop Performance Plan
IMPLEMENTATION	12. Obtain Appropriate Approvals 13. Monitor and Evaluate Implementation Efforts 14. Track Key Performance Indicators

EXHIBIT 39-4 (CONTINUED)
PROCESS EVALUATION TEAM WORKBOOK EXAMPLE
GENERAL TEAM INFORMATION

PROCESS NAME		
Purchase Requisition		

TEAM MEMBERS	PHONE/MAIL
Chuck	4773 – E5
Steve	3462 – C1
Lisa	2119 – B2
Nancy	7411 – D3
Dave	6211 – D2
Mike	4771 – E5

PROCESS PURPOSE
To provide timely procuring of capital and operating material and equipment

TEAM MISSION
To identify, evaluate & recommend improvements to the system that will provide timely procuring of equipment.

TEAM CHAMPION	Joe

TEAM LEADER	Paul

EXHIBIT 39-4 (CONTINUED)
PROCESS EVALUATION TEAM WORKBOOK EXAMPLE
DRIVING FORCES ANALYSIS

DRIVING FORCE	COMMENTS	EFFECT ON PROCESS		
		HI	MID	LOW
OUTPUTS	P.O.'s, Reqs, approvals	✓		
SUPPLIERS	Accounting, Purchasing, Engineering	✓		
TECHNOLOGY	Lack of on-line system		✓	
PRODUCTION				
SUPPORT	Currently, clerks type requisitions		✓	
DISTRIBUTION	Mail system can cause delays		✓	
RESOURCES	On-line system		?	
RETURN	Large ROI possible	?		
EXPERIENCE	Engineering, Operations, Purchasing, Accounting		✓	

341

HANDOUT

EXHIBIT 39-4 (CONTINUED)
PROCESS EVALUATION TEAM WORKBOOK EXAMPLE
CUSTOMERS—OUTPUTS—SUBPROCESSES—INPUTS—SUPPLIERS

CUSTOMERS	OUTPUTS	SUB-PROCESSES	INPUTS	SUPPLIERS
Purchasing	Requisitions	Prepare & approve requisition	Project needs	Engineering
Engineering	P.O./ Material	Order material	Requi- sitions	Engineering

EXHIBIT 39-4 (CONTINUED)
PROCESS EVALUATION TEAM WORKBOOK EXAMPLE
CUSTOMER PROBLEM ANALYSIS

Process: *Purchase Requisition*

Output: *P.O. / Material*

Customer Problems/Dreams	Relative Importance	Customer Experience Ranking			
		Consistently Exceeds	Meets but Seldom Exceeds	Seldom Meets	
Product-Related	60				
1. *Meets specifications*	40		20		
2. *Defect Free*	20		10		
3.					
4.					
5.					
6.					
Service-Related	40				
1. *Timely delivery*	30			0	
2. *Technical support*	10	10			
3.					
4.					
5.					
6.					
Customer Experience Totals	40	10	30	0	

343

HANDOUT

EXHIBIT 39-4 (CONTINUED)
PROCESS EVALUATION TEAM WORKBOOK EXAMPLE
PROCESS WORKFLOW DIAGRAM TRACKING

Process	START	COMPLETED	COMMENTS
Purchase Requisition			
SUB-PROCESS *Requisition approval*	*3/1*	*3/17*	
ASSIGNED TO *Mike*			
SUBPROCESS *P.O. Process*	*3/10*	*3/21*	
ASSIGNED TO *Lisa*			
SUBPROCESS *Exp. Tracking*	*3/21*		
ASSIGNED TO *Lisa*			
SUBPROCESS			
ASSIGNED TO			
SUBPROCESS			
ASSIGNED TO			

EXHIBIT 39-4 (CONTINUED)
PROCESS EVALUATION TEAM WORKBOOK EXAMPLE
COST ANALYSIS

SUB-PROCESS	COST	QUALITY (defects/million)	CYCLE TIME PER *Req.*	COMMENTS
Requisition preparation	$100/ req.	10,000	3 days	
Requisition approval	$800/ req.	5,000	17 days	
P.O. prep.	$100/ P.O.	50,000	2 days	Not enough time to get best deal
TOTALS	$1,000	65,000	22 days	

EXHIBIT 39-4 (CONTINUED)
PROCESS EVALUATION TEAM WORKBOOK EXAMPLE
PROBLEM-SOLVING INFORMATION

PROBLEM STATEMENT (effect, gap, measurable, pain)	DATE _3/21_
Current methods of preparing requisitions are lengthy (3 days) and costly	TEAM _Purch. Req. Team_ **TARGET DATE FOR SOLUTION** ___

	STEPS	INFORMATION NEEDED
	1. Identify	
	2. Analysis	*Process flows, on-line systems costs*
	3. Generate Possible Solutions	
	4. Select Solution	
	5. Implement	
	6. Evaluate	

CUSTOMER EXPERIENCE IMPACT

- *Late delivery*
- *Don't get best deal*

CAST EXPERIENCE IMPACT

FINANCIAL RESULTS IMPACT

SOLUTION IMPLEMENTED

RESULTS

HANDOUT

EXHIBIT 39-4 (CONTINUED)
PROCESS EVALUATION TEAM WORKBOOK EXAMPLE
PERFORMANCE PLAN

PROCESS

IDEAL PROCESS WORKFLOW OVERVIEW	RECOMMENDATION OVERVIEW	PERFORMANCE INDICATORS
Input Requisition — To Pur.	Increase Eng. App.	1. Rush 24 hour
Place order	Install auto requisition tracking	2. Normal 48 hour
		3. Savings $10,000/ mo. reg. goods
Check for additional App.		
		COST/BENEFIT OVERVIEW
		$30,000 Requisition tracking system
		$500,000/ year reduced purchasing cost

EXHIBIT 39-5
PROCESS EVALUATION TEAM SAMPLE SCHEDULE

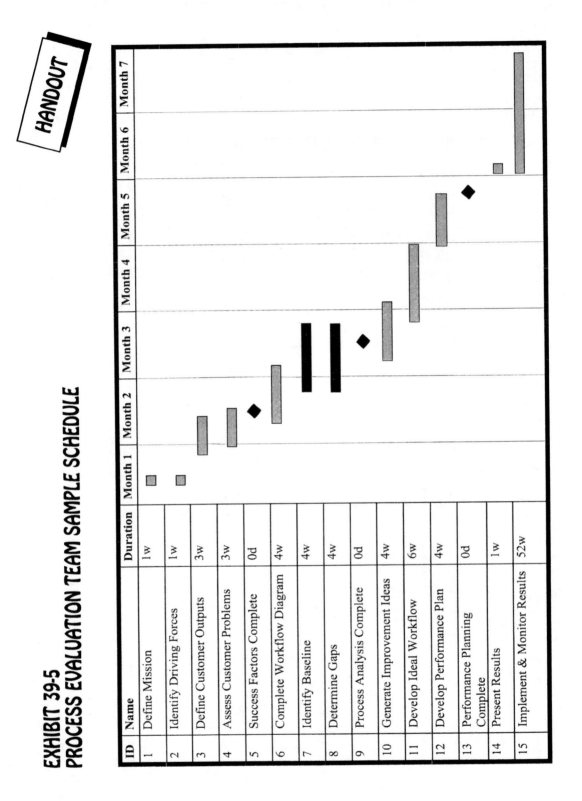

ID	Name	Duration	Month 1	Month 2	Month 3	Month 4	Month 5	Month 6	Month 7
1	Define Mission	1w							
2	Identify Driving Forces	1w							
3	Define Customer Outputs	3w							
4	Assess Customer Problems	3w							
5	Success Factors Complete	0d							
6	Complete Workflow Diagram	4w							
7	Identify Baseline	4w							
8	Determine Gaps	4w							
9	Process Analysis Complete	0d							
10	Generate Improvement Ideas	4w							
11	Develop Ideal Workflow	6w							
12	Develop Performance Plan	4w							
13	Performance Planning Complete	0d							
14	Present Results	1w							
15	Implement & Monitor Results	52w							

EXHIBIT 39-6
PROCESS EVALUATION TEAM CHECKLIST

CHECKLIST	COMMENTS
1. Mission defined	
2. Driving forces defined	
3. Customers problems and dreams defined	
4. Workflow diagrams include • Interviews to capture various perspectives • Records actual, not designated, behavior • Errors and rework routines	
5. Gap analysis, look for • Activities and policies that cancel each other • Duplication of effort • Weak links between information flow and tasks • Lack of flexibility • Long wait and queue times • Lack of accountability and ownership • Use the *"Five W's & H"* questions • Activities that have no customers	
6. All relevant time accounted for • Cycle time • Breakeven time analysis • Customer response time • Rework • Incomplete deliveries • Inventory turns • Engineering change notices	
7. Ideal workflow • Customer requirements met or exceeded • Are competitive benchmarks met or exceeded? • Were compromises made or win–win agreements?	
8. Performance plan • Do all key people understand results? • Are resource requirements stated? • Are performance indicators customer, cast, and financial driven?	
9. Timetable for implementation • Early milestones – early successes • Responsibilities understood • Contingencies investigated	

EXHIBIT 39-7
"GOING TO WORK" WORKFLOW DIAGRAM OVERVIEW

HANDOUT

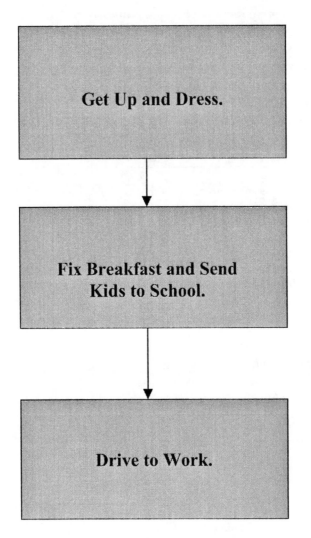

EXHIBIT 39-8
"GOING TO WORK" WORKFLOW DIAGRAM
"GET UP AND DRESS" SUBPROCESS DETAIL

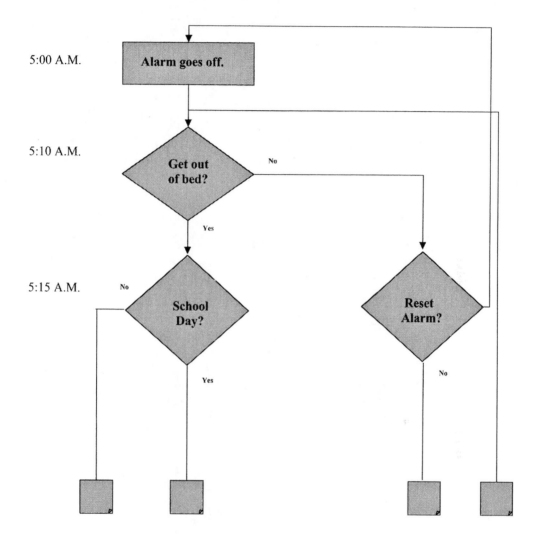

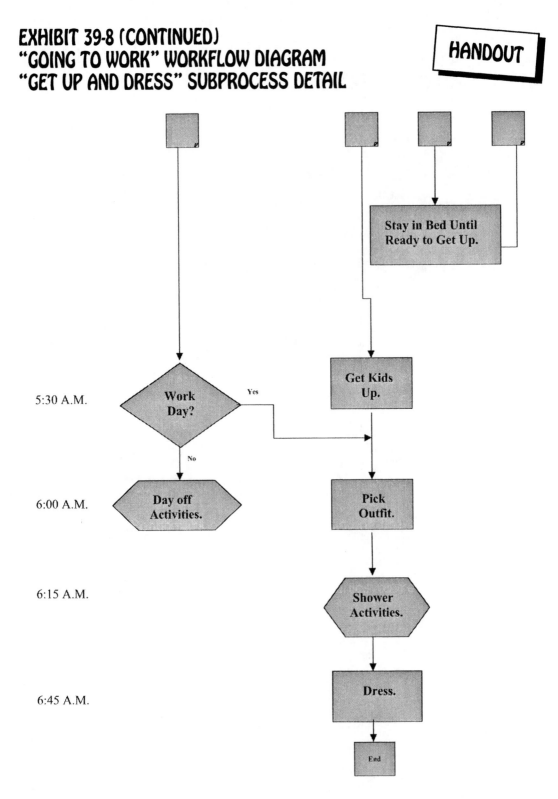

5:30 A.M.

6:00 A.M.

6:15 A.M.

6:45 A.M.

PET Costing

WHY THE COSTING PROCESS IS IMPORTANT

- PET process maximizes value.
- Value is defined as:

Value Created = Value of the Output—Cost of the Output

- Value of the output is determined by the customer.
- Cost of the output is:

Output Cost = Input Cost + Process Cost

COSTING GUIDELINES

- Obtain the average compensation cost from accounting.
- Estimate time allocations by departmental output.

  Example:

  Department: Accounting

  Output: Credit Approval

  Average Clerical Compensation: $20/hour incl. Benefits

  Time Allocations: 4 Accounting Clerks:

  - One clerk 90% dedicated to credit approval
  - Three clerks 25% dedicated to credit approval

  Cost: 2000hr x .90 x $20/hour + 2000 hours x 3 x .25 x $20 = $66,000

  Cost Per Output: $66,000 divided by # of credit approvals

- Confirm that the cumulative cost of all activities approaches the total cost of the process.

  - Use the workflow diagram to verify that all activities are costed.
  - Remember indirect costs such as material handling, transportation, approvals, inventory, etc.

Need to Be Accurate, Not Precise!

Time Is Money

THE 5% RULE

Less than 5% of the process time is spent doing value-added activities.

WAIT TIME RULE

Wait time is equally divided between:

- waiting for previous batch to be completed;
- waiting for rework to be completed;
- waiting for management approvals.

CYCLE TIME REDUCTION RULE

For every 25% reduction in cycle time:

- Labor productivity often doubles.
- Overall process cost can be reduced by as much as 20%.

CYCLE TIME REDUCTION BENEFITS

Companies with the best cycle times:

- Grow at 3 times the industry average.
- Earn 2 times the average industry profit.

Analyzing the Workflow Diagram

Questions for each activity on the diagram

WHO

- Who performs the activity?
- Who should perform it?
- Who else can perform it?
- Who is promoting waste?

WHAT

- What is being done?
- What should be done?
- What else can be done?

WHY

- Why perform the activity?
- Why perform it there?
- Why perform it then?
- Why perform it that way?

WHERE

- Where is the activity being performed?
- Where should it be performed?
- Where else can it be performed?
- Where is waste occurring?

WHEN

- When is the activity being performed?
- When should it be performed?
- When else can it be performed?
- When is waste occurring?

HOW

- How is the activity being performed?
- How should it be performed?
- How could it be performed better?
- How can it be performed better in other areas?

Guidelines in Selecting Key Business Process Priorities

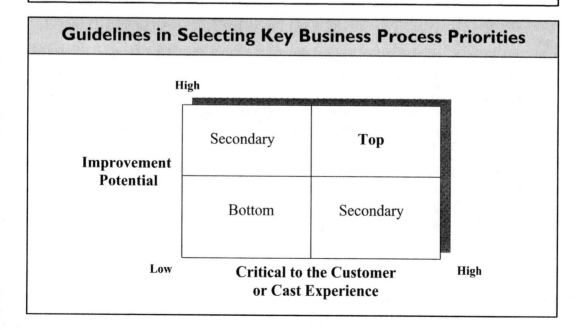

The Six Steps to Problem Solving

1. Identify the Problem—Write a problem statement.
2. Analyze the Problem—Gather and study data.
3. Generate Possible Solutions—Brainstorm alternative actions.

   This is the creative and fun part of problem solving. List all solution ideas, regardless of how crazy or impractical they seem.
4. Select a Solution—Choose the most viable action.
5. Implement the Solution—Begin the action.

   Great solutions are worthless without well-focused, concrete action.
6. Evaluate the Solution—Measure the outcome; confirm achievement of desired results.

*After all the years of 3- to 5-day problem-solving workshops, employees continue to tell us these are the most practical steps to solve most business problems.

Causes of Waste

Method
- Is the work process understood?
- Is the method safe?
- Is the sequence of work adequate?
- Is the setup adequate?
- Are appropriate temperature and humidity levels maintained?
- Are the lighting and ventilation adequate?
- Is there adequate communication with the previous and next areas of the process?

Causes of Waste

Material
- Are there any mistakes in volume?
- Are there any mistakes in the grade of material?
- Are you mixing suppliers' raw material?
- Is there any wasted or scrapped material?
- Is the material handling adequate?
- Are the inventory levels adequate?
- Is work-in-process inventory excessive?
- Is the layout adequate?

Causes of Waste

Machine
- Does it meet production requirements?
- Does it meet process capabilities?
- Is the preventative maintenance (PM) adequate?
- Is production stopped because of downtime?
- Does it make any unusual noises?
- Is the layout adequate?
- Are there enough machines?

Causes of Waste

People (Operator)
- Does the operator follow standards?
- Is the operator's work efficiency acceptable?
- Is the operator problem-conscious?
- Is the operator responsible?
- Is the operator accountable?
- Is the operator qualified?
- Is the operator experienced?
- Is the operator assigned to the right job?
- Is the operator trained?
- Is the operator willing to improve?

Categories of Waste

- Non-value-added activities
- Excessive effort or strain
- Discrepancy in methods or procedures
- Clutter in the workplace

SCENE 40: BENCHMARKING THE BEST

We'll switch places for a day.
—The Prince, *The Prince and the Pauper*

AUTHORS' NOTES

Your best is always yet to come when you are always striving to improve. Benchmarking—the search for best-in-class processes—can help you greatly in doing that.

Xerox has been benchmarking for over 20 years, but most other companies haven't even started.

Why not? Perhaps they think it's too expensive and time-consuming to be worthwhile. Perhaps they think they already are benchmarking, when in fact they're just "industrial tourists" cruising competitors' market data. (If they traveled to Europe they'd tick off seven countries in seven days. A true benchmarker would live in Paris for two years.)

We've observed that many companies confuse benchmarking with competitive market analysis. To set them straight, here's a comparative review:

Benchmarking measures processes and practices.
Competitive market analysis measures finished products and outcomes.

Benchmarking is ongoing.
Competitive market analysis is a one-time event.

Benchmarking requires a continuing financial investment.
Competitive market analysis is funded in a single shot.

Benchmarking compels companies to revise and to update paradigms.
Competitive market analysis documents the status quo.

Benchmarking spurs dynamic action leading to breakthrough improvements.

Competitive market analysis yields voluminous reports.

Is benchmarking for you? Consider that successful benchmarking companies have raised customer satisfaction by over 40 percent, cut returns by 30 percent, reduced lead times by 50 percent, and brought employee turnover rates to new lows.

In light of these bottom-line results, the time, effort, and money required for benchmarking seem a reasonable price to pay.

PLOT

To organize a Benchmarking Study to compare critical company processes against the best-of-the-best. In so doing, to address:

- how you compare to the competitor's best practice;
- how you compare to the industry's best practice;
- how you compare to the best practice regardless of industry;
- opportunities for improvement and actions to accomplish results.

RUNNING TIME

One to two hours for organization of the activity.

(The actual benchmarking will involve considerable additional time.)

KEY PLAYERS

- Leadership Team
- Benchmarking Team Leader

PROPS

- Benchmarking the Best Workflow Diagram (one per participant) (Exhibit 40-1)
- Benchmark Planning Meeting Agenda (one per participant) (Exhibit 40-2)
- Cast experience data
- Guest experience data
- Storyboard materials (see Scene 30)
- Process evaluation study results (if available)

DIRECTOR'S SCRIPT

LIGHTS ...

1. Pre-distribute to the Leadership Team the Benchmarking the Best Workflow Diagram and the Agenda for Benchmark Planning meeting.

CAMERA ...

2. Assemble the Leadership Team.
3. Review the Benchmarking the Best Workflow Diagram and the Agenda for Benchmark Planning meeting.
4. Storyboard all key business processes.
5. Use the priority dotting technique to determine the three processes from the Benchmarking Study that will benefit the guest experience or the cast experience the most.
6. Ask the team to consider and discuss possible team leaders for the Benchmarking Study.
7. Select a Benchmarking Study leader who has proven leadership skills and will directly benefit from the improvements in the process.
8. With the team, discuss preliminary budget considerations for the Benchmarking Study.
9. With the selected Benchmarking Study leader, share the key business process storyboard.

10. Schedule a follow-up meeting with the Benchmarking Study leader to discuss in detail the Benchmarking the Best Workflow Diagram.

11. Assemble the Leadership Team and the Benchmarking Team Leader.

12. Review the workflow diagram. The first part of the processes is complete, as the Leadership Team has by now done the following:

    ■ selected the key process to benchmark;

    ■ chosen a team leader; and

    ■ prepared a preliminary budget.

13. Have the Benchmarking Team Leader select a team to assist in the study. Advise the Leader that:

    ■ Team members should be those who have the most at stake in the process, and who will have the ultimate responsibility for making the actual changes.

    ■ Team members chosen should have hands-on experience in the process being benchmarked.

    ■ This is not the place for upper management personnel.

14. Prepare the Benchmarking Team Leader to lead the Benchmarking Team by providing these instructions:

    ■ The preparation of detail workflow diagrams for the process being benchmarked is critical.

    ■ The team should not go on a "fishing expedition" just to see what pops into their boat.

    ■ Pick a specific area you want to improve and do your homework. Study your own process thoroughly. Ask yourself:

    ■ What changes would you like to see in the guest experience?

    ■ What changes would you like to see in the cast experience?

    ■ When the workflow diagrams are completed, let the team determine the performance variables they want to measure. If measurement information is not readily available, the team must determine a means of capturing the needed information.

- Benchmarking must respond to three questions:

1. Who is your toughest local competitor? (i.e., with whom do you compete head-to-head in the same market?)

2. What company in your industry does the best job of performing the benchmarked process? (This company may or may not be a head-to-head competitor, but should be providing products or services similar to yours.)

3. What company out of all industries, regardless of product or service, does the best job of performing the benchmarked process? (For example, Xerox once benchmarked outdoor wear merchant L.L. Bean's order filling process.)

The companies identified as top performers are the "best-in-class."

ACTION!

15. Have the Benchmarking Team Leader begin the benchmarking process by instructing the Benchmarking Team to revise the preliminary budget.

Notes:

Leadership Team approval may be needed if the revised budget is outside the parameters of the preliminary budget.

Obtaining performance measures of direct competitor best-in-class companies will be more difficult than obtaining these of noncompetitors. However, much written material on best-in-class companies is usually available. Most of this can be found on the Internet. Also, professional trade organizations are often an excellent source of industry best practices.

16. Coach the Benchmarking Team Leader in continuing to conduct benchmarking by providing the following instructions:

- If possible, establish a benchmarking partnership with a best-in-class company. If a site visit is possible, develop a questionnaire and interview guide. Send an advance copy of the questionnaire and interview guide to the company to insure the most productive visit.

- Establish a Benchmarking Partnership Code of Conduct before conducting the Benchmarking site visit. The code should include:

    1. *Share*—Be willing to exchange the same level of detail information about your process that you are seeking from your benchmarking partner.

    2. *Be sensitive*—Treat the information as you would treat any confidential internal document. Establish ground rules that ensure neither party is sharing proprietary information unless prior approval has been given by the appropriate corporate officer.

    3. *Prepare*—Understand the benchmark company's background, markets, product lines, and history. Do your homework before the site visit.

- After completing all site visits, identify the gaps between the best-in-class company's processes and yours.

- Develop specific actions to close these gaps.

- Present these proposed actions to the Leadership Team. The Leadership Team will use this information to prepare the Best Show Plan (see Scene 4).

CUT!

17. After the Benchmarking Study has been completed, meet with the entire Benchmarking Team to debrief the experience. Ask:

- What did we do well?

- What could we have done better?

- Was this a worthwhile effort? Why or why not?

18. Organize the study findings for future review and analysis of the process. Working papers for the future review and analysis should include:

- Cast Experience Data
- Guest Experience Data
- List of Key Business Processes
- List of Benchmarking Team Members
- Process Workflow Diagrams
- Key Performance Variables to Measure
- List of Benchmark Companies Considered
- List of Benchmark Companies Selected
- Benchmark Data by Benchmarked Company (e.g., flow-charts, articles, annual reports, interview notes, etc.)
- Gap Analysis
- Recommended Action Plan

CURTAIN CALL

To benchmark or not to benchmark, that is the question.

The answer—if your goal is to become or remain among the best-of-the-best in your industry—is YES.

EXHIBIT 40-1
BENCHMARKING THE BEST WORKFLOW DIAGRAM

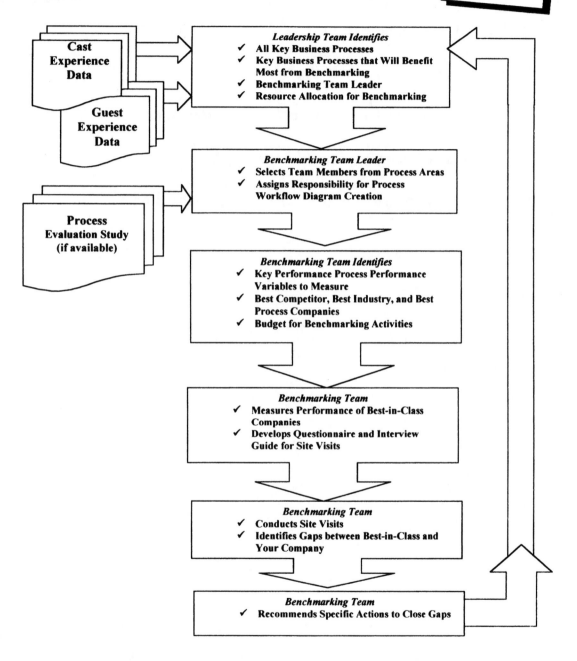

Cast Experience Data

Guest Experience Data

Process Evaluation Study (if available)

Leadership Team Identifies
- ✓ All Key Business Processes
- ✓ Key Business Processes that Will Benefit Most from Benchmarking
- ✓ Benchmarking Team Leader
- ✓ Resource Allocation for Benchmarking

Benchmarking Team Leader
- ✓ Selects Team Members from Process Areas
- ✓ Assigns Responsibility for Process Workflow Diagram Creation

Benchmarking Team Identifies
- ✓ Key Performance Process Performance Variables to Measure
- ✓ Best Competitor, Best Industry, and Best Process Companies
- ✓ Budget for Benchmarking Activities

Benchmarking Team
- ✓ Measures Performance of Best-in-Class Companies
- ✓ Develops Questionnaire and Interview Guide for Site Visits

Benchmarking Team
- ✓ Conducts Site Visits
- ✓ Identifies Gaps between Best-in-Class and Your Company

Benchmarking Team
- ✓ Recommends Specific Actions to Close Gaps

EXHIBIT 40-2
BENCHMARK PLANNING MEETING AGENDA

HANDOUT

I. Review Benchmarking the Best Workflow Diagram

II. Storyboard Key Business Processes

III. Select Processes That Will Benefit from Benchmarking

IV. Select Benchmarking Team Leader

V. Prepare Preliminary Budget for Benchmarking Study

Mirror, Mirror, on the Wall, Who is the Best of All?

A Benchmarking Study begins with researching the best-in-class. Here are some good sources of information:

Internet databases: An excellent place to start. In a few hours you can gain as much data as you would have over several days in the library ten years ago.

Wall Street: Contact the industry specialists for financial information on your target companies. Remember, though, that financial performance is not a perfect indicator of best-of-the-best process results.

Professional associations: Read their journals. Attend conferences where their representatives are scheduled to speak.

Your current suppliers: Ask how they view your competitors' best practices, but don't demand confidential information.

Your customers: Solicit information on competitors in customer focus groups. Customers will readily help you, because whatever benefits you as their vendor will help them, too.

Industry experts: Technical professionals and consultants associated with specific industries or processes are usually knowledgeable about best practices. Do not ignore experts in your own organization. Consult any of your own employees who know a competitor through trade associations or previous employment.

University professors: Many colleges and universities conduct extensive research on specific processes and best practices.

SCORE (Service Corps of Retired Executives): This network of former executives can provide a wealth of firsthand knowledge about many industries and processes.

Award Winners: All winners of the annual Malcolm Baldridge Award consent to share their expertise with other domestic companies. Several of them conduct seminars at which they describe how they became one of the best-of-the-best. Check out other local or trade association award winners.

SCENE 41: BAD SHOW VERSUS GOOD SHOW: THE REAL COST

I want to leave you with this thought, that it's just been sort of a dress rehearsal and we're just getting started. So if any of you start resting on your laurels, I mean just forget it, because ... we are just getting started.

—Walt Disney

AUTHORS' NOTES

Walt Disney delighted in the results of no business like show business, except when he witnessed "bad show." He was a stickler for detail, inspecting every nook and cranny of his "on stage" areas looking for anything that could destroy that Disneyesque "magical moment" for a guest. What constitutes bad? In theater, an empty house. In business, most team leaders just don't know. If you're a team leader who's too much in the dark about your company's costs, our Bad Show versus Good Show Questionnaire will shine a light.

For starters, you'll learn that in a typical manufacturing environment, combined "good show" and "bad show" costs can reach 25 percent of sales. (In a service organization, they can approach 40 percent.) Manufacturers' costs break down as follows:

Bad Show

- 8 percent External Failure—warranty cost, product returns
- 9 percent Internal Failure—rework, scrap

Good Show

- 3 percent Prevention—training and improvement efforts.

The math here reveals that a typical manufacturing company spends $0.17 of every dollar on mistakes and only $0.03 on preventing those mistakes. (Appraisal—inspections, approvals, testing, quality control—accounts for 5 percent, or $0.05.)

What does your own math reveal about your company? The Questionnaire will help you estimate your total costs, and itemize internal and external failure, appraisal, and prevention.

Why crunch these numbers at all? Simply to make management and frontline employees realize the state they're in so they'll start to make improvements. Indeed, several world-class manufacturing and service companies have reduced "cost of show" to just 5 percent, with most of that going to prevention. Your own "cost of show" may rise initially, but don't be alarmed. It's normal to spend heavily on prevention before failure and appraisal costs can start to fall.

There is a cost, however, that sheer numbers do not immediately depict: that of customers lost due to "bad shows." This is not an expenditure so much as a squandered opportunity, which can be recouped by transforming "bad shows" into "good shows."

PLOT

To calculate "bad show" and "good show" costs, and to recognize (and ultimately reduce) their large contributions to "total show" costs.

RUNNING TIME

30–45 minutes

KEY PLAYERS

- Leadership Team Leaders
- Natural Work Team Leaders

PROPS

- Cost of Show Questionnaire (Exhibit 41-1)
- Cost of Show Questionnaire Interpretations (Exhibit 41-2)

DIRECTOR'S SCRIPT

LIGHTS, CAMERA ...

1. Assemble the Leadership Team. Review and discuss the Cost of Show Questionnaire.

2. Determine whether the scope of the questionnaire should be limited to:
   - the company in general;
   - key business processes; or
   - specific departments.

3. Determine whether the questionnaire should be completed either in a team setting, or by individual team members and summarized.

Note: Strong, opinionated leaders generally get more reliable results if the questionnaire is completed individually and then summarized.

ACTION!

4. Instruct the participants to complete the questionnaire.

5. Plan a subsequent meeting to review the results.

CUT!

6. At the subsequent meeting, review the results of the questionnaire by discussing:
   - Cost of Show Questionnaire Interpretations.
   - Are we spending enough on prevention activities?
   - What improvements need to be made to reduce our "cost of show"?

CURTAIN CALL

The "good show" must go on.
The "bad show" must be closed before opening night.

EXHIBIT 41-1
COST OF SHOW QUESTIONNAIRE

Following are several statements about your company. Indicate whether you "Strongly Agree," "Agree," "Somewhat Agree," "Disagree" or "Strongly Disagree" with each one.

In the space before each question, note your response by entering the number (1-6, see below) that corresponds to your opinion. Add the numbers and record subtotals at the end of each section.

1. Strongly Agree
2. Agree
3. Somewhat Agree

4. Somewhat Disagree
5. Disagree
6. Strongly Disagree

Section 1
PRODUCT/SERVICE

____ 1. Our product/service is considered the standard of our industry.

____ 2. We have a 70% or better customer retention rate.

____ 3. Our warranty periods are as long or longer than our competitors'.

____ 4. We conduct formal benchmarking studies to improve key
    business processes.

____ 5. We conduct formal customer focus groups at least once per year for
    all major products.

____ 6. Our product development personnel (marketing, research and
    development) spend more than 50% of their time in the field with
    customers.

____ 7. Our customer service employees are trained in interpersonal relations.

____ 8. Our customer service employees are considered a key source of
    customer and new product information.

                    Section 1 Subtotal _____

EXHIBIT 41-1 (CONTINUED)
COST OF SHOW QUESTIONNAIRE

Section 2
ORGANIZATION

____ 1. Our company is structured around key business processes, not traditional departments. The key business process has total profit and loss responsibility for that process.

____ 2. We have identified our key suppliers and have established sole-source partnerships with at least 50 percent of them.

____ 3. Our employee turnover rate is less than our industry's average.

____ 4. We are trained in and use formal problem-solving tools to improve our processes.

____ 5. Receiving adequate vendor quality data lets us eliminate more than 50 percent of our incoming inspections.

Section 2 Subtotal _____

Section 3
PROCESS

____ 1. We use complaint data plus scrap and rework information to determine where improvements should be made.

____ 2. We are all aware of our customers' needs, problems, and dreams. We are empowered to assist customers in any legal, moral, and ethical way.

____ 3. Our traditional performance appraisals have been replaced by proactive developing planning.

____ 4. Every employee has a yearly training plan.

____ 5. Within the first 3 weeks on the job, every new employee attends a formal orientation program that is at least 8 hours long.

EXHIBIT 41-1 (CONTINUED)
COST OF SHOW QUESTIONNAIRE

___ 6. Traditional time card supervisor tracking has been replaced with employee recording.

___ 7. Our policy manual is no longer than two typed pages.

___ 8. Training is coupled with a focused experience that reinforces training.

Section 3 Subtotal _____

Section 4
MEASUREMENTS

___ 1. Everyone knows the goals and measurements for guest experience, cast experience, and financial results. Measurements are reported to all employees on a monthly basis.

___ 2. We report scrap, rework, and customer complaints monthly to all employees.

___ 3. Our key business processes are benchmarked against our best competitor, the best process in our industry, and the best-of-the-best regardless of industry.

___ 4. We have replaced in-process inspection with statistical process control charts for all key operations.

Section 4 Subtotal _____

Summary
Product or Service _____
Organization _____
Process _____
Measurements _____
Grand Total _____

EXHIBIT 41-2
COST OF SHOW QUESTIONNAIRE INTERPRETATIONS

HANDOUT

25-50

- Your company is prevention-focused.
- If all your answers are in the 1-2 range, your "cost of show" is low.
- You are already benchmarking and studying many key business processes.
- Fine-tuning of improvement efforts will keep costs low.

51-75

- If your subtotal for the "Product" questions is high and subtotals for all the others are low, your company is prevention-focused.
- If your subtotal for "Measurements" is high, your company is appraisal-focused.
- Your "cost of show" is moderate.
- Although your costs are moderate, you may be spending too much on appraisal and internal failure. A formal improvement effort will help reduce costs.

76-100

- If most of your answers are in the 3-4 range your "cost of show" is in the moderate to high range.
- You are not spending enough on prevention. A formal improvement effort will help refocus your cost on prevention.

101-125

- If most of your answers are in the 4-5 range, your company is failure-focused.
- You spend little on prevention and appraisal.
- Your "cost of show" is high. A formal improvement effort will reduce your failure cost.

126-150

- Your "cost of show" is very high. An extensive formal improvement effort is imperative.

Survey Total	Category	Cost of Show % of Gross Sales
25-50	Low	2-5%
51-100	Moderate	6-15%
101-125	High	16-20%
126-150	Very High	21-40%

SCENE 42: CARDS 'R' US EXERCISE

Whatever we accomplish is due to the combined effort. The organization must be with you or you don't get it done ...
—Walt Disney

AUTHORS' NOTES

No departmental work team is an island, though many work teams act as if they were. They boost their own outputs at the risk of reducing productivity for the entire organization. They drain rather than share resources, leaving other teams scrambling and often failing to meet their own goals.

These self-serving teams are like the baseball batter who swings for the fences (and strikes out) instead of laying down a sacrifice bunt to move the runner into scoring position. Such selfishness will cease only when "sacrifice" no longer implies giving oneself up for the team, but instead means exchanging personal glory for an even greater collective reward, in which each individual's share is larger, too.

By comparing continuous improvement efforts undertaken within natural work teams to process improvements pursued jointly by multiple cross-functional process evaluation teams—and contrasting the respective results—the Cards R Us exercise teaches a holistic and more profitable approach to team play.

PLOT

To improve both intradepartmental work processes and cross-functional team processes, and to recognize the relative benefits of each.

RUNNING TIME

Two to three hours

KEY PLAYERS

Teams with 18 members
For teams with 15 to 17 members, combine the following:

■ Tool room and storeroom roles
■ Material handling and finished goods roles
■ Accounting and quality control roles

For teams with 18 or more members, add the following:

■ Additional layout workers
■ Additional material handling workers
■ Letter operators

PROPS

■ "Happy Birthday Card" example
■ At least two Cards 'R' Us Specification Sheets (Exhibit 42-1)
■ Cards 'R' Us Production Accounting Report Template (Exhibit 42-2)
■ Cards 'R' Us Workflow Diagram (one for every three participants) (Exhibit 42-3)
■ Cards 'R' Us Accounting Log (Exhibit 42-4)
■ Cards 'R' Us Production Orders (Exhibit 42-5)
■ Cards 'R' Us Rework Log (Exhibit 42-6)
■ Cards 'R' Us Organization Chart (Exhibit 42-7)
■ Card stock (for workstation signs)
■ Cards 'R' Us Inventory Record (Exhibit 42-8)
■ Cards 'R' Us Tool Room Log (Exhibit 42-9)
■ Two 12- to 18-inch rulers
■ One box of red and one box of blue water-soluble 1/4-inch felt-tip markers

- At least one ream of white copy paper
- At least two pink pearl erasers
- At least two #2 lead pencils
- One bottle of White-Out
- Flip chart
- 11 tables

DIRECTOR'S SCRIPT

LIGHTS ...

1. Using the Specification Sheet, create a Happy Birthday Card example.

2. Using card stock, prepare a workstation identification card for each job title on the Cards 'R' Us Organization Chart.

3. Fold each card in half so it can stand upright on the table like a tent.

4. Place each of the tent cards on a separate table to designate individual departmental workstations. Cards can be placed at random, except that:
   - "H," "A," "P," "Y" Operator Cards should all be at one table. (HAPY Department)
   - "B," "I," "R," "T," "D" Operator Cards should all be at one table. (BIRTD Department)
   - For groups smaller than 18 where one participant is assuming two departmental roles, include both of these departments at one table.

5. You, the director, will take the role of Vice President of the "Happy Birthday" Division. Place your tent card at its own separate table.

6. Place the following:
   - The ream of copy paper on the Storeroom table.
   - The Cards 'R' Us Production Orders and an the Cards 'R' Us Accounting Log on the Accounting table.
   - The specifications, a ruler, pencils, and an eraser on the Layout table.

377

- A red marker at each of the "H," "A," "P," "Y" operator stations.
- A blue marker at each of the "B," "I," "R," "T," "D" operator stations.
- Specifications and a ruler on the Quality Control table.
- The bottle of White-Out on the Rework table.
- An eraser and the Cards 'R' Us Finished Goods Inventory Record on the Finished Goods table.
- Tool Room Log on the Tool Room table

7. Copy the template of the Cards 'R' Us Production Accounting Report onto the flip chart.

CAMERA ...

8. Position the entire team so members can move from table to table in a production line fashion.

9. Explain the exercise's objective: to experience the difference between pursuing improvements as a work team per se, and as a team operating as part of a cross-departmental process.

Note: The exercise has purposely been set up inefficiently to provide opportunities for pursuing improvements.

10. Assign each team member to a departmental workstation where he or she will assume the appropriate departmental role.

11. Explain each department's role.

Layout
- Folds raw material.
- Pencils "Happy Birthday" as per specifications.

Accounting
- Assigns batch numbers.
- Issues Production Orders (lot size 10).
- Maintains Cards 'R' Us Accounting Log.

- Summarizes results on Cards 'R' Us Production Accounting Report at the completion of each round.

Tool Room

- Maintains the tools needed for the lettering machines (red and blue markers), and additional tools (rulers, erasers, etc.).
- Issues replacement tools as tools wear out (e.g., markers that run out of ink); exchanges tools for new setups (e.g., moving from red Y to blue Y).
- Records exchanges and replacements on Tool Room Log.

Quality Control

- Reviews completed product for conformance to specifications.

Rework

- Corrects or scraps rejected products.
- Reports scrap and rework on Rework Log.

Finished Goods

- Receives finished product and erases all pencil marks.
- Records inventory on Production Order and sends to Accounting.

Material Handling

- Moves WIP (work in progress) and finished goods inventory between departments when participants raise their hands.

BIRTD

- Fills in the following: "B," "I," "R," "T" and "D."

Note: These operations should be imagined as being performed by a lettering machine; the marker represents the tool to be used with the machine.

HAPY

- Fills in the following: "H," "A," "P" and "Y."

Note: These operations should be imagined as being performed by a lettering machine; the marker represents the tool to be used with the machine.

Storeroom

■ Issues material for production by batch.

12. Explain the workflow, but *do not* reveal the actual Cards 'R' Us Workflow Diagram to the team at this time.

ACTION!

13. Begin the production process by instructing Accounting to issue enough work orders to keep the storeroom busy. Remind departments to raise their hands when they are done, to signal Material Handling to collect their cards.

14. Allow the exercise to proceed for about 15 minutes, or until the first few batches of cards have arrived in the Finished Goods inventory.

15. Suspend the process and ask Accounting to calculate for Round 0:

■ WIP = Total # of Batches Issued (from all rounds) *times* 10 (# of cards in each batch) *minus* Scrap (from all rounds) *minus* Finished Goods (from all rounds).

■ Scrap (from Accounting Log for the Round).

■ Rework (from Rework Log for the Round).

■ Finished Goods (from Accounting Log for the Round).

16. On the flip chart, complete the Cards 'R' Us Production Accounting Report for Round 0.

17. Begin production for Round 1. Let the process run for 15 minutes.

18. Suspend the process and ask Accounting to complete the Accounting Report for Round 1.

19. Announce the following:

■ Management is concerned with continuous improvement.

■ Each department will be given the chance to make improvements to its own department.

380

- Departments may not make any changes that affect other departments or disrupt the workflow.
- Each department will make a 1 to 2 minute presentation to the Vice President.
- The Vice President will only allow changes within the department of the presenter.

Allow 10 minutes for departments to discuss intradepartmental changes and to prepare their recommendations.

20. After presentations have been made and the teams have made their intradepartmental changes, begin Round 2.

21. After 15 minutes, suspend production.

22. Ask Accounting to complete the Production Accounting Report for Round 2.

23. Ask Accounting to calculate the "% Changes" from Round 1 to Round 2. (Round 1 WIP *minus* Round 2 WIP; the difference is *divided* by Round 1 WIP; this result is *multiplied* by 100 to convert to a percentage.)

24. With the entire team, discuss the impact of the implemented recommendations on the operation's productivity.

- Was there more production?
- Was there less WIP?
- Was there less scrap?

25. Display the Cards 'R' Us Workflow Diagram.

26. Announce that management is serious about reengineering the entire process.

27. Invite the overall team to discuss changes to the process. If the team has 20 members or fewer, allow the entire team to discuss changes to the entire process. If the team is larger than 20, divide the team into two or three subteams to discuss possible changes.

After 10 minutes, allow all subteams to discuss their ideas together.

Allow 15 minutes for the discussions.

28. Request that all ideas be presented to the Vice President.

29. Allow time for implementation of ideas to change the process.

30. Begin Round 3.

31. After 15 minutes, stop the process and ask Accounting to complete the Cards 'R' Us Production Accounting Report for Round 3, and to calculate the "% Change" between Round 2 and Round 3.

Note: After the productivity changes have been implemented, there will be significant improvements in productivity in most teams.

CUT!

32. Debrief and discuss:

- How can optimizing departmental productivity affect the productivity of the entire process and the work of other company teams?

- What can you do to become more holistic in your approach to process improvements?

CURTAIN CALL

Written 400 years ago in England, John Donne's Meditation XVII, in *Devotions,* powerfully conveys the holistic—as opposed to myopic—view of life that we apply to American business today:

> No man is an island, entire of itself; every man is a piece of the continent, a part of the main; if a clod be washed away by the sea, Europe is the less, as well as if a promontory were, as well as if a manor of thy friends or of thine own were; any man's death diminishes me, because I am involved in mankind; and therefore never send to know for whom the bell tolls; it tolls for thee.

EXHIBIT 42-1
CARDS 'R' US SPECIFICATIONS

HANDOUT

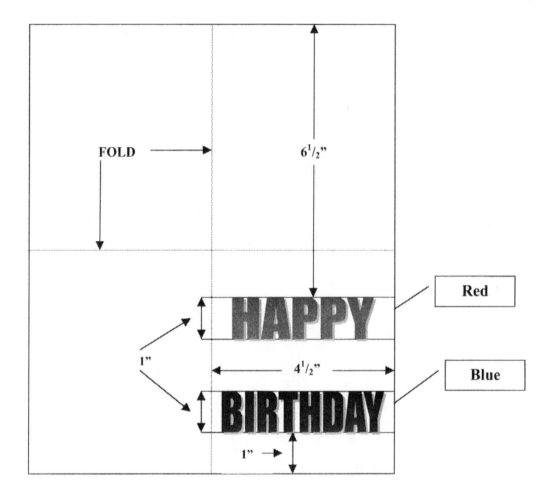

FOLD

$6^{1}/_{2}$"

Red

HAPPY

1"

$4^{1}/_{2}$"

Blue

BIRTHDAY

1"

EXHIBIT 42-2
CARDS 'R' US PRODUCTION ACCOUNTING REPORT TEMPLATE

HANDOUT

	Round 0	Round 1	Round 2	Round 1 to 2 % Change	Round 3	Round 2 to 3 % Change
WIP						
Scrap						
Rework						
Finished Goods						

EXHIBIT 42-3
CARDS 'R' US WORKFLOW DIAGRAM

HANDOUT

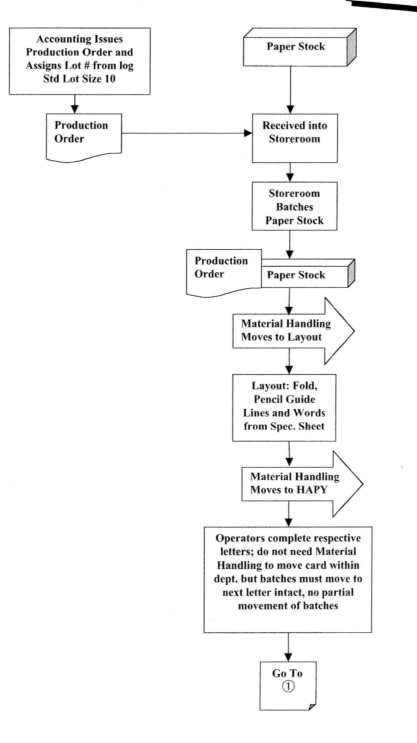

EXHIBIT 42-3 (CONTINUED)
CARDS 'R' US WORKFLOW DIAGRAM

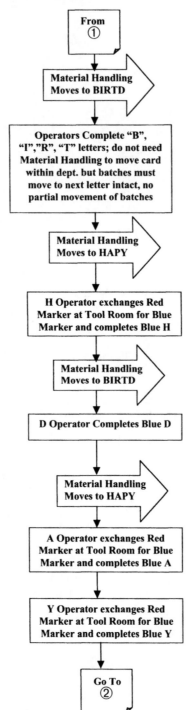

From ①

Material Handling Moves to BIRTD

Operators Complete "B", "I","R", "T" letters; do not need Material Handling to move card within dept. but batches must move to next letter intact, no partial movement of batches

Material Handling Moves to HAPY

H Operator exchanges Red Marker at Tool Room for Blue Marker and completes Blue H

Material Handling Moves to BIRTD

D Operator Completes Blue D

Material Handling Moves to HAPY

A Operator exchanges Red Marker at Tool Room for Blue Marker and completes Blue A

Y Operator exchanges Red Marker at Tool Room for Blue Marker and completes Blue Y

Go To ②

EXHIBIT 42-3 (CONTINUED)
CARDS 'R' US WORKFLOW DIAGRAM

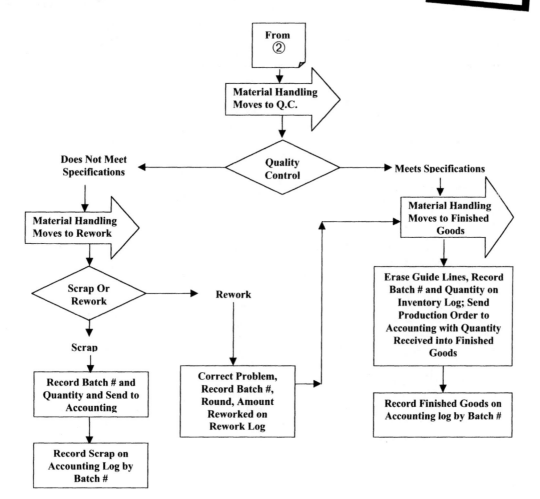

EXHIBIT 42-4
CARDS 'R' US ACCOUNTING LOG

Batch #	Round Issued	Finished Goods		Scrap	
		Quantity	Round	Quantity	Round

EXHIBIT 42-5
CARDS 'R' US PRODUCTION ORDER

PRODUCTION ORDER	
Batch #	
Issue Quantity	
Finished Goods Quantity	

EXHIBIT 42-6
CARDS 'R' US REWORK LOG

HANDOUT

Batch #	Round Rework Completed	Amount Reworked

EXHIBIT 42-7
CARDS 'R' US ORGANIZATION CHART

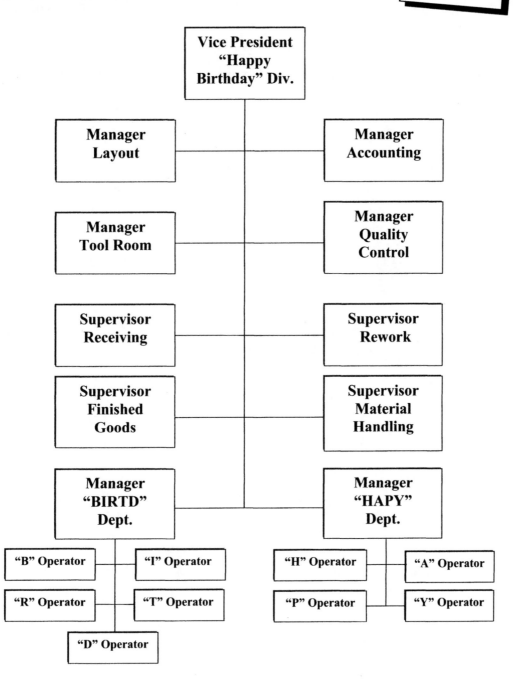

EXHIBIT 42-8
CARDS 'R' US FINISHED GOODS INVENTORY RECORD

Batch #	Amount Received	Cumulative Total

EXHIBIT 42-9
CARDS 'R' US TOOLS ROOM LOG

HANDOUT

Name	Dept.	Tool Issued	Tool Returned	Reason E=Exchange R=Replacement

SCENE 43: GETTING THE BEST RESULTS FROM MEETINGS

It's very rude to sit down without being invited.
—March Hare, *Alice in Wonderland*

AUTHORS' NOTES

Why is it that meetings continue to be one of the top causes of tension headaches in American business culture today? Do those who schedule meetings truly believe that the collective intelligence of a team is more powerful than any one single individual? Probably not; in our opinion, it's all based on habit, on mandates, and on yes, you guessed it, culture!

We're not against meetings. We believe that two heads can be better than one, it just depends on the heads. If they're aligned, focused, and ready to address issues in good faith, we say more power to them. But how do they become aligned and focused so that they can address the issues effectively?

Turning those mandatory meetings into results must be your goal.

The late humorist Will Rogers was once a guest observer at a corporate board meeting. Afterward he remarked, "I agreed to repeat nothing, and I'll keep my promise. But I gotta admit, I heard nothing worth repeating." In his opinion, everyone in that boardroom had wasted their time.

Today more than ever, time is a highly precious commodity. Wasting it in meetings is not just unacceptable, it's a crime. Here's what to do:

- Start on it.
- Optimize it.
- End on it.

So, how do you as a meeting leader achieve these simple steps? Well, let's take it a step at a time.

PLOT

To communicate a method to plan, conduct, and conclude effective, time-efficient meetings.

RUNNING TIME

One hour or more

KEY PLAYERS

- Any individual in a position to conduct meetings

PROPS

- Flip chart
- Markers
- Agenda
- Additional supporting documents

DIRECTOR'S SCRIPT

LIGHTS ...

1. Write the following on the flip chart:

   Ground Rules for Effective Meetings
   Meeting Time Frame
   Team Roles
   Decision-Making Consensus
   Conflict Resolution
   Commitment

CAMERA ...

2. Assemble the team.

ACTION!

3. Present the three critical elements of successful meetings:

Planning

Purpose and expected outcome

- Why do we need to have this meeting?
- What result do we seek?
- Can the result be achieved without a meeting?
- Do we need supporting material?

Agenda

- What issues must be addressed?
- In what sequence should the issues be addressed?
- How much time should be allotted to each issue?
- Who will facilitate the discussion?
- What information should be presented? By whom?
- How will the agenda and supporting material be distributed to attendees? By what date?

Attendees

- Who is essential to the success of the meeting?
- Have they been invited? Will they attend?

Logistics

- Where should the meeting be held?
- What supplies or materials will we need? (E.g., flip chart, markers, audiovisual equipment, food, etc.)

Conducting

Timing

- Begin and end the meeting on time.

Ground Rules (see flip chart)

- Meeting Time Frame
  - ✓ State the projected length of the meeting.
  - ✓ Have someone act as timekeeper, or time the meeting yourself.

- Team Roles
  - ✓ State and explain the roles of leader, facilitator, minutes-taker, and timekeeper.
  - ✓ Determine and clarify any other essential roles.
- Decision Making or Consensus
  - ✓ Determine if and when consensus is mandatory.
  - ✓ Define consensus as: "all of us being able to live with the decision even if all of us do not agree."
- Conflict Resolution
  - ✓ Separate business from personal conflicts.
  - ✓ Use the tension in business conflicts as creative energy to generate positive results.
  - ✓ Resolve personal conflicts by restating the viewpoints of both parties and reaffirming their value to the process.
- Commitment
  - ✓ Underscore attendees' vested interests in staying focused on the issues of the meeting and seeking a mutually beneficial result.
  - ✓ Insist on respect for all attendees' points of view.
  - ✓ Establish, clarify, and confirm responsibilities for follow-up actions.

Notes:

After presenting the Ground Rules at the start of the meeting, you may need to review one or more of them as the discussion goes on.

Ground Rules may seem restrictive to some well-seasoned professionals. Convey to these people that the rules are not to limit, but to facilitate a frank and productive exchange of views.

Agenda Items
- Discuss all items on the agenda.

Consensus on Actions

- Reemphasize the importance of ultimate consensus.
- Agree upon follow-up actions and who will be responsible for carrying them out.
- Have the minutes-taker record who is responsible for the follow-up actions, and who will monitor the progress of their work.

Concluding

Minutes Review

- With the minutes-taker, determine how and to whom the minutes will be distributed.

Meeting Evaluation

- Ask all attendees:
- What did we accomplish today?
- What can we improve upon in future meetings?

Next Agenda

- Reconfirm follow-up actions, individual responsibilities, and any next steps.

CURTAIN CALL

In recognition of your successful acquisition of Planning, Conducting, and Concluding skills, and in anticipation of all your future meetings being successful ones, we hereby award you your M.M. (Master of Meetings) degree.

Encore

We hope that our *Fieldbook* inspires you to launch your very own style of *Dream*ovations—a high-flying journey into business blue sky, as we say.

The *Dream*ovations principles apply to every business, from investment banking to hotel management to building skyscrapers. To achieve success in any venture, you must dream of new ways to do business, believe in your people and your partners, dare to take risks to grow, and do whatever it takes to make it all happen, *Dream, Believe, Dare, Do.*

Our mission is "to help organizations discover the magic of *Dream*ovations." We offer the following unique services to introduce, plan, and implement the *Fieldbook* concepts and assist companies to develop holistic, long-term strategies to strengthen their cultures:

■ ***Dream Retreat***—a strategic team initiative focused on all four *Dream*ovations principles. If you are ready for strategic planning that gets results, forming a brand new team, restructuring or redirecting your team, or embarking on a new team initiative, the *Dream Retreat* is an opportunity not to be missed.

- **Keynote Presentations**—Bill Capodagli, internationally acclaimed management expert and presenter, sparks organizations to build strong cultures based on the *Dream, Believe, Dare, Do* principles.

- **Customized team and leadership development**—evaluation, planning, coaching, and implementation sessions focused on any or all of the following: developing new missions, identifying core values that guide decision-making, and overcoming barriers to success.

We are committed to long-term partnerships in working with organizations, and look forward to learning how we can help you build and truly live the *Dreamovations* culture.

We also invite you to share your success stories with us as you unleash the potential of your organization, and inspire your team to participate in the *Dream.*

Capodagli Jackson Consulting
5845 Lawton Loop East Drive, Suite 201
Indianapolis, IN 46216
1-800-238-9958/317-547-5390
email: capojac@aol.com
web: capojac.com

Bibliography

Albrecht, Karl. *At America's Service: How Your Company Can Join the Customer Service Revolution*. New York, Warner Books, 1988.

Albrecht, Karl, and Ron Zemke. *Service America*. New York, Warner Books, 1985.

Auvine, Brian, Betsy Densmore, Mary Extrom, Scott Poole, and Michael Shanklin. *A Manual for Group Facilitators*. Madison, WI, The Center for Conflict Resolution, 1978.

Barker, Joel Arthur. *Paradigms: The Business of Discovering the Future*. New York, HarperCollins, 1992.

Blanchard, Ken, and Sheldon Bowles. *Gung Ho!* New York, William Morrow and Company, Inc., 1998.

Blanchard, Ken, Bill Hybels, and Phil Hodges. *Leadership by the Book: Tools to Transform Your Workplace*. New York, William Morrow and Company, Inc., 1999.

Blanchard, Ken, and Spencer Johnson. *The One-Minute Manager.* New York, William Morrow and Company, Inc., 1982.

Blanchard, Ken, and Terry Waghorn. *Mission Possible: Becoming a World-Class Organization While There's Still Time.* New York, McGraw-Hill, 1997.

Capacchione, Lucia. *Visioning: Ten Steps to Designing the Life of Your Dreams.* New York, Penguin Putnam, Inc., 2000.

Capodagli, Bill, and Lynn Jackson. *The Disney Way: Harnessing the Management Secrets of Disney in Your Company.* New York, McGraw-Hill, 1999.

Collins, James C., and Jerry I. Porras. *Built to Last: Successful Habits of Visionary Companies.* New York, HarperCollins, 1994.

Deming, W. Edwards. *Quality, Productivity, and Competitive Position.* Cambridge, MA, Massachusetts Institute of Technology, 1982.

Disney's Add a Little Magic: Words of Inspiration. New York, Disney Press, 1999.

Disney, Walt. *Walt Disney: Famous Quotes.* Lake Buena Vista, FL, The Walt Disney Company, 1994.

Fleenor, John W., and Jeffrey Michael Prince. *Using 360-Degree Feedback in Organizations: An Annotated Bibliography.* Greensboro, NC, Center for Creative Leadership, 1997.

George, Jill A., and Jeanne M. Wilson. *Team Member's Survival Guide.* New York, McGraw-Hill, 1997.

Hirsh, Sandra Krebs. *Using the Myers-Briggs Type Indicator[r] in Organizations, 3d ed.* Palo Alto, CA, Consulting Psychologists Press, Inc.

Jung, C.G. *Psychological Types.* Princeton, NJ, Princeton University Press, 1971.

Kohn, Alfie. *No Contest: The Case against Competition.* Boston, MA, Houghton Mifflin, 1986.

Kohn, Alfie. *Punished by Rewards: The Trouble with Gold Stars, Incentive Plans, A's, Praise, and Other Bribes.* Boston, MA, Houghton Mifflin, 1995.

Kroeger, Otto, and Janet M. Thuesen. *Type Talk at Work.* New York, Dell Publishing, 1992.

Kuczmarski, Thomas D., *Innovation: Leadership Strategies for the Competitive Edge.* Lincolnwood, IL, NTC Publishing Group, 1996.

Labovitz, George, and Victor Rosansky. *The Power of Alignment: How Great Companies Stay Centered and Accomplish Extraordinary Things.* New York, John Wiley & Sons, Inc., 1997.

Lundin, Stephen C., Harry Paul, and John Christensen. *Fish!* New York, Hyperion, 2000.

Myers, Isabel Briggs, and Mary H. McCaulley. *MBTI Manual: A Guide to the Development and Use of the Myers-Briggs Type Indicato®, 3rd ed.* Palo Alto, CA, Consulting Psychologists Press, Inc., 1998.

Nelson, Bob. *1001 Ways to Reward Employees.* New York, Workman Publishing, 1994.

Nierenberg, Gerald I. *The Art of Creative Thinking.* New York, Barnes & Noble, Inc., 1982.

Peters, Tom. *The Circle of Innovation: You Can't Shrink Your Way to Greatness.* New York, Knopf, 1997.

Peters, Tom. *Power + Action50: Reinventing Work.* New York, Knopf, 2000.

Reddy, W. Brendan. *Intervention Skills: Process Consultation for Small Groups and Teams.* San Diego, CA, Pfeiffer & Company, 1994.

Rohnke, Karl. *Silver Bullets: A Guide to Initiative Problems, Adventure Games and Trust Activities.* Dubuque, IA, Kendall/Hunt, 1984.

Rohnke, Karl. *Cowstails and Cobras II: A Guide to Games, Initiatives, Ropes Courses & Adventure Curriculum.* Dubuque, IA, Kendall/Hunt, 1989.

Senn-Delaney Leadership Consulting Group. *Senn-Delaney Leadership Programs*, Long Beach, CA, 1985.

Sheridan, Bruce. *Policy Deployment.* Milwaukee, WI, ASQC Quality Press, 1993.

The Disney Approach to Quality Service. Walt Disney World Company Seminar Productions, Lake Buena Vista, FL, November 1995.

Vance, Mike, and Diane Deacon. *Think out of the Box.* Franklin Lakes, NJ, The Career Press, 1995.

Woods, John. *The Quotable Executive.* New York, McGraw-Hill, 2000.

Walton, Mary. *The Deming Management Method.* New York, The Putnam Publishing Group, 1986.

Wetherbe, James C. *The World on Time: The 11 Management Principles That Made FedEx an Overnight Sensation.* Santa Monica, CA, Knowledge Exchange, 1996.

Wiersema, Fred. *Customer Intimacy: Pick Your Partners, Shape Your Culture, Win Together.* Santa Monica, CA, Knowledge Exchange, 1996.

Wilson, Jeanne M., and Jill A. George. *Team Leader's Survival Guide.* New York, McGraw-Hill, 1997.

Zemke, Ron. *The Service Edge.* New York, NAL Books, 1989.

Zemke, Ron, and Thomas Kramlinger. *Figuring Things Out: A Trainer's Guide to Needs and Task Analysis.* Reading, MA, Addison-Wesley Publishing Company, Inc., 1982.

Index

ABOUT THE AUTHORS

Bill Capodagli, Managing Partner of Capodagli Jackson Consulting, brings managerial experience at several top consulting firms and graduate-level teaching experience to the firm. He is a popular speaker at both national and international conferences where he teaches audiences the *Dream, Believe, Dare, Do* Business Model.

Lynn Jackson, Bill's partner in Capodagli Jackson Consulting, holds graduate degrees in organizational development and counseling, and she has successfully implemented the *Dream, Believe, Dare, Do* principles in numerous organizations.

Bill Capodagli and Lynn Jackson have amassed over 2,700 hours benchmarking the Disney organization, trained over 7,000 people in *Dream, Believe, Dare, Do* methods, and spent over ten years compiling information on Disney practices.

For more information, you can call 1-800-238-9958 or email Bill and Lynn at quality@evansville.net